AF588355

AWAKENINGS

AWAKENINGS

Gabriel Marcel

A translation of Marcel's autobiography,
En chemin, vers quel éveil?
by

Peter S. Rogers

Introduction by Patrick Bourgeois

MARQUETTE STUDIES IN PHILOSOPHY

NO. 30

ANDREW TALLON, SERIES EDITOR

Library of Congress Cataloguing-in-Publication Data
Marcel, Gabriel, 1889-1973
[En chemin, vers quel éveil? English]
Awakenings : a translation of Gabriel Marcel's autobiography / Gabriel Marcel ; [translation] by Peter S. Rogers ; introduction by Patrick Bourgeois.
p. cm. — (Marquette studies in philosophy ; #30)
Includes bibliographical references and index.
ISBN 0-87462-653-6 (pbk. : alk. paper)
1. Marcel, Gabriel, 1889-1973 I. Title. II. Series.
B2430.M253 E513 2002
194—dc21

2002014652

Fourth printing 2020

A translation of
Gabriel Marcel, *En chemin vers quel éveil?* Paris: Gallimard, 1971

MARQUETTE UNIVERSITY PRESS
MILWAUKEE

The Association of Jesuit University Presses

Contents

Translator's Acknowledgements 7

Introduction by Patrick Bourgeois 9

Marcel's Dedication 27

Preface by Jacques de Bourbon Busset 29

Marcel's Foreword 31

Awakenings 33

1 33
2 48
3 61
4 67
5 79
6 84

[Neither a table of contents nor chapter titles appear in the original. Numbers were added to set off what could be considered chapters—Series editor's note.]

7 89
8 107
9 110
10 130
11 138
12 143
13 149
14 160
15 165
16 178
17 180
18 201
19 205
20 211
21 216
22 227
23 233

Biographical Note on Gabriel Marcel 240

Selected Studies of Gabriel Marcel 242

Philosophical and Dramatic Works Translated into English 244

Selected Works by Gabriel Marcel 247

Index 250

Translator's Acknowledgments

I would like to thank Anne Marcel, K. R. Hanley, Kay Labauve Rees, Ann Begley and Cassandra Mabe for having read the manuscript at different stages of the translation. Terese Lyons, Tom Zamparelli, Bob Dewell, Peter Bernardi, Eileen Doll, and Robert Gerlich answered questions as did Laura Dankner of the Monroe Library at Loyola University New Orleans and Victoria Blanchard of the Maxwell Music Library at Tulane University. The French Cultural Services in New York provided funding for the publication of this project. I am grateful to Debbie de la Houssaye of the French Consulate in New Orleans for help to secure my participation in a seminar on translation held at the Université de Nice in the summer of 1995. My thanks are also due to Anne Maryse Gratade and Elisabeth Rosemberg for their support of my interests in things French.

According to Marcel Proust, the task and duty of the writer are those of a translator. Translation of any writing thus becomes quite removed from an original text. A keen reader of Proust, Gabriel Marcel offers his own perspective on the translator's task: "Of course I was to notice quickly the nearly insurmountable obstacles that beset the translator, and it happened to me more than once to associate myself directly with the rewriting that was necessary for a translation that was done too hastily, at the expense of a text that should have been transposed without altering it." While I may not have avoided every obstacle, I hope that the reader will enjoy encountering Marcel in his own response to Proustian duty.

As Patrick Samway reminded me, Gabriel Marcel had spoken at Loyola University New Orleans in 1965. I am grateful to one of its teachers, Patrick L. Bourgeois, for proposing this project.

I dedicate the translation to my Jesuit companions and teachers Youree Watson, Edward Romagosa, Paul Beauchamp, Charles O'Neill, Leo Nicoll, Robert Rimes, Jerome Neyrey, J. Fillmore Elliot, and John Edwards.

Peter S. Rogers

Introduction

The time is ripe, as we move into a new millenium, for publishing an English translation of Gabriel Marcel's autobiography, *En chemin, vers quel éveil?*, because of the renewed relevance and importance of his life and his creative productions to the contemporary world and to the post-modern situation. Since creativity is the primary dimension of the mystery of being, giving rise to all three instances of his creative production, music, drama, and philosophical reflection, the relation of his autobiography to his entire productive projects is clearly tied to the unifying thread of creativity. For creativity produces the life and the account of that life in his autobiography, just as it gives rise to musical compositions, to dramatic works, and to philosophical reflections and their expression in writing. The renewed need for his call to a sense of being is made more acute in light of the serious danger of suppression of the sense of being today in a way more threatening than in Marcel's own time. This renewed relevance of Marcel's invitation to reflect on the sense of being is what I intend to establish, thus showing indirectly how this autobiography, and indeed, his entire work, can serve as a call to us all today to be, to think, and to create artistically.

One cannot help being impressed with Marcel's familiarity with the history of philosophy, especially that in the nineteenth and early twentieth centuries, with a special reference to the idealism in France in the early part of the twentieth century. And to some extent, it is precisely his struggle with this form of idealism that makes even his earliest work relevant at the brink of the new millenium. His book on Schelling puts him at the core of the recent post-modern dialogue, since the romantics and idealists between Kant and Hegel serve as the grist for much thinking today. And, although Royce is little known among continental thinkers in America, Marcel's presentation of Josiah Royce's metaphysics likewise can serve to put him at the core of the post-modern situation. For today, as was the case when Marcel began his own creative and recollective philosophical reflections, we in the post-modern situation suffer the extreme danger of a serious, and I might add culpable, loss of the sense of being. His works, then, and this autobiography, can provide an opportunity and appropriate time or propitious moment (Kairos καιρός), for the retrieval of this sense of the mystery of being, and a reorientation of philosophy in a post-modern situation, not as a return to the historical beginnings of existential thinking as such, but, rather, a reawakening of the creativity at the heart of this sense of being that is so precarious today.

This autobiography makes a special contribution precisely in that it affords a narrative account of the sense of Marcel's life and work as he himself envisions it. Such narrative, as is clear from much recent writings on the role and nature of narrative, entails a serious and creative interpretation, making a unified sense of a life and life-work. Marcel is seen in this work to narrate his life and to choose certain events, relations, and works, thus weaving together a unified story of his life out of the many concrete situations, events, and relations. This in itself is an exercise in interpretation that could be studied as one interpretation of his life, done by himself, and lending itself to further use in other narratives about his life. Certainly, as a well thought-out and creative autobiography, it enjoys a place of priority as an expression of a life recollected in second reflection.

Such secondary reflection as one of the most central and essential themes of Marcel can be understood to be at the heart of philosophical issues intensely discussed today, thus showing a continued point of the relevance of his thought. In showing the place within secondary reflection of such an interpretation, and even of narrative in general and of art, not only is a place made for the role of his autobiography as an instance of narrative, but also for his other works of drama and philosophy within recent philosophical movements. In this context the place in the work of Marcel of the ever-important productive imagination in second reflection emerges, just as it does in much recent contemporary thinking, but without the balance that Marcel offers.[1]

Second reflection, belonging to methodology, is a recovery guided by a quasi intuition, distinguishing it from a copy or representation. For Marcel, participation cannot be an object of thought. And this secondary reflection is an immediate but blind intuition on the part of humans, reminding us of Kant's third Critique in that it is not mediated by thought or conceptual knowledge. However, this intuition can be made the focus of conceptual analysis, which is where reflection begins, but not without a loss of immediacy. And this is the precise place of interpretative and/or narrative dimensions, as Thomas Busch so insightfully pointed out, thus allowing to emerge the positive construction operating in drama and in narrative through the imaginative presentation. It is clear that art, narrative, and especially drama have a role to play, because in these areas we can almost recreate complex experiences in which the audience can be participants and not simply spectators. "In a sense, art, narrative, and drama come closest to bridging the gap between experience and thought, a gap which is identified and analyzed by philosophy."[2] This reveals the central importance in the relation between literature or drama and philosophical reflection, which today has been so badly treated in the post-modern situation. In this context Philosophy is too often reduced to literature, and truth and insight are dissolved. The healthy-mindedness of Marcel is that the relation between philosophy and literature is kept alive and active, but also distinct, so that one does not dissolve and absorb the other. Rather, they are two activities that can feel one another, and that can help to close the gap between experience and thought. This insight thus reveals a central positive role and relevance of Marcel's writings as we move into the next millenium. His works can be seen to thwart the regressive direction of much post-modern thought today. For, in a special way today, when the emphasis on the end of metaphysics puts the very possibility of philosophy into question, these philosophical reflections of Marcel can shed light on the philosophical enterprise for the future as we move into a new millenium. And it is precisely the positive role of limit in the concrete philosophy of Marcel that can serve as a response to the recent challenge from post-modern deconstructive thinkers, a response which must be made for the redirection of continental philosophy in this country.

The existential turn of phenomenology and of much twentieth century philosophy has revealed the richness, fullness, and ambiguity of human existence, which entails the mystery of being at the heart of human existence, as seen above. In turning to lived existence in the break-away from the dominance of the modern Cartesian world view, these philosophies rediscover the richness of lived existence underlying any scientific model which is found only to schematize the concrete, allowing the human gaze to become blinded by the clarity and assurance of these derived and second level accounts. Thus it is in this return to the fullness of concrete existence, following the turn of Kierkegaard and Nietzsche, and even of Jaspers, that leads to the focus and emphasis on the depth of mystery at the heart of human existence, especially in those philosophies in which there is a religious dimension. The philosophy of Gabriel Marcel explicitly develops in interpreting human existence in terms of the mystery of Being and at once questions the limits of reflection upon it.

Marcel's philosophical reflection on the mystery of existence and being expresses the question of limit or end only obliquely. For Marcel, in this context of limit, the objectivity and characterizablity of the problematic are surpassed in the notion of mystery. And access to the mystery is gained in second reflection attuned to existence in such a way as to bring it to thought. For Marcel, existence as mystery eludes any problematical treatment, for it is irreducible to that tendency to characterize. It is not a problem before me, but one which involves me, if it can be spoken of at all in terms of problem, as he does in saying: "A mystery is a problem which encroaches" upon itself.[3] I cannot abstract myself from the mystery of my own being. Thus, this dimension of mystery cannot be considered merely to be a problem that cannot be solved. Rather, I am precisely what (who) is being reflected upon. On this level there is an ontological exigency at the heart of human existence that should prevent me from closing myself off into the problematic and the objective. And it is on this level that the "thou" is encountered in presence. If second reflection were to allow itself to begin other than with this realization, i.e, the presence of the other, it would not be possible to get the "other" precisely as person back into reflection. This presence is closely linked to *availability* (*disponibilité*) or readiness for the other. The unavailable person is not *really there* for the other, but maintains a certain closedness and distraction toward something else.

With this move in second reflection to existence as mystery, Marcel has turned toward the fullness of existence which eludes first reflection and which is irreducible to it. This concretely situated being is not able to be approached in a philosophical reflection which is detached, epistemologically oriented, instead of involved and immersed in the concrete situation. Thus, in this critique of the primacy of objectivity, Marcel has overcome the primacy of epistemology, and at once, found its source: "...But what is more important for me is the affirmation that existence is not only given, but it is also giving—however paradoxical that sounds. That is, existence is the very condition of any thinking whatsoever."[4] Existence as giving encompasses creativity. This giving as creative is the central motif of Marcel's whole philosophy, as he himself says, in agreeing with Gallagher's interpretation: "... as soon as there is creation, in whatever degree, we are in the realm of being (p.84). But the converse is equally true: that is to say, there is doubtless no sense in using the word 'being' except where creation, in some form or other, is in view."[5] Marcel says that this insight grew as he concentrated more on the relations among his philosophical thought, his dramatic work, and his musical compositions.

We see here that Marcel, in his own rich and concrete way, has turned to lived existence in its concrete fullness in a unique reflection different from and going beyond that of first reflection. It is on this level that all of his celebrated themes, mystery, participation, presence, communion, fidelity, creativity, charity, faith, and hope, must be interpreted, for first reflection, oblivious to this level, would reduce them to an abstraction or an objectivity. Thus mystery is Marcel's manner of bringing into focus the attempt to think, beyond the boundaries of knowledge, the wholeness of existence in the questions that most vitally concern human life, interest, and heart. It is somewhat an attempt to reach the ineffable in a reflection that will never be adequate because of the richness of existence and of being. For this he invokes faith. And this faith, intimately related to hope and charity, is not exclusive of a philosophical faith in God. And it does not exclude the possibility and actuality of Christian Faith, but rather, uncovers its condition of possibility as its place in experience.

In this context, Marcel seems to admit or to hint at the need for an indirect access to the question of the whole, in thinking beyond the boundaries of knowledge and of problematic reflection. In fact, most of his primary reflection on the mystery of being takes place within a certain domain going beyond the boundaries of the Kantian limit—i.e., the total and full existence beneath and beyond the realm of primary reflection—the domain of existence, which for Kant must remain unknowable. And, in certain contexts, Marcel speaks of the need for images, for myth, in order to prevent making an idol out of that which is reflected upon here. He says concerning knowledge of the historically human: "a thought which cannot be embodied without the help of myth—the price we have to pay for our own condition which is that of incarnate beings."[6] Further, Marcel refers to the need for images that really serve as symbols of something richer, with two levels of meaning for the one for whom they speak in a certain way:

> Must not the philosopher admit that we cannot really free ourselves from some key-images—for example that of heaven as the abode of the blessed—provided that he shows that these images are bound up with the conditions of existence which belong to a wayfaring creature, and that they cannot accordingly be considered as literally true. In this sense I would say, for example, that heaven can hardly appear to us, who are of the earth, as other than the sky above; but in so far as the bond which holds us to the earth is relaxed or changes its nature, it will be bound to present a different aspect to us. We are fated to undergo a metamorphosis whose nature we can foresee only very imperfectly, and it is just on the idea of this metamorphosis that rests the revival of orphism whose imperious demands must be familiar to many of us today. Hence again it follows that salvation can also be better conceived by us as a road rather than a state; and this links up again with some profound views of the Greek Fathers, in particular St. Gregory of Nyssa.[7]

Marcel's philosophy is quite relevant today for all who, following his lead, appropriate the philosophy of mystery incorporating it into a concrete reflection as a hermeneutic of existence, thus well responding to the challenges from recent movements of continental thinking. His philosophical "*élan*" gives an indirect access to concrete existence in its mysterious fullness and to the totality in its elusiveness. Such treatments of philosophy, initiated in intimation by Marcel, and explicated by one of his own best disciples, Paul Ricoeur, allow for continual and ongoing reflection on the mystery of existence in spite of the challenge from recent philosophies. But, due to the limit of human experience, and to the quest for the totality in thinking (and in action), philosophy will never be completed. Thus, one could perhaps say that philosophy culminates precisely in its attempt to stay attuned, and to "see" or to interpret, at the limit, the ultimate significance of the mystery of being. With all this in mind, we can now turn to a further consideration of the relevance of his thought and life to Catholic higher education today.

Today the situation of philosophy and of the religious identity of Catholic colleges and universities in the United States, and the unique role of Marcel in philosophy and in Catholic culture, are such that a further relevance of his work can easily be established.

In recent years, many Catholic universities and colleges in the United States have begun programs of Catholic Studies and Catholic Institutes in the attempt to preserve and express their Catholic identity in the context of Theology Departments that have become pluralistic and more broadly based in their transformation into Departments of Religious Studies. This fostering of interdisciplinary programs of Catholic Studies pushes some scholars to focus anew on Catholic authors who can speak to the present generation. In this context, the literature, philosophy, and life of Gabriel Marcel enjoy a special place. For they are centrally religious.

Gabriel Marcel's contribution to such programs of Catholic Studies can be significant. For, as a Catholic philosopher of the twentieth century, he was one of the first to present the contributions of existential philosophy as a serious and positive movement in continental philosophy. His article of 1924, published even before Heidegger's work containing an ontological focus on human existence, reveals a real possibility for a Catholic philosopher. With more of his plays now translated into English, the students in such programs can read and study his provocative plays, incorporate their dramatic dialogues and relations into a philosophical reflection with Marcel. One such work that comes to mind is the ensemble of *Le Monde cassé* (*The Broken World*) and the philosophical reflection to which it gave rise, "Concrete Approaches to Investigating the Ontological Mystery," formerly translated as "Ontological Mystery."[8]

Since these Catholic Studies programs are interdisciplinary, the role of Marcel's works is unique. For his plays and essays, with one author, are already interdisciplinary. And the relation between the plays and the philosophical reflections is such that several goals of these programs are realized at once. The student confronts contemporary drama, with surprising and thought-provoking endings, leading to philosophical reflections that can be called in some sense spiritual. Thus, the role of Marcel's work in Catholic studies programs makes a unique contribution, and nourishes serious thought on the part of students coming to grips with their Catholic identity, belief, and commitment.

This is not, however, to reduce his philosophy to theology, or to prerequire Christian belief or events. For, although some of his philosophical terms are illuminated for those who believe in the Christian mystery, such as presence in relation to Eucharist and creative fidelity in terms of faith and of the Church, these terms stand alone and are illuminative independently of such Christian belief.[9] Thus even though their intelligibility can be clarified by Christian terms, they are strictly philosophical insights that are intelligible as such. They are conducive to real human commitment, while also possibly leading to and deepening Christian commitment. Thus, although much of his philosophy may be occasioned by Christian belief and life, it does not require this belief and can stand alone as philosophy. And, by the same token, he wants seriously to maintain the distinction between the natural and supernatural, showing clearly that no amount of reflection can allow us to attain to the mysteries of the Incarnation and Redemption. His point is that such "supernatural life has to find some connections and points of insertion in natural life—which in no way means to imply that supernatural life is merely the flowering of natural life … ."[10]

Turning now to his own account, one can see the formative stages of Marcel's dramas, of his philosophy, and of his music, as they unfold in his own hindsight narratives. He himself, at the very beginning of his autobiography, indicates that this is his journey or vocation and its meaning that he is attempting to make clear in this work. One could suspect that Marcel is attempting, in accord with his own unique use of the term, to situate his way in various phases of its development. And at the outset of this work, Marcel returns to some of the questions raised in *Le Mystère de l'être* (*The Mystery of Being*) about the relation between life and the person, and the difficulty in attempting to take a distance in order to think about one's life. He admits that this questioning developed "from my experience and not, properly speaking, about it" (10 February 1971). It would be fair to say that this book is thus not *about* his life as much as it is *from* his experience. It is rather more a question of his re-living those experiences that came to make up the life of music, drama, and philosophy in this person, Gabriel Marcel.

Marcel indicates in the context of his play, *Le Coeur des autres* (*The Rebellious Heart*), that dramatic creation takes root in a lived life, so that sometimes what the creative writer develops in the experiences of his characters brings about a transformation in his own life. The thoughts developed in this book "tend, in effect, to shed light on the narrow relation that binds my work to my life and my characters to myself" (38-39). This book, then, truly expresses the labyrinthine way of the awakening of Gabriel Marcel and its polyvalent creative activity and expressions in music, drama, and philosophy. Two qualities stand out in the account of the process of this awakening: the singularity of its situation over a life; and creativity. And, just as Marcel's drama, music, and philosophy were aimed at an awakening in each concrete individual within a situation of at least a quasi interpersonal relation with him, so too, this very book aims at a creative awakening in the singular individual, resulting from the reader's availability and attuned listening in reading Marcel's autobiography. For Marcel, creativity is the ontological root that is so often stifled, but which, once awakened, seeks creative expression. What is reached is the singular creative source of the individual that is so radically intersubjective. We must reflect further on the sense of this book as Marcel himself understood and expressed it.

What Marcel states about the playwright's aim in relation to the spectator applies to his role as a musician and philosopher as well. The spectator should be treated as an awareness to be awakened, or as an "awareness to be opened up to a higher degree of lucidity" (147). Such an awakening detaches "the spectator from his prejudices, from the received opinions that weigh him down and keep him from entering into himself and communing with another. In short, the theater should help to renew him interiorly" (147). Such an aim shows the intentional unity of Marcel's creative life of music, drama, and philosophy. It also shows the fundamental proximity of his philosophical attitude to his drama in that both aim as such at quickening the human spirit, effecting a break-away from one's prejudices and received opinions. This is truly the Socratic element of his philosophical project. And it shows why Marcel considered his work not only to be non-systematic, but also not able to be conceived as an intelligible whole removed from time. Thus he rejects such tendencies to systematize his work or to reduce it to an intelligible whole transcending time. He states further that he has "never wanted, not only to create a system, but even to write a treatise in the philosophical sense of the word"(169). He has not wanted to write a "philosophical treatise" as such.

It is worth noting that Marcel considers the autobiography to have no meaning unless it also be regarded as an "examination of conscience" (163, 171). In such an undertaking, he has attempted throughout to be "faithful to life and its movement." He refers to the "spiral movement" that he felt obligated to follow here, "as is so often the case" (233). Indeed, this spiral movement must mean the development of the work along the lines of its aim to awaken within the reader the creative process that overcomes one's prejudices and received opinion.

Marcel ends this examination of his "rocky road" by dwelling on his physical and moral dependence. After mentioning certain practical dependencies on specific people, he indicates the painfulness of physical life, which is "sharpened by the news of death" of friends. This intense and heartfelt reference to the death of friends provokes a last invoking of mystery. In this context he states: "This clearly means that the incomprehensible can shed light from the moment it becomes the place for authentic communion. If I am still a Christian, it is, I believe, in spite of everything, because I espouse this mystery of the Communion of the Suffering and of its being rooted in the life and person of Christ" (239). And he ends these reflections with a further elaboration, reaching a quasi musical crescendo of the autobiography: "It is there, at this point attainable only with the greatest difficulty, that the highest music bursts forth. This is the music of the *Missa solemnis* and of the last *Quatuors* (*Quartets*). It is the music of the *Quintette à cordes* (*String Quintet*) of Schubert and of so many other works that I have passionately loved and that have always nurtured me. The hesitant and rather trembling meaning of my dramatic or philosophical effort will have consisted in translating into the language of thought, and more still into the language of existential dialogue, the kind of implicit assurance, and finally triumphant assurance, that these grand intercessors, as though preparing the Revelation, will have granted me with the passage of time"(239). Let us take a further look at this work, relating it more clearly to his life and to the understanding of the reader.

At the beginning of this autobiography, Marcel, in explicating the question "developed from my experience and not, properly speaking, about it," addresses issues most fundamental to his philosophical reflection. He insists again that a "life that is lived" (33, 34) resists a reduction to objectification or items in a file. These remarks throw into focus his famous second reflection as recollection at the heart of his style of philosophy. In this context, he goes on to quote Goethe's words "*Wahrheit und Dichtung*"—*truth and poetry* – as applying to every worthwhile autobiography. And, while affirming his inability to present this poetic element in an autobiography as a "true novel," he admits a certain connection between some of his characters in his drama and what he is (35). This will reveal something of his life at the junction of his being. But he immediately indicates an extreme caution that is needed.

Marcel uses the character of Daniel Meyrieux, a playwright in *Le Coeur des autres*, to show a character that he himself as a playwright might risk becoming "if my dramatic creation developed in a certain direction" (35). He indicates that he intended to highlight in this play what his relation with his wife could have become. Thus this was a "possible me." Marcel goes on to mention that this is one of the better plays, and that it is meaningful for discovering the "point at which dramatic creation takes root in a lived life?" (36).

Marcel is quite aware of the extreme difficulty in this approach to the characters of an author. He goes on to indicate in *Le Regard neuf* (The new look) that: "At the heart of the character Maurice Jordan, there is, I think, something of an affective imagination which I might have experienced had I been able to have a son. It seems to me that it is this affective imagination which animates the work with a kind of rhythm that I still feel when I happen to reread this play" (38). Yet the play cannot be reduced to this element, for the concrete situation of this character comes into play. At this point, Marcel makes a keen remark central to the sense of this autobiography: "What I can say is that, by writing this play and the others grouped with it, I was aware of removing myself from the world of thought at the heart of what my philosophical reflection was until then centered" (38). This reveals several important points.

First, it might be clear here that in Marcel's writings his dramatic creations preceded his philosophical insight and expression. In this play he begins to move away from a certain kind of philosophy to which until now he had adhered in favor of the great mystery of being, recollection, and second reflection that became so central to his unique philosophy. To confirm this point, we need only to recall the relation between *Le Monde cassé* and the article on ontological mystery. The play preceded and gave rise to the philosophical reflection expressed in the essay. Thus, we must not mistakenly interpret this as an instance of philosophical drama. His plays do not express philosophical insight, and they cannot be considered philosophical plays as perhaps those of Sartre can be considered. Rather, they lead to philosophical recollection that seeks expression in his essays and lectures.

Finally, the character of Maurice Jordan shows an important correlation to the author, but only about the element of the character, not his particular situation. One must be careful not to confuse the plot, its unfolding in events, and the rest of the character, as also belonging to Gabriel Marcel, the author. We thus return to the acute problem of the relation between the author and his characters. It is extremely difficult to see which possibilities of Marcel are expressed in his myriad characters and which simply are the fruit of his fertile creative imagination—not expressing any real possibility of himself emerging within his own lived experience. This point leads to an extremely important significance of this autobiography. Throughout the process of narrating this story of his lived life, Marcel indicates some real possibilities for his own existence that were expressed in the fictional characters. Concerning this thought, Marcel says "They [these thoughts] tend, in effect, to shed light on the narrow relation that binds my work to my life and my characters to myself" (38-39).

Another connection of which he takes account is his relation to his philosophy professor, Monsieur Colonna d'Istria, who first inspired him. After the first class with this teacher Marcel decided that he would become a philosopher. This enchanted world of philosophy, where thought was "encouraged at every level" was something that came easily to him, and something at which he excelled. This year of philosophy is the only year at the Lycée that he fondly remembered. At this point, however, he did not separate the philosopher from the professor of philosophy, nor question the notion of having a teacher of philosophy (67-68). And, later, Marcel was much influenced by Henry Franck, with whom he felt a great affinity, and by Royce and Hocking, especially regarding the move from the monadism that he sensed in the work of Proust to an accent on intersubjectivity (72). It must be added that none of these relationships means a philosophical agreement with these friends. It is the case, however, that Marcel considered "concrete dialectic" as the "very core of my personal destiny" (88). In fact, in this context he refers to his first philosophical essay, "Les conditions dialectiques de la philosophie de l'intuition" ("The dialectical conditions of the philosophy of intuition") (88).

There is no need in a brief introduction such as this, placing Marcel in his own context and showing his extremely important relevance today, to go into detail about many events which had transforming influence on him, such as World War II and his inevitable non-combat status, and his experience with the ouija board, which, at the same time, profoundly influenced him regarding the possible importance of the parapsychical. However, one event must be mentioned: that of his engagement and marriage to Jacqueline Boegner.

Marcel states that his marriage to Jacqueline was immediately placed under the "sign of music," because it was music that brought them together, and it was Jacqueline who later put his improvisations into musical script. And the relationship pervaded his whole creative work, as he indicates: "But what I insist on mentioning is that the appearance of Jacqueline Boegner in my life was most certainly at the origin of a kind of inner renewal which was to be translated very quickly in my work, and I think especially here in my theatre and in the plays which I alluded to at the beginning of this journal." Marcel goes on to affirm the intensely positive impact of her entire family on his life. As a lonely only child, he found the membership into a family such as that of Jacqueline quite welcome and wholesome. He considered his close friendship with Henri Boegner, Jacqueline's brother, as first awakening him to the thought of her as a possible companion (111).

Marcel attributes special importance to *Le Monde cassé* and the conference bearing the title "*Position et approches concrètes du mystère*" ("*Concrete Approaches to Investigating the Ontological Mystery*"), which he published together, with the later as an appendix to the play. These plays from the early thirties mark the beginning of the period that follows Marcel's conversion to Catholicism in 1929. And it is in this context that Marcel begins reflecting on his experience of conversion to Catholicism, and the role of mediator that François Mauriac played by writing a note that gave Marcel peace. "It seemed to me that Mauriac simply played the role of a mediator between myself and an invisible power which, certainly, was not unknown to me but, on the contrary, I would say, using the words of Saint Augustine, more interior than myself" (123). This letter of Mauriac led him to make his actions and explicit commitment conform to his thoughts and writings, ending up in an explicit faith commitment. This entailed what he considered a commitment to the fullness of the Christian message, which he considered to be embraced by Catholicism. He then sought our Fr. Jean-Pierre Alterman, who had been a spiritual director of Charles Du Bos, a good friend, who had spoken well of the priest. The fact that this priest was born into a Jewish family helped win him over to Marcel (125).

Marcel gives a significant place of importance to the role of the broken world in the experience of the living, concrete, existential subject, a subject in strong contrast to the subject for idealism. He himself was quite aware of living in a broken world. Marcel indicates that the play, *Le Monde cassé*, allows one to see what was going on inside him at a level that philosophical reflection can reach only with great difficulty (134). And he especially refers to the last two scenes of act 4. Setting the stage for explicating the last two scenes of this play, Marcel shows an important connection of the characters of this play with individuals whom he knew, giving rise to the characters of Christiane and Laurent. The lady of his acquaintance was an intelligent and beautiful young woman much appreciated by all of her friends, while her husband received little attention. He was a self-effacing and good man, but one more involved with his own self-love than in his love. It is she who proclaims that they exist in a "broken world." She is intensely conscious of the separation and of a world that does not touch the heart. But at the end of the play this all disappears and is replaced by a light leading to unity and life. Marcel puts the best twist on this ending and on his experience at this time: "It is certain that, if I had not already, as I said earlier, acquired through my own experience the certainty that there exists a dimension at the heart of which separation disappears, I would not have been able to write the last two scenes of *Le Monde cassé*" (136). And it is this attunement to the concrete, lived, singular experience that makes Marcel's recollection so relevant today.

His constant concern for the singular, for the other, and for moving away from the dominance of the products of first reflection mark Gabriel Marcel as a philosopher attuned to the issues of a post-modern era. While he promotes the positive elements of post-modern thinking, he does not succumb to the negative and regressive reductionism of post-modern deconstruction. This is obvious from his treatment of lived time and of the present and from his view on language, both of which mark deconstruction as reductive and regressive. Rather, Marcel's constant concern to focus on lived time and lived personal relations in the intersubjective situation, and his preoccupation with the singular and concrete situation prevent him from losing the gains of twentieth century philosophy for the popularity of passing fads. Thus, there is a sense in which Marcel's philosophy is perennial, since his gains should not ever be lost. They are the subtle products of the development of contemporary philosophy out of the contrast between and interarticulation of ancient and modern philosophy, emerging in the twentieth century as a gigantic gain, not to be lost in the post-modern era. Such contemporary thinking moves forward, but precisely as rooted in its present situation that emerges from its past, gaining new vistas for thinking from that present latent with its own possibilities. Such contemporary thinking can profit greatly from those gains of Gabriel Marcel.

Patrick L. Bourgeois
13 September 2000

Notes

1 Marcel's treatment of this question ultimately led to the well developed position of one of his faithful followers, Paul Ricoeur. I am following here some points I made by way of summary of the paper read to the Gabriel Marcel Society in March of 1997 by Thomas Busch, and the summary and commentary by Brendan Sweetman. See: Gabriel Marcel Society Newsletter, March, 1996, edited by Robert Lechner. The paper read by Thomas Bush bore the title: "Gabriel Marcel: Secondary Reflection as Interpretation." An article which covers some of the same points, but not as explicit as this paper read at the Marcel Society, is Bush's article: "Secondary Reflection as Interpretation" in *Bulletin de la Société Américaine de Philosophie de Langue Française*, vol. VII, No. 1-2, 1995, pp. 176-183.

2 Thomas Busch affirms this in his paper, and Brandon Sweetman in his response agreed with him.

3 K. R. Hanley, *Gabriel Marcel's Perspectives on the Broken World*, followed *by Concrete Approaches to Investigating the Ontological Mystery*, translated by Katharine Rose Hanley, introduced by Ralph McInerny, (Milwaukee: Marquette University Press, 1998), p. 178.

4 Gabriel Marcel, *Tragic Wisdom and Beyond: Including Conversations Between Paul Ricoeur and Gabriel Marcel*, translated by Stephen Jolin and Peter McCormick (Evanston, Northwestern University Press, 1973), p. 221 (in conversation 1).

5 Kenneth T. Gallagher, *The Philosophy of Gabriel Marcel*, forward by Gabriel Marcel (New York: Fordham University Press), 1962. See Marcel's foreword to Gallagher's book, p. vii, and referring to page 84 of Gallagher's text.

6 Gabriel Marcel, *The Mystery of Being*, translated by (Chicago: Henry Regnery Company, 1960), vol. II, p. ix. "The Hegelian idea of history, which is the source of the vilest idolatries of our time, is only a counterfeit or a perversion of a much more profound thought, a thought which cannot be embodied without the help of myth—the price we have to pay for our own condition which is that of incarnate beings. Here it is that philosophy reaches it boundaries, and awaits the first glimmers of the fires of revelation."

7 Ibid., Vol. II, 204-205.

8 These two works, the play and the philosophical essay, form a very good ensemble for such a Catholic Studies program. The play raises certain fundamental religious and personal questions about human existence, upon which the philosophical essay reflects. And they have recently been translated and published under one cover: See: K. R. Hanley,"*Gabriel Marcel's Perspectives on the Broken World*, mentioned above in note 3.

9 K. R. Hanley, *Gabriel Marcel's Perspectives on the Broken World*, p. 195.

10 K. R. Hanley, *Gabriel Marcel's Perspectives on the Broken World*, p. 196.

For Siegfried Foëlz, to seal the
unforgettable encounter
(Dresden, April 1969)
and
for Father Marcel Belay
whose understanding is only
equalled by his charity.

Their friend,
Gabriel Marcel.

Preface

In an article on Gabriel Marcel titled "Un exemple" (An example), Étienne Gilson wrote: "In philosophy as elsewhere, only what is authentic endures, and that is why, like Montaigne, Pascal, and Maine de Biran, unquestionably Gabriel Marcel will always attract readers. Person speaks directly to person in his work, which will always have readers because he will always make new friends."[1]

That is also why it is practically impossible to single out one book, or certain passages from any one of them, no more than it is possible to separate the philosopher from the playwright or from the musician. His work is an organic whole that cannot be fragmented. This is undoubtedly the essential quality of any thought that is profound and bound to endure.

This does not mean that every reader interprets Marcel's thought in precisely the same way, nor that he favors the same aspect, however unified the thought may be.

As for myself, I was especially sensitive, and still am, to the fact that Gabriel Marcel is a thinker on the move, an itinerant philosopher. Chance has frequently provided a writer with a fine title, but that is not the case with the book called *Homo viator* (*Homo Viator*). At a time when dogmatisms of every sort flourish (nihilism being only one of them), it is refreshing to come into contact with a work that is like a spring of living water.

What is most surprising is that this vital thought, which is formulated as it were under our eyes, sets itself off from fashionable ways of thinking and current events. I believe that this apparent paradox explains the impressive force that his thought has had throughout the years.

The freshness, the vitality of the work (which particularly concerns me because it touches upon my fundamental theme) has to do, I think, with the intuition that the infinite is reflected in one's private life.

The emphasis that Gabriel Marcel has placed upon personal relationships and on intersubjectivity has certainly contributed to dispelling the clouds of what one could call the false universal. To be sure, there is still much to be done in this area. All who continue this work are indebted to him. Ever questioning his own thought in order to approach more closely the mystery of the person, he wrote these lines: "Drama as well as music must bring about—beyond what is called discursive knowledge—a superior consciousness where our being can be found in all its integrity, and which transcends abstract statements that satisfy pure intelligence."

In my view, those who are rightly worried about the contemporary rift between the rational and the vital will profit by meditating on this observation of a philosopher who is at the same time an artist and, better still, a poet.

Jacques de Bourbon Busset

Note

1 Gilson's article may be found in *Existentialisme chrétien: Gabriel Marcel* (Christian existentialism: Gabriel Marcel). *Présentation de Étienne Gilson de l'Académie française. Textes de Jeanne Delhomme, Roger Troisfontaines, Pierre Colin J.-P. Dubois-Dumée, Gabriel Marcel.* Paris: Librairie Plon, 1947. *Trans.*

Foreword

This morning I dictated the last lines of this work, and now I feel compelled to write, without further delay, a foreword clearly addressed to those close relatives and friends of mine whom I haven't mentioned in the book. I hope that, as I have passed them over in silence, they don't misunderstand my feelings for them. For many I have great affection and at times even genuine tenderness.

The truth is that I didn't want to write my memoirs. I don't possess the essential qualities of a memoirist. Moreover, I would have failed horribly had I tried to portray those whom I knew and loved best.

If they appear in my work at all, it is indirectly and imperceptibly in my characters.

The title of this work reflects my journey or, if you will, my vocation, which I wish to make as clear as possible. If I have felt it imperative to undertake this task, it is, above all, because of the apparently composite character of my work. Experience has sufficiently shown me the difficulty that commentators have had in getting through it.

On the other hand, I have desired to react against a too frequently noticed tendency to remove my work from time, that is to say to take it out of its "factual" context. It seemed to me indispensable to situate it once again but, this time, to accentuate the call of the transcendent which I think I felt from the time of my childhood, through the trials of premature mourning, but which I also heard through the kind grace of music.

Thus, with all these hesitations, repetitions, and omissions, often involuntary, and with some promises forgotten along the way, this book is obviously flawed owing to extremely poor eyesight which has made it painfully necessary for me to dictate the text in its entirety.

Nevertheless, I would like one to feel that it is directed towards the other, towards the unknown brother to whom I confide myself with all my uncertainty, all my tears, but also with this invincible hope, this force of all my being, towards what great light and what great awakening!

10 February 1971

1

A man who has come to the last stages of his earthly existence reflects on his life. First of all, this means that he distances himself from it. Otherwise, how could he think about it? Yet, at the same time, he questions himself about this act, and this means that he wonders how it is possible. Is he truly capable of freeing himself sufficiently from his own life in order to consider it and, even, to judge it? Is he not rather afraid of being a prisoner of some fiction since, after all, this very act of *distancing* is in some way a part of his life?

I asked myself these questions explicitly some twenty years ago in the lectures given at Aberdeen, which appeared under the title: *Le Mystère de l'être* (*The Mystery of Being*). But now I realize that this questioning developed *from my experience* and not, properly speaking, about it.

This is all the more understandable since I was not then aware of having entered upon what I called the final stage of my own existence. Today things are different.

I should note that, for me, this question of the relation of a person to his life had come up earlier, in a theatrical setting. It's the question Geneviève Forgue asked the heroine in act 4 of *Le Monde cassé* (*The Broken World*).

By virtue of the authority with which she feels herself mysteriously invested by her brother Dom Maurice, who has just died in a Benedictine monastery, Geneviève asks Christiane the following question: "Don't you think that an entire part of yourself, the most precious part, the only precious part ... your soul ... has it occupied your life?" And Christiane answers, "No, it hasn't. Rather, some caricature of it has. A false charity that only dictated its lies to me."

As it frequently happens in my work, under the pressure of a dramatic situation and by means of characters with whom, of course, I did not identify, but who were sustained by a kind of sap coming from my inmost depths, I asked myself this question which was only to be articulated philosophically much later: does a person confuse himself with his life, and if the two are not identical for him, what are the relations which unite them? Today, at a time I may call vesperal, I question *my life*, not knowing with any certainty which answer it will be able to give me. So I undertake this book as an adventure whose outcome seems uncertain to me.

My life: and I immediately see that the very meaning of these words is vague.

Reflecting upon these two words: *my life*, I immediately come up against an antinomy.

There is a sense in which it is true to say that every life can be recounted. And there is another more profound one by which we should affirm, on the contrary, that a life cannot be retold.

How do we account for this contradiction? Certainly by recognizing the ambiguity of the term life. In the first meaning, I am referring to chronology: I was born in such a place, on a given day, born of particular parents; I did my studies in a given high school, then in some university, and so on. To provide these details to an interviewer or in answer to a questionnaire is to speak of myself as of someone, a unity among others. There is hardly any need to say or recall that, in our world today, this aspect dominates. We are assured that each of us, in a foreseeable future, will have his surrogate under the form of an index or filing card.

But it is quite clear that an irrepressible protestation surfaces from the depths of my being against this substitution, or more exactly against this pretended equivalence. Though perhaps not able to immediately justify this denial, I deny that my life can be put on a file card; and that is what I mean when I affirm that a life cannot be recounted. What I am in effect saying is that there is in a life that is *lived* something which resists being reduced to entries placed one after another.

It would probably be good to note here that the fact of relating cannot be reduced to a simple chronological exposé. We could say that to say something again is not simply to tell again. Otherwise we would not explain the fact that certain people possess a narrative faculty which others just do not have. To account for one's life is not simply to recount a series of circumstances which followed one another historically.

But personally, when I had to compose, some time ago, an autobiography for a volume that was to be dedicated to me in the USA in the collection Living Philosophers, I encountered the problem, which I don't think I completely resolved, of giving the reader a set of chronological markers; I felt that this was insufficient, and that it would have been necessary to become somehow the novelist of myself, without, of course, there ever being a question of giving myself over to any kind of fantasizing. Goethe's words —*Wahrheit und Dichtung, truth and poetry*—must be applied to every autobiography worthy of the name. But it is precisely this poetic element that I found myself incapable of putting into a work whose only merit is honesty.

I wouldn't even be able to pretend to compensate for this lacuna. On the contrary, I must recognize that I could in no way write this kind of *true novel.* On the other hand, it should be noted that those who will later want to know what I was will have to look for many indications in my dramas and apply some kind of radioscopic analysis upon my characters. This will permit them to perceive—although it has not been recorded—something of my life, something, one should perhaps add, at the juncture of my being.

In such a study, of course, it is advisable to proceed with extreme caution. I'll give a particularly significant example: Daniel Meyrieux of *Le Coeur des autres* (*The Rebellious Heart*). He is a playwright. Can I say, in all truth, that he is myself as a playwright? I think it would be quite wrong to do so. What is true is that, in this play, I have tried to capture the characteristics of the man I would risk becoming if my dramatic creation developed in a certain direction. But even more essentially, I intended to underline as intensely as possible what my relations with my wife would subsequently have risked becoming. I think that, to a certain extent, she recognized herself in this figure that has remained especially dear to me, this combination of a certain modesty, delicateness and sharpness of observation which she possessed. In this play, I was not overly gentle with this possible *me*. Quite the contrary. One generally agrees, I think, that I portrayed him as being truly hateful, especially in his relations with Jean, his natural son, whom Rose pushes to receive in their home after the death of his mother.

I should add, though I am less sure about it, that when I wrote *Le Coeur des autres* in Sens, I was thinking perhaps more or less confusedly that my wife and I would one day be led to adopt a child. But now I must say that it was more than a transposition. It was rather a radical transformation, since I didn't have any natural child, for us to even think of welcoming one into our home.

Le Coeur des autres, which was staged in 1921 at the Théâtre Montmartre and which has never since been performed, is probably one of my least studied plays.[1] Yet I believe that it is, if not one of my better plays, at least one of the more meaningful ones for anyone who tries to discover the point at which dramatic creation takes root in a lived life. The play is a part of an ensemble of plays that I wrote during the three years we spent in Sens, when teaching provided me with great leisure because my class in philosophy at the lycée had very few students in it. We might remember at this time that Robert Brasillach[2] was then my student, not in philosophy, but in the ninth and tenth grades, in those rather absurd courses on morality (an hour a week) which were (unless I am mistaken) done away with some years later.

These years in Sens with my wife were some of the happiest moments of our life.

After my appointment, my aunt, with tireless zeal, went to Sens to try to find lodging for us while we remained in Lugano, in this Ticino to which I have always vowed a veritable predilection. She found an apartment for us which was quite bright and like a house, for on one side it gave onto a shady walkway that surrounded the city and, on

1 This play was performed in 1974 at Le Moyne College, Syracuse, New York. *Trans.*

2 Robert Brasillach (1909-1945), French writer and collaborator tried and executed during the Liberation of France. *Trans.*

the other side, onto a courtyard. The owner was an old madwoman of sorts whom I "portrayed" in my *Divertissement posthume* (The posthumous joke)—the very same one who forbade the renters to dry their feet on the outdoor carpet, because its only use was decorative. With nostalgia, I recall the many hours we spent there reading and listening to music. We were not concerned about the future. We would have to be able to express with words what Schumann translated into music, in an immortal manner, in order to render the intimate happiness that was then our own. The clouds which were to form so quickly on the political horizon were not yet clearly discernible. Certainly the thought of the ruins left by the war did not leave me. I am still shaken when I recall the anguish and indelible sorrows of that time, as illustrated in *Le Regard neuf* (The new look), *Le Mort de demain* (Tomorrow's dead), and *La Chapelle ardente* (*The Votive Candle*), but it seemed to me that, by virtue of my marriage, I had gone "out onto the open sea."

Although these words may come as a surprise to some, they nevertheless translate an essential experience and one which those who study the works I composed at that time will have to consider. By this I mean that, in the years 1919-1922, I had the liberating feeling of being able to give myself without any ideological or metaphysical ulterior motive to the characters who presented themselves to me. And by talking about them here, I come too clearly up against the very mysterious question as to which type of relation truly binds the writer of theater to his characters. That is the question, one recalls, which, almost simultaneously, Pirandello was to treat with extraordinary brilliance in *Six personnages en quête d'auteur (Six Characters in Search of an Author)*. I admire this formidable work, but I would not dare say that it translates in a perfectly faithful way the experience that I had in dramatic creation. I truly think that here there is a mystery that the brilliant dialectic of Pirandello does not, cannot, fully take into account. I elaborated on this point, some years later, in a brief article entitled "Tragique et personnalité" (Tragic and personality), which *La Nouvelle Revue française* published in 1925.

The character of Maurice Jordan, in *Le Regard neuf*, now comes to mind. This passionate father trembled during the war for his son who was fighting on the front, as would a wife for her husband or lover. Here, we are somewhat removed from the stereotyped and, ever since Sartre, all too frequently faint images that have tended to be associated with the word "father." It is evident that in this character's origins one finds the anguish I experienced when I worked for and directed a section of the Red Cross at the time of the war; families desperate for news about their loved ones would seek me out hoping to hear reassuring words. At the heart of the character Maurice Jordan, there is, I think, something of an affective imagination which I might have experienced had I been able to have a son. It seems to me that it is this affective imagination which animates the work with a kind of rhythm that I still feel when I happen to reread this play. But I must immediately add that from this "element"—the word is even improper—it would be quite impossible to deduce the play which cannot in any way be reduced to it. I would not at all be able to say how the idea of the sad Jordan household came to me, this half-starved tutor who had previously married, out of self-interest, a vulgar and rich woman, without taking into account what she would become, without truly expecting that he was chaining himself to a future harpy. He did not foresee, of course, the passionate attachment that would bind him to his son or the ensuing conjugal conflict which would somehow claim the young man as a victim or pawn. What I can say is that, by writing this play and the others grouped with it, I was aware of removing myself from the world of thought at the heart of which my philosophical reflection was until then centered. This kind of innovation was not, however, absolute. Up to a point it was already prepared for by the *Quatuor en fa dièse* (Quartet in F#) and by the first version of *L'Iconoclaste* (The iconoclast), as well as by the two unfinished plays *L'Insondable* (*The Unfathomable*) and *Un juste* (The just one) which were to be published some forty years later. Here and there I turned my back on philosophical drama. I had denounced its erring ways in the preface to *Le Seuil invisible* (The invisible threshold) in 1914, but I did not go so far as to say what this condemnation implied.

Please excuse the somewhat meandering character of these thoughts. It would be wrong to think that they are unrelated to my fundamental proposition in this little book. They tend, in effect, to shed light on the narrow relation that binds my work to my life and my characters to myself. And, if I insist on this point, it's because I want to criticize rather directly the very unclear image of those who look upon me simply as an "existentialist philosopher." What is even more absurd is the conception of me as a Christian opponent of Sartre who would emerge, after him, during the years that immediately followed World War II.

I will certainly have the opportunity to explain clearly my motivation for refusing to be called an existentialist, but I must still emphasize right now the central importance of the theatrical *given* in my life. I must say this despite a kind of continuous frustration I suffered from as a dramatist while the philosopher, on the contrary, profited in the very beginning from a fullness of sympathetic comprehension which I was far from expecting when in 1927 I published the *Journal métaphysique (Metaphysical Journal)*. It was then that, on the insistence of Jean Paulhan, I published a collection of Notes which I had not previously considered worthy of publication, but which was merely to be used in the near future for the writing of a philosophical work which would be my doctoral thesis.

I must add, however, that probably in 1927 I had become aware of what was specific in my contribution to contemporary philosophy. I had probably taken into account that it would have been contrary to any deep tendency on my part to try to construct anything which might resemble a system; and under these conditions the publication of the *Journal métaphysique* gave the impression of taking a particular stand.

On the other hand, I am not at all sure that I accounted for, at least clearly, the essential connection which linked my dramatic work to, what I would prefer not to call, my philosophical endeavor. Such words seem pretentious and shock me. It was more a question of adventure than of some undertaking. Though there were interruptions, it was during these moments that I realized I was committed to a search where all that was essential to me was at stake, as was the case, for example, in 1932. I once again experienced, though transposed, of course, the joy of discovery which I had experienced during so many walks ever since the time of my childhood. In this perspective, it doesn't seem useless to say that my first childhood dream concerned my future and the possibility of one day becoming an explorer. Of course, to realize this dream, I would need to acquire physical attributes which I entirely lacked. Nevertheless the direction to which this childlike wish corresponded was unquestionably mine. As proof I need only mention my taste for reading music, which I enjoyed for so many years—and in an all together different area, the constant care I was to reveal as director of the series Feux croisés through which I wanted to find new authors.

I must always emphasize the word *find.* But I must add, it seems to me, that it wasn't simply a question of finding for myself and for the pleasure that the find gave me, but conjointly of having others benefit from the fruits of my discovery. I was, of course, bitterly disappointed when another didn't seem to appreciate sufficiently this *good* which I had believed him worthy to share with me. I not only clearly remember but I feel quite literally the disappointment in the precise meaning of the word that I then experienced. In some way I remained appalled. For me it was as though the very being of what I had wanted to communicate had been profaned, even desecrated, by the lack of understanding I had encountered. It would perhaps be more exact to say that it was the intimate relation between myself and this melody, this poem or this landscape which presented itself to me as though altered by the fact that the other had shown himself unworthy to recognize what I considered its irreplaceable and unique quality. And, of course, my relation to this other was subsequently affected affected.

This is the first time, I'm quite sure of it, that I happened to think about the kind of disappointment that I often experienced, especially, it seems to me, during my adolescent years. It was then, of course, one of the ways by which I became aware of a vulnerability which, upon reflection, I would be led to think, was one of the most characteristic dispositions of my being.

Yet, on the other hand, what I think I see is that experiences of this type called into play the triadic relation that I was to concentrate upon during World War I under conditions that I will probably have to clarify later on.

As regards these same experiences, I also noticed the need I always felt, when I had made a discovery, of associating myself with someone to whom I felt close, instead of keeping this treasure all to myself or burying it. Today I question the true nature of this need. Was it not, at least in a few cases, as though I needed to have a confirmation of the approval that I expected to find from him or her in whom I had confided my discovery. Then, were the approval denied, I saw myself thrown into some unbearable doubt, at least until the time when a better opportunity would arise and free me from it.

This is a plausible interpretation, and yet I am rather certain that it is inadequate. And I wonder whether it does not ignore what is essential, that is to say the fact that I have always, yes always, ever since my early childhood, wanted to feel myself in harmony with the other. This musical image is, I think, the only apt one.

Upon reflection, it seems to me clear that this aspiration has its origin in the very conditions in which I grew up. I am emphasizing the fact that I was an only child and that, for a very long time, though I had some playmates, I had no friends. I distinctly remember the strong regret I felt, from my early childhood, of not having a brother or sister. For me this was a frustration which aggravated another one which was much less expressly felt and which followed my mother's death on 15 November 1893. Three weeks later, I was to celebrate my fourth birthday.

I say that this frustration was not and could hardly be expressly felt, because I was immediately taken in by my grandmother and my aunt who showed me a tenderness and care that could not be surpassed.

But I think that what I discern today is the somewhat passionate—by this I mean nearly boundless—character of the attachment my aunt gave me from the moment she took charge, not only of my education, but of my very being.

It would be quite exact to say—and perhaps I see this rather clearly for the first time—that she felt herself passionately responsible for me, that is to say responsible for what I would be and for what would happen to me.

Responsible towards whom? Should I say that it was towards her deceased sister whose child she had taken in? Possibly. But I tend to think that the truth is at once more hidden and contradictory: the more I think about it, the more it seems to me that she felt herself responsible for me towards a God in whom, however, she didn't think she believed. How can one otherwise explain that, early on, she demanded that I make in her presence an examination of conscience where I would reveal every thought and deed. How can I not then conclude that, though she never admitted it to herself, she seemed to be the one and only mediator between Transcendence and the child to whom she felt she had given herself entirely. In return, she felt he should give himself over entirely to her.

Would it be fair to say that, in adopting such an attitude, she showed herself unduly possessive? I am convinced that had she so been reproached, she would have judged it iniquitous. For she was convinced, no doubt about it, that it was *not for herself*, for her personal satisfaction, that she was so demanding, even to the point of being intransigent, but that it was for me, to protect me from myself. Some will probably conclude that it was an illusion and that she was not clear as to the nature of the domination she intended to exercise over me. Even today I feel myself incapable of deciding whether this depreciative interpretation is or is not justified. In it I rather see an example of the fundamental ambiguity which appears to me to be inseparable from every situation where the self prevails. That is what Antoine Sorgue was to express some fifty years later in the final scene of *L'Émissaire* (The emissary). I'll discuss this later, since it is perhaps there more than anywhere else that one may find formulated the fundamental assurances which painfully emerged for me from my life.

But how did I react to the demands made upon me? When I look over this distant past, this is what I clearly see: to her passionate demands I responded passionately. From that time on, I detested ingratitude. I was too clearly aware of all that had been given me not to respond, unreservedly, to what was certainly more of an injunction than a request. But how could I have, in my inner most being, questioned myself about the legitimacy of this injunction?

The circumstances were to notably accentuate what I will call the tragic character of the situation, and I now wonder whether it was not foundational for my later development. Now, as I look back, the contours appear with a sharpness and *firmness* that they didn't seem to have when I was a child, since I was so given over to sadness and nostalgia.

Reflecting on what I have just written, I would say that this situation probably appeared at certain times of crisis much like a precipice that one has walked along in the mist but which a sudden break of light reveals, and suddenly the walker is overcome with vertigo, then presently the mist reforms and the vertigo ends.

I was six and a half years old when my father and my aunt decided to get married. Thus, in a certain way, the unity of a broken household was reconstituted. I would no longer visit my father on Rue Général-Foy; he had come to live with us on Rue Meissonier.

Certainly, I don't have to question myself here about the nature of the feelings the newly married couple had for each other. But I became very quickly aware, it seems to me, not only of the profound differences which existed in their ways of seeing and feeling, but also of their antagonism, in a given situation, as in the Dreyfus Affair. That is something I will have to return to. Given these circumstances, I decided that they had married because of me and, quite unwillingly, I thus held myself responsible for a marriage that was, in the end, unhappy. Today I tend to think that the truth was not so simple, but it is no less evident that, had I not been there, they would never have thought of getting married.

I am almost certain that this premature awareness of being at once responsible and not responsible for an event was at the origin and center of the tragic vision which was eventually to take shape in my plays. In 1913 I was even to write a play about this, *Le Petit Garçon* (The little boy), which has never been performed, nor even published, but which will have to figure in my "Complete Theatrical Works."

The situation around which the play gravitates is not identical, but only analogous to the one I myself suffered.

Geneviève Rimbert, deceived by an unworthy husband, has not wanted to divorce him because of her son André. Again, out of devotion to her son, once she becomes a widow, she gives up the possibility of having another life with Philippe Crozant, who loved her and with whom she would probably have been happy. Thus, without realizing it, André has contracted a burdensome debt towards his mother and she will remind him of it at every opportunity, since his future is at stake. Well, André, who probably takes after his father, is not very serious—already he is confusedly sensual, and certainly far from resembling the ideal image of himself to which his mother thought she was sacrificing herself. How could he not revolt against the kind of enslavement in which a tyrannical mother, because of her rights as creditor, intends to keep him until the (desired?) day when he will be able to fly the coop. But André hasn't much courage; it is out of the question for him to blatantly go against her wishes. He even knows quite well that he is indebted to her, but with this awareness he feels a certain gratitude mingled with an obscure resentment.

He is hardly twenty years old and lets himself be seduced by Colette, the wife of the same Crozant, to whom his mother remains all the more attached since she reproaches herself, confusedly, for having previously rejected him. You can imagine then Geneviève's chagrin and indignation when she discovers what can hardly be called a liaison between Colette and her son.

From then on, André will have but one idea, to act in such a way that Crozant will be forced to seek a divorce and then be able to marry Geneviève. Thus will she no longer be, or so André thinks, the sacrificial victim who constantly points to the life she has led for him, the indebted son.

I won't go into the details of the plot: the scandal André willingly provokes will not have, of course, the consequences he expected. Philippe Crozant is now too carnally attached to his wife to have her infidelity, however patent, make him break up with her. Besides, he is no longer thinking about Geneviève for whom he nurtures a secret resentment. And at the end of the play, mother and son find themselves in a torturous tête-à-tête that death itself could not end. I think it useful to reproduce here the greater part of the final scene: whatever the transposition I had recourse to in writing the play, it contains lines which throw light onto what, I dare say, has been my own drama.

ANDRÉ: What's going to become of me?

GENEVIÈVE: We shall be fine together, the two of us. You'll see. I have forgiven everything.

ANDRÉ: Each time you forgive me it seems as though I am smothering.

GENEVIÈVE: I have understood, don't you see, that I had asked for too much and not given enough.

ANDRÉ: Yes, Maman, you have given me too much, much too much.

GENEVIÈVE: No, no, I realize it now.

ANDRÉ: I can't bear your giving me any more.

GENEVIÈVE: You don't understand. I won't ask you for anything more. You will live your own life, André, your own life. Now I will live only for you.

ANDRÉ: No, Maman, I feel that that would kill me. It's too much, you understand, to be someone for whom one lives. You must have other tasks, other thoughts. I'm not strong enough to support so much love.

GENEVIÈVE: You only want to bring us together, Philippe and me, so that you could be rid of me .... My little boy, you still don't believe me, you need only to let yourself be loved.

ANDRÉ: You are still asking too much of me, I was not made to be loved so much, don't you understand ... I was made to be a child among many others, whom one loves, whom one kisses in his bed and cares for when he is sick, and then who gets on with his life— a mediocre life amidst millions of others. Maman, it isn't my fault, you see, if you didn't have other children.

GENEVIÈVE: My little boy, you will get married, you will have children, you too; and I .... Why are you looking away? Oh, it's horrible, I have guessed your thoughts: you see me as the importunate mother-in-law, the tyrannical and odious grandmother ... all I have to do now is disappear.

ANDRÉ, *crying out*: Maman, that would be more terrible than everything; my reason would not survive, it would be madness ...

GENEVIÈVE: Madness!

This play, written at the time of *La Grâce* (Grace) and *Le Palais de sable* (The sand castle), published in the volume entitled *Le Seuil invisible*, in a certain way prepares more directly for the following plays, such as *Le Regard neuf.* My parents who had accepted to pay Grasset for publishing these first plays had agreed that *Le Petit Garçon* be grouped with the other two. But Grasset found the volume too large, and so *Le Petit Garçon* was not included. I think that my aunt either was not truly aware of the play's reference to the drama that had been actually lived or that, had she recognized it, her feelings were not hurt. Needless to say, I was pleased about that.

When I recall the shape of the family milieu in which I grew up (and this often happens to me, especially for some time now), my thoughts turn to my father and to the part he played. There can be no doubt that he had a very real affection for me. But besides being the least demonstrative of men, he considered children as strangers with whom he was truly unable to communicate. For him they were only the embryos—in themselves little worthy of interest—of the adults they would later become. I believe I can say, without exaggeration, that he always intimidated me, although this timidity somewhat decreased from the moment I became more independent and aware of who I was. His intellectual superiority and his immense culture could not but command one's respect; but when he judged something mediocre, he could not hide his feelings. I have never known anyone so radically bereft of hypocrisy. In this sense he had something of Alceste, and one shouldn't be surprised to know that he made a lot of enemies. But, from a distance, how I admired this rightness, this basic integrity. He was in no way vain. It seemed to me that he was really not much concerned about himself or given over to introspection. I add that in the very high positions he held successively at the Council of State, then as minister plenipotentiary in Stockholm, later as director of the Beaux-Arts, as administrator of the Bibliothèque Nationale, and finally as director of the Musées Nationaux, he showed the greatest concern for service to the state. Though he was necessarily liberal and an individualist, he nevertheless had the strictest and most rigorous sense of what his responsibilities were. Today I feel myself all the more committed to remembering him since I am unfortunately quite aware that I did not know how to show him the admiration he merited when he was alive.

Of course I don't want to "canonize" him. While he did have his faults, his weaknesses, which I needn't insist on and which are in part due to the fact that he himself had a very deficient family life—it seems to me that his father was not around much for him, and I am not sure that there was a great intimacy between him and his mother, the great-granddaughter of Mirabeau. He was proud of that family relationship. He had inherited a very beautiful portrait of the great political figure which, after his death, if my memory serves me correctly, we gave, not to the Museum of Aix-en-Provence, but to the Méjane Library which, I think, was still directed in 1926 by Monsieur Aude.

With great emotion I remember the long trip my aunt and I made in a car from Tréminis, where we were on vacation, to Aix-en-Provence, which I then saw for the first time, and where I had the feeling, not exactly of the déjà vu, but of coming to some fraternal shore. Some cousins of my father, the Lucas-Montignys, had always lived in this city where, much later, I was to make the acquaintance of Maurice Blondel.

Sisteron, where my father ran for the National Assembly in 1893, was on our way to Aix. My mother had accompanied him in his electoral campaign and had written her relatives some extraordinary letters full of life and color during what had been such an adventure for her. I can see my aunt placing a flower on a window sill of the hotel where they spent the night and the unspeakable emotion that this gesture gave me is, forty-four years later, still with me. 1893-1970: between these dates, between these moments, separated by such long intervals and by the nearly inconceivable transformation of the context in which my life passed, a kind of very mysterious musical consonance rises up in me, a kind of melody of silence which words cannot express. And I also see myself as a child, in the garden of the grand hotel at Aigle, in Switzerland, where I had come with my aunt and grandmother, and where my parents met us after such a predictable defeat and which I have every reason to believe my father accepted rather matter of factly. But six months later, my mother was taken away from him in two days by a sickness against which one then had, it seems, no recourse.

2

This summer day of 1899 was a terrible date in the life of a child, as I learned that we were going to leave Stockholm and return to Paris. How can I ever forget the heavy heart with which I received this news? As my father suffered somewhat from the Swedish climate and didn't much care for the worldly and formal aspects of diplomatic life, he was going to switch positions with a senior member of the Council of State, Monsieur Catusse. This meant first of all that I could no longer hope to spend vacation in Finland or in Norway. What may seem peculiar is that nothing, or almost nothing, attracted me in the Paris where we were to settle definitively. I also felt that our return would be, sooner or later, followed by my entrance into the lycée, something I vaguely feared since, until then, I had been educated at home. I can't recall whether it was immediately before or after our stay in Stockholm that, for some months, I attended classes at Rue Royale where my fellow students were mainly young girls.

What had I most appreciated in the Swedish capital? Without hesitation I would say the landscapes. I remember a discussion with my father on the topic during a boat ride on the Saltsjön. He was essentially a man of the Midi, the French South, and this somewhat uniform and sad nature bored him. Yet there was something in it that exalted me. But what words could I use to translate that emotion?

I must have expressed myself rather awkwardly. But when I think about what I had lived during that year in Stockholm, I see this: it was as though I had been removed from the humdrum life I was to suffer from so much later on, by the fact of being far away, and on the edge of countries that were still farther away and which attracted me. I see myself, on the Strandweg, contemplating with nostalgia the ships which were going to leave for Hernösand and for Luléå. The power that the names of places had upon me was incredible. How thankful I was, much later, to Marcel Proust who had described this power with such miraculous precision at the end of *Du côté de chez Swann (Swann's Way).*

But in Stockholm I also enjoyed the time often given me to meet the children of the other members of the diplomatic corps: the Danish children and the Italian children and also, but less frequently, the son of the Russian minister who was so pale and blond and who, it was said, was destined to have a great musical career. What prestige he had in my eyes! I was to meet him again fifty years later, in the most unforeseeable fashion. A Russian music critic who had looked at my compositions introduced him to me, thinking that he might be able to help me with them. I learned that Stravinsky had placed great hope in him but that, an inveterate gambler, he had wasted his life. In fact, he did not help me, and I even noticed that he had not at all remembered the French child who had admired him so much.

I think there was a touch of snobbery in all of this, in the pleasure I derived from visiting, at my level, this small cosmopolitan society, but I think that what I especially kept was the fact that I was in no way chauvinistic. I think I can affirm that from this period on I felt I was a European. I only wanted to come into contact with different people who, indistinctly, presented themselves to me as being fraternal.

It would probably have been good to take advantage of this disposition in order to have me learn foreign languages. A certain Miss Wackrill—I'm not sure about the spelling—gave me lessons in English; I had learned a little German, with my grandmother when I was a young child, and I knew a few words in Swedish, but nothing of all that was then developed. Yet today I think I recognize that it was above all in the area of languages that I could have excelled. My tastes led me rather towards history and geography. But such interests were to be discouraged and almost smothered by the constant duty to memorize and the perpetual emulation that life at the lycée represented for me.

Let me summarize: in Stockholm, I breathed. In Paris, from the day that I crossed the threshold of the Lycée Carnot, I lived what today I would call a state of chronic moral dyspnea, and this especially because of the regimen of competition that reigned at the school. I remember my aunt's anxiety on the days when we were told our rankings in compositions, something I truly hated. How could such an intelligent woman place so much importance on a classification which truly meant almost nothing? But for me I felt as though my very being was questioned every time. I must add that my father, who had been an excellent pupil, was also inclined to worry about where I placed and not just about the grades.

But under these conditions, I would say that the subjects taught tended to lose their own value; they simply provided times for one to become nervous. This term which corresponds to a psychological reality that is so irrefutable designates quite well the sickness I continued to suffer from until I first began to study philosophy.

That experience has, of course, made me very critical of our school system. I think that, especially during this particular time, the compositions took on too much importance in the life of the class. Should we then conclude that they should have been simply done away with, as well as the numbered grading system? I must admit that I'm not sure. Some people, in their manic horror of any kind of selection, go to another extreme, one that is perhaps definitively more harmful than the one they aim to fight.

All I can say, and which alone is important in my own perspective, is that it was, without the shadow of a doubt, a very serious mistake to submit me to this certainly evil nervousness by placing too much importance on awards and high rankings in composition. I was a conscientious student. I wouldn't go so far as to say I was naturally so; that might be nonsense. But then I had become a good student or rather made myself one. In any case, I would have done my best, even if my family had shown themselves relatively indifferent to my "rankings" in class. It would have been much better for me not to sense the lycée as a place where work was enforced or that what was taught was being imposed upon me.

I stop in this reminiscence, and I can only wonder. How do the different experiences which I have just recalled contribute positively or negatively to *giving form* to what was eventually to become my work? There is certainly not a simple answer, and I would like at all cost to keep from giving one of these *a posteriori* reconstructions whose fallacious character, following Bergson, I myself have often signaled.

As for Sweden (where, strangely, I have never returned) and the image this country has left me, I think I can say that the continued presence in me of this melancholic landscape of water, stones and birches has contributed to forming something of a north pole in my being. The reading of Ibsen's works was to give an intellectual form, of course, and that without any doubt whatsoever, to what was at first only an affective strain.

Here I note the deep and lasting impression I felt when my father, a remarkable reader, read *An ennemi du peuple (An Enemy of the People)* out loud to me.

I remember that the main character, Dr. Stockman, the director responsible for the thermal establishment to which a little Norwegian village owes its prosperity, discovers that, because of a series of seeps, the waters of the establishment are permanently polluted. It will be necessary to close the house down while waiting for an end to the long and costly repairs that alone could correct the situation. But he encounters the bad will and the bad faith of the town authorities, who refuse to face this situation and to draw the necessary conclusions. From that moment Stockman enters into open conflict with them.

It is evident that, given my age, I understood the play literally and missed its symbolic and ideological character. But what I am certain about is that not only did this case of conscience fascinate me but it also made me discover, in light of the indictment made by Stockman against his enemies, that the majority or mass of people always risk being impermeable to the truth.

I have every right to think that in my mind a rapprochement took place between the Stockman case and the Dreyfus Affair, whose development I had carefully followed, because my professor of music, the sister of the mathematician Hadamard, was a distant relative of Dreyfus.[1] My aunt was herself an impassioned Dreyfusard, and how could I not have been shaken by the thought that an innocent person had been a victim of a kind of military conspiracy and sent to Devil's Island, instead of the really guilty man? I must add that my father,

[1] Jacques Hadamard (1865-1963). *Trans.*

under the circumstances, without properly speaking taking a stance against Dreyfus, adopted a position that was rather different from what then seemed to me the only possible one: he was especially worried about the immoderate disorder into which the Affair was going to throw the country. Did he go so far as to admit that, in order to safeguard public order, it was necessary to sacrifice an innocent person? I am not sure. His thought must have been more complex and more subtle; but for the child that I was, the evidence was simply that he was on the other side. However, as I could not doubt his fundamental integrity, I became very aware of the complex character of human situations. Here again the essentially dramatic aspect of human life appeared. And I found myself rather directly prepared to recognize the irremediable ambiguity of the concrete given, as it was to be the case in my principal works, be it *Un homme de Dieu* (*A Man of God*), or *Le Chemin de crête (Ariadne)*, *Le Dard* (The sting) or *L'Émissaire.*

A little later I was to come across an illustration of this ambiguity at the heart of my family life, when I learned that one of my mother's brothers, Ernest Meyer, then counsel of the Council of State, was going to get a divorce.

His wife, who was to me aunt Aline, was a fine musician, and their shared love of music was at the root of a real friendship between her and my father. He, on the other hand, had the least sympathy for his brother-in-law. Hence his position, which deeply hurt my grandmother. A little blinded by her affection for her son Ernest, she naturally sided with him. She reproached, and somewhat reasonably so, her daughter-in-law for being a rather negligent mother. It was true that she didn't take much care of her daughter, my cousin Madeleine, for whom I had much affection.

I thus had the opportunity to note very directly the radical difference of perception that can exist between people of good faith who are confronted by a situation that is quite difficult and perhaps even impossible to judge objectively. I must add, however, that it was public knowledge that my uncle was an extremely inconstant husband and that his wife's complaints were fully justified—which doesn't mean that she was beyond reproach.

Here again, I found myself initiated into the complexity of life at an age when, ordinarily, at the period about which I am speaking, children normally lived with simple ideas.

I should, however, introduce a related remark here: isn't it especially in believing families, whatever the confession of beliefs they profess, that the child could benefit from this simplified vision of human relations. Well, my father and my aunt were both free thinkers. My father had been reared in the Catholic faith, but had rejected very early on the beliefs in which his teachers had been perfectly incapable of grounding him. I think I can say without exaggeration that the only merit he recognized in the Christian religion was to have inspired, in all domains, countless works of art which he most religiously and fervently admired. Of course he thought a certain anticlericalism à la Homais to be grotesque and despicable.[2] His intellectual guides had been Renan, Taine and Spencer.[3] He was an agnostic. Here again, I should probably express myself with some nuance. I don't doubt for a second that, after the death of my mother, from which I think he never recovered, he suffered most truly from not being able to uphold the idea of an after-life where those who love one another would meet for eternity. The verses he had inscribed on her tomb bear irrefutable witness to his suffering. Nevertheless, with this reservation we may say that this agnosticism gave him some kind of spiritual peace, if not of the heart.

It was quite different for my aunt. The pessimistic poets of the nineteenth century, from Vigny or Leopardi to Jean Lahor and Madame Ackermann, had deeply marked her.[4] This pessimism which

2 Homais is the name of the anticlerical pharmacist from the novel *Madame Bovary. Moeurs de province* by Gustave Flaubert (1821-1880) that was published in 1857.

3 Ernest Renan (1823-1892), Hippolyte Taine (1828-1893), Herbert Spencer (1820-1903). A former priest, Renan is known for his questioning of the divine inspiration of the Bible. After the publication of his *Life of Jesus* in 1863, he was dismissed from his chair at the renowned Collège de France. Later becoming its head, Renan figured greatly in the intellectual life of the latter part of the century. Taine was a literary critic, philosopher, and historian, especially known for his determinism and its application to the study of literature. *Trans.*

4 Louise Choquet Ackermann (1813-1890), French poet, author of *Pensées d'une solitaire* (Thoughts of a solitary woman). Jean Lahor is the pen name of Henri Cazalis. *Trans.*

her reason could not handle was in her, I am sure, like a permanent brand. She would have wanted to be a sincere believer, but she could not. She greatly admired Christians, she found that they alone held an answer which would have been acceptable *if one had been able to admit it without cheating*—and this cheating was impossible for her.

While I recall this set of circumstances which have unquestionably had a deep impact on my life, I tend to be scrupulous, because I risk giving the impression that I was a child who was continually haunted, like a young Hamlet, by thoughts which, all in all, were not of my age. In no way whatsoever would I want to paint here anything that might resemble a romantic and stylized portrait of the child whose decidedly unsettled features I am now trying, at the end of my life and with some anguish, to discern. It would certainly be illusory to try to see him or to think of him in some unified way. As so often happens these last twenty years, I have been using words that come to mind from a foreign language. The epithet *ungeschickt*, better than the French word *maladroit* (awkward) translates, I believe, what was poorly harmonized in me: a kind of perpetual misunderstanding with things, much more than with people, from which I have suffered my entire life. I can still hear the best professor I had at the lycée, the only one along with my professor of philosophy whom I truly loved, Maurice Roger, cry out while seeing me tackle some problem where I seemed to get stuck: "How complicated you are!" It was a kind way of saying, "How gauche you are!" I detested all the games where the body needed to play a major part. In the recreation area of the lycée, I kept to myself, wishing that I would be left alone. My family made praiseworthy efforts to counteract this weakness: I participated in gymnastics and took boxing as well as fencing lessons. During vacation, I later learned to ride a bicycle and to swim, but all these exercises, which I didn't deem suitable, bored me.

Should I conclude that I was a purely cerebral person? I am certain that it would be wrong to think so. What is true is that during my childhood I certainly led a life that was much too *cerebral*. But it was precisely against this life that something in me never ceased to protest. I loved nature; I was a tireless walker. During the school year, I lived for the upcoming vacation that we would spend every year in a different place, and always in the mountains. The doctors forbade my grandmother to go beyond 1200 meters, and I see myself looking feverishly in the Swiss Hotel Guide for some tempting and new place to spend our vacation. It was only later, from the moment I began to travel alone or with friends, that I visited places at a higher altitude I had only dreamed of seeing: Pontresina, Sils Maria, Saint-Luc, Saas Fee ... This dream of being outdoors in the mountains was so intense that for some years I lived in an imaginary kingdom with these valleys, mountain tops and villages. I would find it every night, in going to sleep, but I believe no one ever knew anything about it.

I didn't live in the clouds, and I wouldn't even suggest I was a dreamer. But as I remember my years in the lycée, the image that comes to mind is that of my pulling a cart day after day without complaining.

Here again, I would like to keep from exaggerating. My life was not that of some slave on a boat. I was allowed a few distractions, but less frequently, much less frequently, did I get to the theatre. Each time it was a celebration that I looked forward to far in advance. At first there was an extravaganza: *Les Sept Châteaux du diable* (The seven castles of the devil). The following year, *Les Fourberies de Scapin* (*The Trickeries of Scapin*) and *Le Malade imaginaire* (*The Hypochondriac*), at the Comédie-Française. A little later, *Cyrano de Bergerac*. I broke into tears when I heard Coquelin Aîné tell Maria Legault in the last act:

> *Non, non, mon cher amour, je ne vous aimais pas!*
> (No, no, dearest Love, I didn't love you.)[5]

The books I read, at least until I was twelve or thirteen years old, were like those of all the children belonging to my milieu. Then came the time when I asked for collections of plays as birthday presents: Greek tragedies that I wanted to have for myself. The complete works of Marivaux, but also the twenty-five volumes of Alexandre Dumas

[5] The line is from act 5, scene 5, of Edmond Rostand's play. Coquelin Aîné played the role of Cyrano and Legault that of Roxanne in 1897 when *Cyrano de Bergerac* was first performed. See Edmond Rostand, *Cyrano de Bergerac. Comédie Héroïque en Cinq Actes, en vers*. Paris: Fasquelle Éditeurs, no publication date given. *Trans.*

père's theatrical works. When it was a question of theatre, I was omnivorous, or nearly so.

I probably dreamed of being a playwright, since I would eventually write plays. I certainly did not think that this could be a profession—but rather an avocation, and I wondered what my main work would be. I liked Greek and even imagined for a moment that I could be a Hellenic scholar. If only one day I could discover some lost plays of Sophocles, or of Euripides, or better still of Menander!

Today I think that nothing truly prepared me for such activity. Of course, I was what one then called an excellent pupil, winning a good number of awards every year, but I wonder whether the exhausting effort that I paid for such success did not in some way go against my nature. Though some family members certainly thought the contrary, I am quite sure that I was not a precocious child. The plays I alluded to revealed no real gift, except perhaps, if need be, *La Lumière sur la montagne* (The light on the mountain), which my parents sent to the poet and critic Fernand Gregh, who found it interesting.[6] Ibsen's influence was noticeable, the Ibsen of *Rosmersholm*, rather than that of *Un ennemi du peuple*. I was then fifteen years old.

I have given to understand that my parents were somewhat concerned about my intellectual gifts and my future. I suffered, no doubt, from being treated as an object. Could I myself be sure that I would distinguish myself in some manner? But I vitally needed someone to have confidence in me. It was like a warmth I could not do without.

I have mentioned my piano lessons. They were very important to me, to the extent that they were lessons on how to read music. My teacher had rightly observed that I would never be a performer. I didn't play that well, and I didn't have enough time to improve on what I could hardly call my technique. On the other hand, I was a good reader, and my curiosity knew no limits. I would add that I was certainly gifted with a musical sensibility that was, if not exceptional, at least not ordinary.

[6] *La Lumière sur la montagne* is preserved in the Carlton Lake Collection of the Harry Ransom Humanities Research Center, the University of Texas at Austin. *Trans.*

I remember rather distinctly what the main stages were on the way which, although I didn't notice it, was to lead to a liberating awareness.

First of all there were the sonatas of Mozart and Beethoven for piano, and this even before I could play the piano myself. With Mozart, I had the strange feeling of being on an equal footing in daily life. In the adagio of the *Pathétique* symphony or in the *Appassionata,* I recognized the voice of our incurable sorrow. It was then, it seemed to me, that for the first time I felt the mysterious thread between the most elevated music and the most deeply lived experience. Later, short melodies of Bach which were within my reach as a beginner initiated me into a work that would play an important role in my spiritual development. Then, after Stockholm, I tackled the Romantics, especially Schumann, whom my father fervently admired, but also Grieg for whom I had an inordinate attachment, because in him I seemed to discover once again that Nordic soul which had revealed itself to me on the banks of the Saltsjöm and of the Maelar.

I take this occasion to note that my father, with his beautiful baritone voice, revealed to me Schumann's *Les amours du poète* (*Dichterliebe*), *La Vie et l'amour d'une femme* (*Frauenliebe und leben*), etc. My aunt accompanied him at the piano, and much later I was to do the same for him. He later expressed the desire to have the score of *Faust* by Schumann placed in his coffin, and that was done. It seems to me that from the distant past I can still hear him sing the celestial melody of *Pater Marianus,* exalting the Eternal Feminine. His desire expressed his unchanged love for the one who had been taken away from him so early on in life.

My aunt was not a musician but she was quite intelligent. By thoughtful effort, she tried to come to some understanding of what was foreign to her immediate sensibility. It was in that frame of mind that she asked Alfred Bachelet, the future author of *Scemo* (Scemo), to come explain certain scores of Wagner. I must have been eight years old then. I would listen seated in a corner of the large living room of the Rue Meissonier, and I discovered the incantatory force of certain Wagnerian themes.

I write these words "incantatory force," and suddenly it seems to me that the very words enlighten me. I have felt the power of incantation since my early childhood in music as in certain landscapes. More rarely in poetry. However, I remember the shock I felt on reading a verse of *L'Énéide* (*The Aeneid*):

> *Et dulces moriens reminiscitur Argos,*
> (... dying, he remembered the sweet land, Argos,)[7]

and I also remember having been aware that, for the first time, at that moment, Latin poetry spoke to me.

I continue to question, to examine this distant past, in order to try to expose this fragment of my being, or if you will, the seed of what, so slowly, I would say today, so much later, has become my work and probably, through it, my true self. And I wonder whether it isn't through my sensitivity to incantation that my reflection helps me to identify it.

Since then, I am not at all surprised that there was a time, when I was about fourteen or fifteen, when I seriously wondered whether my true vocation was not in the field of music. Of course, I was thinking of a life as a composer and not as a performer.

Naturally I shared, somewhat timidly, this thought with my music teacher. The response was disappointing: "Of course you are a musician," I was told, "but nothing allows me to say that you have the makings of a creator." After all, the answer was common sense. Not only did I not insist but I think I felt some embarrassment in the idea that I could have nurtured such a fantasy.

Strangely enough I later learned from a friend, Pierre de Mouÿ, whom I had not seen since my childhood, out of sight for almost fifty years, that my father would have wanted me to become a musician.

With this assertion as a base, I will say that I can see my father later, probably around 1910, listening attentively to my first impro-

[7] This is verse 782, Book 10. Antarës remembers his homeland as he has been struck by a spear that was meant for another. *Trans.*

visations on the piano. I even remember that he promised, if I obtained the agrégation,[8] to give me a machine that would let me record them. But he didn't keep his promise. And besides, since the tape recorder didn't yet exist, I wonder how he could have kept it.

So, among the possible existences which were refused me, there was certainly that of the musician. But how can one be sure that it would have materialized? I would later have proof that the gift of melodic creativity had been given to me, and I'll have the opportunity to talk about it; but in the area of counterpoint or of the fugue I would probably have come up against insurmountable obstacles.

I rather think that music must have remained in me as a nurturing and unexplored source. What I now glimpse, rather than discern, is that at the origin of my work there is a conjunction that is rather difficult to pinpoint between the meaning of dialogue and that of incantation.

In my lectures I have frequently suggested the prestige that the expression "to dialogue" had for me very early on. No doubt this is due, in great part, to my unique childhood situation, which made me suffer so much, during boring walks taken with a German maid along the avenues that lead to the Étoile: I would invent imaginary brothers and sisters, my first characters. The fact of being both myself and my imaginary interlocutor, or even of being him while not being him, gave me a pleasure I never tired of. It was then, of course, that I became a playwright. I think I would be right in saying that in this I experienced rather strongly something like the translation of a need to be everywhere: the fact of being here set off in me the need to be also elsewhere. But it was necessary for this elsewhere to become itself a here. Such is, I am quite certain, the origin of that *Homo Viator* (*Homo Viator*), under whose sign I was to publish one of my most significant books.

But I should probably also add that dialogue could not suffice unto itself, although I was definitely not able to explicitly recognize this weakness. Dialogue was as though magnetized by anticipation, should I say by a "beyond," which would only be freed through a kind of melodic apperception, through a presence which could truly only be

8 A national competitive examination taken in order to receive a teaching position in France. *Trans.*

a song and, without words, comparable, I would say today, to these *Mélodie*s (*Five melodies for violin and piano*), effectively without words, where we find expressed perhaps more perfectly than elsewhere the lyrical soul of a Sergei Prokofiev.

3

In today's ideological climate, however immunized I may be against abuses of Freudian or Marxist thought, there are questions I must answer as I look back upon my past.

The first has to do with what was, in the beginning of my life and even afterwards, my attitude towards society and what one already called the social classes, but also towards money.

My parents were both representative, I think, of the comfortable bourgeois society which didn't question—or hardly so—the right to the privileges it enjoyed.

For my father, at least, I think I can say that it was something he never questioned. In no way was he a man concerned about money. Nor was he what had been called a "sensualist." His life was taken up with, it seems to me, a continuous activity of the mind where reading held a great place, reading that was nearly always serious and which, when it was worth it, he would at times take care to summarize in rather elaborate notes. Every year, and most often alone, he would take a long trip through Europe where it was essential for him to visit in detail both churches and museums. He took no account of the fatigue that such continual travels might cause him. In Spain, for example, he never hesitated to take a round about way on the train in order to see a cathedral.

Other than for books, his only expense was for the paintings he collected in such a way as to create an atmosphere around him that supported his sensibility and even his spirit.

I add that he always carried out in the strictest manner the highest offices he was repeatedly given. His integrity was such that, for example during the brief period that he was the director of the École des Beaux-Arts, he obstinately refused to take into account any recommendations that came to him from every quarter. This was also the reason why he was replaced by a politician who was not at all scrupulous about such matters.

But on the other hand, he could not allow the State to intervene in areas where, according to him, its action would only have been harmful. He was an individualist in the manner of Herbert Spencer, and he was greatly worried about a future that risked being marked by the progress of socialism and turned into some form of collectivism.

My aunt's outlook was rather different. Her father had been a banker before being afflicted with a very serious and long sickness during which my grandmother cared for him with utter devotion. I don't think my aunt ever took a political stance, but I am sure that social inequality deeply shocked her. She habitually practiced that individual charity which today is so severely and unjustly criticized.

As for what concerns me, I think I can say this: I would not have thought, it seems to me, of questioning the social order that I belonged to and which, during the period I am referring to, was stable. Certainly, I knew that poor people existed, and I found it normal for someone to care for them. I must have also suspected that, in a general fashion, the fate of the less fortunate classes left something to be desired, but I had to recognize that judicious social reforms would bring about some solution to the situation. The questions of money, it seems to me, awakened a certain shame in me, and I remember having one day timidly asked, and not without embarrassment, whether we were rich. I was told that we were comfortable.

My parents had me read the *Histoire de la Révolution française* (*The French Revolution from 1789 to 1815*) by Mignet, which was certainly not a good idea. Sometimes this reading provoked a sense of boredom in me and at other times a feeling of horror which must have endured. I could not recognize the faults of the Old Regime. Louis XVI and his family only inspired sympathy in me: I remember the emotion I later felt when I read Lenôtre's study of the "Fuite à Varennes" (Flight to Varennes). Under these conditions, the execution of Louis XVI and of Marie-Antoinette, the death of the young Dauphin, etc., struck me as being horrible crimes that one could not think of justifying. That was, of course, what you would call a touching image of life, but it is impossible to exaggerate the influence that such pictures can exert on a child's sensibility, and it seems to me that I would be lying to myself if I did not truly recognize that they were probably at the root of the sympathy that the royalist cause inspired in me. My father was a Republican in the sense that he regarded the monarchy as irrevocably condemned by history. But he kept a tenderness for the July Monarchy and for those who had been its most enlightened and intelligent supporters, for example, Tocqueville. As for myself, I must say that the Republic meant nothing to me. In it I saw only a set of abstractions that I could not see myself getting upset about.

I must say that this kind of attitude in some way announced or even prefigured one of the salient features of what would become my mature thinking.

French political life of that time seemed bland to me. My father didn't think too highly of the politicians who were in the forefront of things. I am thinking in particular of the radicals and of the anticlericalism of Émile Combes, which he detested. Needless to say I reacted like him at the time of the famous quarrel of the inventories.[1] As absurd as this may seem in hindsight, I then had the impression that we lived in a grayish zone where nothing happened that truly got our attention. I can hear myself saying that we had only some disorder in the Hungarian Chamber to get our attention. It doesn't even seem that the Moroccan crisis of 1905 moved me as much as I was to be by the one in 1911.

I don't think I am wrong when I say that it was at the time of the annexation of Bosnia by Austria-Hungary and of the Balkan wars that I began to take a keen interest in foreign affairs. It was as though I then had the feeling that we were leaving a disgusting period of stagnation. And it is quite true that these events prepared the way for the cataclysm of 1914, but I can't honestly say that I had the least premonition of the upheaval we were going to witness.

[1] This is a reference to the on-going separating of Church from State. Government officials were instructed to inventory movable property of the Catholic Church, a policy that was not easy to implement. See Adrien Dansette, *Histoire Religieuse de la France Contemporaine* (Religious history of contemporary France) Paris: Flammarion, 1965. Pp. 613-616. *Trans.*

My father often met important military leaders at the home of Monsieur Chesneau, director of the French engineering school, the École des Mines, where he enjoyed going on Sundays. From these conversations he reaped a general feeling of anguish. Was it really conceivable, I would wonder, that, in a time of high civilization such as ours, war was possible along with waves of attendant horrors? That seemed almost unthinkable to me. Needless to say I could in no way sympathize with the bellicosity that began to show itself in a small nationalist fraction of the youth. Of course I understood quite well that the loss of Alsace-Lorraine was always felt by some of the best among the French as an incurable wound, but I didn't feel that we could reasonably wish for "revenge." Perhaps—but I wouldn't dare affirm it, because on this point my recollections are not clear—I deluded myself with the hope that, one day, Alsace-Lorraine would be able to obtain a privileged status, indeed, a certain form of autonomy within the German empire.

But if war seemed to me to be a terrible evil that no reasonable man could desire, the relative peace that Europe then enjoyed carried with it no particular luster. It vaguely seemed to me that we were living in an age where mediocrity prevailed.

This probably means the same as saying that I leaned towards romanticism, but, paradoxically, this disposition did not express itself in the political arena by any adherence to either a reactionary doctrine or, on the contrary, to a revolutionary ideology. My state of mind then, to the extent that I can reconstitute it, appears to me finally as an expression, at a rather modest level, of the *unhappy conscience.*

Needless to say this characteristic did not imply, in my mind, that one could apply rigorously to my situation of that time the definition that Hegel gave to the unhappy conscience in his *Phénoménologie de l'esprit* (*Phenomenology of Mind*). Here the words must be taken in a more vague sense; they nevertheless seem precise to me, particularly when I try to answer the second question concerning sexuality. Two points seem essential to me: I was reared in an almost superstitious fear of microbes. Of course, my father not only did not experience this fear, he regarded it with scorn, considering it absurd. While it was also foreign to my grandmother, for reasons that escape me, my aunt neglected no precaution to protect me against the omnipresent and imperceptible enemy.

But in another area and at a time one would have judged totally divorced from the first, in the area of morals, the opposition between what was proper and improper arose at every possible moment. I remember, for example, that when I read with pleasure the two volumes of Molière which figured in the Bibliothèque rose series, I was told that other plays by Molière, such as *L'École des femmes* (*The School for Wives*) and *Amphitryon* (*Amphitryon*) were not suitable, and that I would only be given permission to read them much later. That is but one example among a host of others.

To be completely sincere, I will add, without insisting too much, that the intestinal weakness I suffered from for some time, and the measures taken to fight it, had created an obsessive state in me which was to last for many long years in the domain of the imagination. I wouldn't want to insist too much on this point of my life about which, I can assure you, no psychoanalyst would have anything to teach me. The reading of *Introduction à la psychanalyse* (*Introduction to Psychoanalysis*), at the time following World War II, was to give me the necessary lights to understand my own case in an unexpected and somewhat harmful manner.

But what I must especially retain from all this is the carelessness in the educational domain which contributed, no doubt about it, to awakening and nurturing this obsession in me. I can see myself on certain evenings when my parents dined in town, devouring certain articles in the Larousse dictionary on indecent subjects and, as such, forbidden. I always did admit to my aunt during the examination of conscience the fault I was guilty of and of which I was ashamed.

I shudder retrospectively when I remember the errors that had affected my education. It is certain that during the time I am alluding to I would never have allowed myself to make any judgment about my aunt and the way she treated me. I could almost say that for me she was a sacred figure, and it seemed to me that I owed her everything.

Today, of course, I can see things more clearly, and I note that such mistakes have had an effect on my life that she could not have imagined. But this observation in no way alters the tenderness and admiration that I have always had for her and which remains with me as when she first took charge of me. If somehow miraculously she were to open the door and come to me, I would run to her and hold her against my heart. And that all the more since her life was filled with sorrow. After the death of her mother, in 1919, she often reproached herself unjustifiably and with anguish, even though she had been so attentive to her. After my father's death, it was again the same thing, or nearly so. I think, however, that she learned much in the course of her life and that she liberated herself little by little from a kind of moral rigidity that had been at the origin of her faults. She gave herself increasingly to those who were marginalized, to the unfortunate; she was detached from herself to such an extent that she would not let anyone give her the smallest gift. She never understood that she thus imposed a privation upon those who loved her.

I don't think that I have expressed anywhere else all that I have just written and, yet, it is essential. Just the idea that, in the world to come, I could be separated from her would be intolerable to me. I reject it with horror.

4

If I have felt the need to describe in such detail the moral climate in which I spent my childhood, it is because these clarifications seem indispensable in order for me to understand the situation by which I threw myself into philosophy.

True, my readings had hardly prepared me for what was really a decisive and overwhelming discovery. I vaguely remember having read during the vacation which preceded my entry into philosophy class (in 1906), or perhaps even a little earlier, the *Manuel d'histoire de la philosohie* (Manual of the history of philosophy) of Alfred Fouillée, which my aunt had read one or two years earlier. This reading left me with a poor impression; the history of philosophy resembled a game of massacre where finally nothing made sense.

All that changed once I found myself in the presence of Monsieur Colonna d'Istria, to whom I am still deeply grateful.

Physically, he was not the most handsome man, a dwarf with deformed members. Yet his face shone with blue eyes which, when he smiled, gave forth a strange light.

I can't remember exactly what he told us during this first class, certainly nothing extraordinary. And yet, from that first day, home from the lycée, I told my parents that I now knew what I was going to do: I would be a philosopher. It was only much later that I came to separate the philosopher from the professor of philosophy and even to question in some way the notion of having a teacher of philosophy.

Today when I think about the kind of explosion that my entrance into the study of philosophy meant for me, I believe I especially see this: it's as though I had been suddenly removed from the static world that teaching at the lycée, associated with the rather particular conditions of my family life, had made me a prisoner of, a world where I was smothering. I saw myself transported into an enchanted land where thought—as such—was encouraged everywhere and at every level. Unlike my classmates, I don't think I found any part of the philosophy class boring, except perhaps at the very end, where ethics was covered. Unimaginable perspectives opened up everywhere, and I also discovered that what had seemed to be a given, the *das Selbstverständliche*, was in reality becoming the place for impassioned questioning.

It wasn't that Monsieur Colonna d'Istria was a particularly captivating teacher. Perhaps the best among us found him to be too reasonable or in general ready to adopt moderate solutions which to us smacked of being a compromise. The solutions were in no way exhilarating, but I had in some manner too much of a tendency to criticize the spirit or the letter of such teaching. Later I would see whether I had or had not rallied myself to these lukewarm thoughts. I should add that, generally, at that time, pupils were not allowed to argue with a teacher in class.

But I will add that if, during my years at the lycée, the year of philosophy truly is the only one I fondly remember, it is in great part because, for the first time, I was not obsessed by the idea that I had to outdo my classmates. There was no questioning my superiority. Had I become vain? I can't say, but I don't think so. Then I wasn't so concerned about myself. I mostly concentrated on what was taught, especially when it was not just a question of swallowing ready-made formulas or when some appeal was made to the personal involvement of my mind.

If I had not disliked my teachers in the area of mathematics, I think that mathematics would have been able to satisfy me in much the same way, but unfortunately I found out too late its essential value during the optional classes that Monsieur Chalory gave to a classmate and me. I can still hear the cry of admiration that I let out one day, after an explanation regarding, I think, analytical geometry. Alas! It was too late. I had to take note of it the following year when I tried to take the courses in general mathematics taught by Paul Appell at the Sorbonne. Very soon I had to give up. One of my many complaints against secondary teaching of the time has to do with the radical lack of pedagogical skills which then characterized the teachers of mathematics. They were incapable of understanding why a student didn't understand—they couldn't put themselves in his place—and help him in some way.

It's evident that that is one of the most regrettable lacuna of my intellectual formation. Yet I don't want to say that it hurt my philosophical work. I don't think so. I believe, in any case, that my personal contribution could only be situated in quite a different field and almost without any contact with mathematics, properly speaking. Nevertheless I have always found it humbling to sense that I was so distant from the sciences of my time.

But, as I have said, that isn't the only reproach I make to secondary education at the beginning of the century. Modern languages were not taken seriously and, in the study of history, too much instance was placed on rote memory, etc.

Of course, it is difficult for me to reconstitute the adolescent I became when, to my great relief, the doors of the lycée were closed for the last time. It now seems to be that virtually nothing of what I learned really took any root in me. Perhaps my mistake, and that was excusable, had been to want to sacrifice nothing, and nothing, with the distance I now have, seems less justifiable to me than the kind of encyclopaedic rubbish which then governed the programs. For example, I am thinking of the chemistry formulas that were stuffed into our heads. I have retained nothing of them. Much later, towards the end of the 1930s, when I undertook a study of what I and others called the mishandling of education, the chemistry professors at the Sorbonne with whom I had talked were the first to attack this kind of teaching. According to them, it was not only useless but harmful. And it was precisely in the field of chemistry that I had suffered so much.

When I began my studies at the Sorbonne, in early November 1906, I experienced a kind of bewilderment at the thought of all the courses in the program among which I would have to choose. The licentiate program was then so vast, but also very flexible! Of course, as preparation for the tests in French and Latin, I took some courses of Lanson[1]

[1] Gustave Lanson (1857-1934) was known for his *Histoire de la littérature française* (History of French literature). *Trans.*

and Courbaud. But the essential was elsewhere. I particularly remember the lectures of André Lalande,[2] whose colleague at the Institut I was to become almost a half century later. Some of the pupils were called upon to present a given theory of a great philosopher; others were to make a critique, not of the presentation, but of the theory itself. I was modest by nature, and I would have preferred to present the theory rather than to criticize it. But I went about things too late, and I was given the task of criticizing Schopenhauer's theory of free will. I think this was my first public presentation. I tackled it with some timidity.

I believe I lost a lot of time that year. I would sometimes go to the Sorbonne library. I would rummage about looking for something to interest me but I couldn't settle on anything, and that was painful since I was naturally conscientious.

I would have conversations with several students. I remember Pierre Dufet, a big reddish boy, very much taken with Renouvier and who was later killed during World War I. There was also Émile Schloesing, a future minister, more quiet and astute, who was later to be the godfather of Anne Boegner, before she married my son and converted to Catholicism.

It seems to me that it was during this first year at the Sorbonne that I was invited to the Sunday meetings given by Xavier Léon, director of the *Revue de métaphysique et de morale*, in his apartment on the Rue des Mathurins. His wife and he were hospitality itself, and I will always think of them with gratitude. It was there that I especially met the major philosophers of the time and especially Léon Brunschvicg who was a close friend of Xavier Léon.

Was it there that for the first time I met Henri Franck, the future poet of *La Danse devant l'arche* (The dance before the ark)? I can't affirm it. I had heard my uncle, Édouard Meyer, who had cordial relations with his father, say that he was an exceptional person. I approached this rather young man with respectful fear since everyone thought he would have a glorious career as a philosopher and probably as a poet. Next to him, I thought I was nothing: I was only a bundle of mixed desires while he was already a master of his form.

[2] French philosopher (1867-1963), author of *Théorie de l'induction et de l'expérimentation* (Theory of induction and experimentation). *Trans.*

He was a student at the École Normale, whereas I had absolutely refused even to consider preparing for the entrance tests. Once again that would have meant competing, something I so hated. I also thought, and with reason, that were I ever accepted into the school, I would have been taking the place that should have gone to a young man from the provinces whereas my family already lived rather nicely in Paris.

Good Henri Franck! He was never condescending towards me and, finally, I found myself on the same level as he, as the letters we wrote each other indicate and which were published posthumously.

He had been the student of Alain, who in no way encroached on his independence. Goethe, it seems to me, had marked him early on. In him there was the harmony of lyricism and of a certain smiling reason, perhaps rather close to that of Montaigne. He was the first to reveal to me the Claudel of *L'Arbre* (The tree), and the Gide of *L'Immoraliste* (*The Immoralist*) and of *La Porte étroite* (*Strait is the Gate*), and even, I now remember, the Giraudoux of the *Provinciales* (The provincials). For me Henri Franck was an opening onto something else. He had certainly been a brilliant student at the lycée but, it seems to me, without ever having taken much trouble to succeed. Is it an exaggeration to say that, next to him, I had the air of being a scholarship winner.

I don't think it's an exaggeration to say that at that time, between 1906 and 1912, the date of his death, he was the one who, before Bergson, exercised the greatest influence over me. And yet, as I write these lines, if I ask what this influence was, I remark that we are in the area of the indefinable. What I can say is that I can still see that sharp face, those gray-green eyes—at least it seems to me—which were sparkling with intelligence, and I can still hear that voice which was marvelously clear and yet not too high. He was the first among several friends who were for me remarkable companions.

What characterized him, and he loved to let it be known, was his dual heritage: he declared himself to be both Jewish, and proud to be Jewish, and French, and proud to be French. Had he not fallen victim to pulmonary pneumonia in 1912, I am convinced that he would have died as a second-lieutenant in the reserves, killed at the head of his section in the first battles of 1914.

Here again, I must ask: why do I need to remember this companion, whose friendship I lost so early in life, whereas what I am pursuing here is a meditation on myself and on my work?

But that is exactly why I cannot and do not want to separate myself, even in thought, from those whom a mysterious fate or providence incorporated into my life.

If I have been led much later on to emphasize, perhaps I must even say place, such a provocative accent on intersubjectivity, it is in the name of an experience that was reinforced or confirmed by the reading of Royce and of Hocking, and which has challenged Proust's monadism.

Of course today the word *presence* is often wrongly used, but if beyond this more than half a century, beyond this universal upheaval, I still salute Henri Franck and declare him present, I am not resorting to a literary artifice which would seem disparaging to me: what I utter is an invincible existential assurance.

I don't want to say, of course, that there are not times of weakness when such an assurance grows faint and tired. But to the extent that I remain faithful to the thoughts which have sustained me, and which, I will add, have aided many people scattered throughout the world to fight their difficult fight, I hold that this weakness can be imputed to the mortal part of myself; and I concentrate myself on what is a *sursum*, more than on a *sum*.

What we were to tell ourselves, in 1961, W.E. Hocking and myself, in the solitude of New Hampshire, when we recognized ourselves to be "companions of eternity," I say again of Henri Franck and myself; and in saying it, I have the strange feeling of obtaining a kind of victory over this scattering element which is at the heart of all our denials.

Should we then conclude that our ways of feeling and thinking were in unison? Certainly not. This dual belonging about which I have spoken could not quite describe me. How could I have thought myself Jewish when my father was not and when, on my maternal side, no trace of Jewish belief remained? Certainly I was French, but without professing anything which could resemble some kind of nationalism. I will say, while excusing myself for this pedantic expression, that my categories were different and that I truly felt myself to be already very deeply European. But I should add that my own world of thought was then still vague, whereas Henri Franck seemed to me to have emerged into full light: his poem, *La Danse devant l'arche*, testifies to that. Hence my admiration that was like the heart of my friendship for him, but this didn't mean that I felt obliged or could simply join him in his own luminous kingdom.

He had had an infinitely more harmonious childhood and adolescence than myself: he had a beloved country, the province of Béarn, whereas I felt tied down to this Paris that I hardly loved but didn't dream of leaving.

Yet I question what I have just written, and a scruple comes to me: have I not unduly exaggerated the place he has held in my life? After all, we were quickly separated. Of course not; what is undoubtedly true is the admiration he inspired in me and which, however, did not place any distance between us, even when our philosophical differences became evident. It seems to me that he remained in the line of Spinoza, and I, from that period, I was moving towards the recognition of Christ, of the Incarnation at a determined moment of History. Yet I was still quite far from confessing any particular faith.

During a course I was taking to prepare for the agrégation—this must have been in 1909—I remember quite well that I insisted on the distinction of the three stages: esthetic, ethic, and religious. Here I must ask a question for which I have no categorical answer. What did I then know of Kierkegaard? What is certain is that I had not read a line of him. I only knew him through the several pages that Höffding dedicates to him in his rather mediocre *Histoire de la philosophie moderne* (The history of modern philosophy).[3] Well, they did not impress me at all, and I clearly remember that I didn't understand what the qualitative dialectic was that he accentuated so much. Today, however, it seems to me that I probably took from him the distinction of the three stages. Yet it's true that, at that time, I was not trying to know more about the Danish philosopher, whose work, it should be said, was not then readily available.

The true question here—as that is the case in most analogous circumstances—is to understand why the distinction of the three stages made such an impression on me, even though I had had no kind

[3] Harald Höffding, Danish philosopher (1843-1931). *Trans.*

of religious experience. It would be inadequate to say, as one could be tempted to do, that I had been led to it by the readings made at the time of my graduate studies. That would be to hold onto considerations which are, in the end, of little significance and to ignore what, forty years later, one would have quite aptly called the existential character of a search that, it must be said, was not at all easy to articulate.

In the area of real life, it doesn't seem useless for me to remember that after the first six months of student life, during the Easter vacation spent along Lake Geneva, I began to suffer from a cervical adenitis which poisoned my life for years and, at the time of the war, made me unfit for military service.

Nevertheless, I successfully passed the exams for the licentiate and for the diploma for higher studies, and on the first try I passed the exams in 1910 for the agrégation in philosophy.

These four years certainly left me with better memories than those that had preceded. It was truly as though I was letting go.

One may wonder why I chose as my thesis for the diploma of higher studies *Les Idées métaphysiques de Coleridge dans leur rapport avec la philosophie de Schelling* (The metaphysical ideas of Coleridge in their relation to the philosophy of Schelling).[4]

My first idea, after the licentiate, had been to write something on Bradley.[5] But it so happened that the subject had already been taken by Fr. Beauregard, who was to die prematurely and, unless I am mistaken, without completing his project.

What was it that attracted me to Bradley? I can only answer this question conjecturally. I think, without being able to confirm it totally, that what got my attention in the author of *Apparence et réalité* (*Appearance and Reality: A Metaphysical Essay*) was a very vigorous sense of the metaphysical affirmation, accompanied by a reflection which dealt with the traditional given of Anglo-Saxon psychology, but which brought about its true transmutation.

The research I then undertook on the relations between English thought and German speculation during the nineteenth century led

[4] This work has just been published with the title *Coleridge et Schelling* (Coleridge and Schelling). Paris: Éditions Aubier, 1971.

[5] Francis Herbert Bradley (1846-1924). *Trans.*

me to recognize Coleridge's role as a precursor and the place that the borrowings from the author of *Système d'idéalisme transcendantal* (*System of Transcendental Idealism*) held in the *Biographia literaria.*

I then went energetically to work. In my mind, this dissertation was to be something like the first chapter of a history of the relations between English and German thought in the 19th century.

The fact that I was able to conceive this ambitious project, which I was to turn away from rather quickly, shows to what extent I was not yet then clear about the true direction of my philosophical vocation. Certainly I wasn't so pretentious as to believe that one day I would be able to create a work important enough to make me the head of a school of thought or anything like that. My intention, which became much clearer to me during the years that immediately preceded World War I, was to pursue a certain research whose essential task was to clarify, that is to say to make intelligible an order of religious affirmation that presented itself to me as being unquestionable, although I began to clearly understand that it was not necessary to think of integrating it into any kind of Hegelian system.

I had sat for the competitive examinations in August 1910 when it was unbearably warm, and they had left me in such a state of fatigue and exhaustion that I could not think of immediately taking on a teaching assignment. I first had to consider improving my health.

I've kept a clear picture of a solitary excursion I made a few weeks later on Lake Champex, and I can see myself during the long descent towards Martigny, being quite aware of the *here-now*, which was mine at that moment, and of the fact that it would later become a *then*, but on the basis of what other *here-now*? It presented itself to me as though hidden behind some impenetrable fog. This was truly to recognize the mystery of time, should I even say the mystery of temporal distortion, in a dimension that was certainly not one of personal duration. What impressed me even more was the discontinuity of the *presents*. But how this plurality shocks us! Isn't the present dedicated by definition to singularity?

Perhaps this is the place for saying that the mystery of time is certainly at the heart of all that I have ever thought. Yet I have not at all succeeded in encapsulating it in any thing that could resemble a theory. I think this is what Peter Grotzer understood when, towards the middle of the 1950s, he wrote his thesis *La conscience du temps dans la pensée de Gabriel Marcel* (The awareness of time in the thought of Gabriel Marcel) for the University of Zurich under the most comprehensive direction of my good friend Georges Poulet.[6]

Perhaps I will have to come back later to what, in my view, is this ever more enigmatic characteristic that presents in reality what we are inconsiderably led, I think, to look upon as our temporal frame.

Since the doctor recommended a stay along the sea to strengthen my weakened health, I decided, with the approval of my parents, to spend a few weeks on the English coast. Such a stay would at least have the advantage of giving me the opportunity to perfect my knowledge of English. And so I had two vacations: one in Saint-Léonard, the other at Bournemouth, with an interim of a few weeks at Mont Pèlerin, above Vevey. On second thought, it seems that I have inverted the order of these different stays. Little does it really matter. What I clearly remember is the uncontrollable spleen that I experienced in these well-to-do bathing resorts along the English coast. My hosts were qualified representatives of what there could be that was most narrow and insipid in the British mentality. I can still see myself running along the sea and turning to look towards France from which I felt myself exiled. Only walks into the interior, towards Battle Abbey and Bodiam, introduced me to the charm of the English countryside. I have always had a liking for it, and this has been translated by the passionate interest I have for Anglo-Saxon literature that later showed itself in my direction of the collection Feux croisés.

The healthy character that was associated with these stays contributed, doubtlessly, to make them seem odious to me. I hardly cared for my body; it was burdensome to me.

6 Peter Grotzer oversaw the publication of three volumes of the philosophical works of Gabriel Marcel with the publisher Schoningh, Paderborn, Germany. *Trans.*

Considering the different people I was able to meet during these months of forced leisure, the most meaningful encounter was, by far, made at Mont Pèlerin, during Christmas vacation, with Major Piercy. He had arrived with his family some days before. It was on a Sunday morning, in the little salon to which I had escaped, while most of the hotel's guests were at Sunday services, where he found me and engaged me in conversation. He had learned that I was a philosopher, and he wanted to tell me his story, one he judged likely to interest me. Certainly, he was not wrong, and his story was to have the most lasting effect on me. He confided that the person who had accompanied him was his second wife. The first was deceased. He had adored her, and being then without any precise belief in an after-life, he had thought about following her to the tomb. Yet, she had left him with three children that he had no right to abandon. Some friends suggested that he find a medium who perhaps would be able to put him in communication with his deceased wife. To be at peace, he followed the advice without really hoping to attain the desired result. However, he was alarmed by some curious experiences that I won't comment upon. What is important is that he had come to communicate inwardly—while no longer having recourse to a medium—in an almost constant fashion with his wife whose death had at first almost destroyed him. He told me enough about it to make me sensitive to this kind of *con vivencia* he experienced. I purposely use this beautiful Spanish word, which unfortunately has no equivalent in our French language. It was at the request or the express recommendation of his beloved wife—I can't truly say of the dead woman—that he had decided to remarry for the good of the children. This man gave the feeling of being quite happy and of having found his equilibrium. From this second marriage came a child, and the young wife gave the impression of being peaceful and, I would say, profoundly joyful.

A native of Herefordshire, Major Piercy possessed extensive property in Sardinia, on the coast of Golferanci. He invited me to visit him one day. It isn't easy to console myself for hesitating to go. I was afraid of being indiscrete or was held back by some type of shyness.

The young playwright I then was could not keep from wondering about the state of mind of the young woman, in the presence of what one is almost forced to call a case of bigamy. Useless to say that I never had any conversation with her and that, in any case, I would never have dared bring up such a delicate matter. But this situation was to turn up in *Le Porte-glaive* (The sword bearer) that I wrote during the war, and which was only the first version of *L'Iconoclaste* published some years later, and which has never been staged.

5

I interrupt this recollection, perhaps too closely directed by chronology, to indicate the title which came to me two days ago and which, in its interrogative form, states rather well, I think, my intention which has never changed since I started this work.

On the Road, Towards What Awakening?

Or perhaps

Towards What Dawn?
Towards What Light?

What this title infers is the thought of a journey which does not let itself be confused with some kind of wandering about. And here I indicate as clearly as possible one of my principal objections to Heideggerian thought.

Of course, as a physical being, I am drifting towards death, without being able to talk about anything which might resemble a finality. I think that here the idea of a death instinct substantiated by Freud is of such a nature as to mislead the spirit: supposing that it has some foundation, it can only be on the level which is not and which cannot be that of the spirit. Besides, I somewhat hesitate to use a term that is so awkwardly ambiguous. What it designates for me can only be a certain conjunction of reason and love, that our vocation, after all, can only institute, and only under conditions whose precariousness cannot be too clearly acknowledged.

In clear terms, I will say that in a line of Freudian thought, to die is truly to undo oneself, whereas in the other line of thought, it is to accomplish oneself. But the idea of accomplishment is not itself free of ambiguity, far from it, and we should consider more attentively and treat more rigorously than is usually done the thought Mallarmé has expressed in a line that is now famous:

Tel qu'en Lui-même enfin l'éternité le change
(As into Himself at last eternity changes him)[1]

What can we then understand here by eternity? We should be careful about the word being given an infinitely vague meaning that would disappear, in some way, upon reflection. What is aimed at in this verse of Mallarmé, isn't it an absolute judgment which would almost infallibly emerge from the moment that the finite creature has disappeared, whether it be to disintegrate totally or not? But how can this absolute judgment be articulated? What conscience or supraconscience is capable of uttering it? If we hold on to the data of historical consciousness, what we see is quite different and doesn't let itself be schematized in such a way. We see that the historian or, as is the case, the biographer must undertake an infinitely detailed work, examining texts of every kind that are available to him and particularly accounts that he must weigh or, more exactly, counterweigh, since it is a question of appreciating their respective strength whenever there is some discrepancy. It can hardly be a question of going beyond approximations which are not always convergent in order to delimit, rather than attain, the *ipséité* that is being questioned.

These are very general and even banal remarks, but we should always keep them in mind, when we are talking about accomplishment. For after all, to accomplish means, or should mean, to accomplish oneself. And it is the reflexive pronoun which is problematic. I am thinking for example of Bernard Berenson who, at the end of his life, regretted having dedicated himself entirely to research in art.

[1] The first verse from the poem *Le Tombeau d'Edgar Poe* (*The Tomb of Edgar Poe*), by Stéphane Mallarmé (1842-1898). See *Stéphane Mallarmé. Selected Poetry and Prose.* Edited by Mary Ann Caws. New York: A New Directions Book, 1982, p. 51. *Trans.*

Although he had become famous, he let it be understood that he should have followed another path which would have perhaps been more authentically his own. What position could the biographer take when faced with such a declaration? It seems to me that he can only reproduce it, without trying to confirm or, much less, contradict it.

When I look back to the years which followed my success at the agrégation and which immediately preceded World War I, I am led to think that I made the decisive choice on which my entire life was to depend. I don't think I was wrong in choosing the path which was to become mine, but it is certain that I didn't then have the least idea what the conditions would be under which I would pursue the path whose groping beginnings I have such trouble reconstituting today. I remember that there were times when I literally wondered what I was looking for and whether my research had any meaning. My friend Michel Alexandre, who was to become not only a faithful but exemplary disciple of Alain, was then the best of confidants for me. Seeing that he understood me, I found myself reassured. A little later—it must have been in 1913—I submitted a collection of notes to my teacher Victor Delbos for his opinion. The encouragement he showered upon me, and which I so needed, gave me the strength to continue. I truly don't know what would have happened had he told me he was not interested, and perhaps found no meaning, in the texts I had passed on to him with some trepidation. Yet this is the place for me to render homage both to the flawless intellectual integrity and to the extraordinary modesty of this historian who has remained, in my view, an unforgettable example. He believed he saw in my research a prolongation of the thought of Biran, for which, as he was philosopher and believer, he had, I think, a predilection, and, in a certain manner, I don't think he was mistaken.

I won't spend much time here on my first year of teaching at the Lycée de Vendôme which was interrupted for a few months by sickness, nor on the time I then spent at the École Foyer des Pléiades, north of Blonay, where I was associated with the work of the director, Robert Nussbaum, a lively and curious person whose pedagogical ideas owed much to Decroly and to the founder of the *Odenwald*

Schule. Looking back, I can't clearly see how I benefited intellectually from this somewhat aberrant pedagogical experience.

I clearly remember the satisfaction, even the relief, I experienced on my return to Paris after my summer vacation in 1913. I had obtained the renewal of my leave and planned on dedicating myself completely to the preparation of my thesis, not without taking full advantage of the resources that Paris then offered, especially in the area of music and theatre. This entire period was to be filled for me with a euphoric feeling that I would hardly experience later on. This says how far I was from sensing at that time the catastrophe which was in the wings.

Today I would be incapable of rereading what was later to become the first part of the *Journal métaphysique*, and if I forced myself to do so, it would not be without experiencing almost at every page a feeling of irritation that I would not be able to master successfully. Of course I recognize that a philosophical reader, who would have become familiar with my later work, would be able to discover in these notes the beginning of thoughts that I was to develop later on. He would certainly be right to so judge them. But what strikes me is how this research that is so abstract and so awkward depended in the end on the safe and comfortable conditions in which I then found myself.

Of course, in all this there was an attraction that is clearly impossible to ignore. How can we express, without weakening it, the kind of global affirmation that supported, so to speak, what I would be almost tempted to call my wandering, or *divagation* in its etymological sense? I believe I can say that this affirmation became one with me, that it was the deepest part of me, and that at the same time I experienced an uneasiness, or at least some worry, as soon as I detached it from me to consider it. It could not be separated from the invincible confidence that the work of Bach gave me, his cantatas that I would buy on the Rue de la Chaussée-d'Antin, at the store which was then a seller for the Breitkopf publishing house.

Certainly Bach was not the only one to reign in me and over me. In addition to the Romantics, Wagner and César Franck, there was the Debussy of *Pelléas et Mélisande* and also the Dukas of *Ariane et Barbe-Bleue*; I would never be able to describe sufficiently the emotion that the last scene evoked in me, when Ariane definitively turns away from the women whom she has freed and who refuse to follow her because Blue Beard, vanquished, still captivates them and does so forever. I had attended the rehearsal of this masterpiece with my father, a work whose hold over Henri Franck, as on myself, was never ending.

On rereading these pages, I am surprised to see that, if I have mentioned Bergson, I have not yet talked about the passionate interest with which I had taken his courses two years in a row at the Collège de France. I would go there repeatedly with the hope of some revelation. I am indebted to Bergson for having freed me from a spirit of abstraction whose harmful consequences I was to declare later.

6

On the other hand I feel quite certain that, for the period I have just spoken about, the two plays published in 1914, under the title *Le Seuil invisible*, have a way of clarifying rather profoundly the period I have just spoken about and one that is quite superior to what can be found in *Fragments philosophiques* (*Philosophical Fragments*) and probably even in the first part of the *Journal métaphysique*. *La Grâce* had been written in England, at the beginning of 1911. *Le Palais de sable*, which was at first to be called *Le Royaume du ciel* (The kingdom of heaven), was called that a little later, probably in 1912, but I don't remember under what conditions. It isn't enough to say that it presents clearly my religious position at the time; the fact must be emphasized that the dialogue in the two plays, but especially in *Le Palais de sable*, is presented with an existential quality that greatly distinguishes it from what it could have been for philosophers such as Berkeley and many others who have used it for the exposition of their ideas. I haven't mentioned Plato, because with him, at least in certain cases, the dialogue is presented as being something other than a simple manner of exposition. I leave to the care of his most informed and lucid commentators whether it is all right for us to use here the term *existential*.

In *La Grâce*, I particularly wanted to show that a fact as mysterious as a conversion can certainly be given a naturalist interpretation but that, at the same time, such an interpretation can only be rejected by someone who is aware of having been touched and saved by grace. Would I have gone so far as to let it be understood that the two interpretations were equally valid? Certainly not. I could not keep from recognizing in the affirmation of the converted person a transcendent value relative to the false explanation with which his wife Françoise, blinded by her materialist upbringing, seemed to be satisfied. But at that moment, I tended to think that this value of *believing affirmation* was situated beyond truth. Yet, in the final analysis, I feel myself closest to Olivier, Françoise's young brother, when he anxiously looks at the face of the dying Gérard.

It is certainly not surprising that François de Curel liked this play. In his mind, it was perhaps not fundamentally different from *La Nouvelle Idole* (The new idol), or from *Le Repas du lion* (The lion's feast) or at least their author was right to think such to be the case.[1] In *Le Palais de sable*, I was already clearly going to distance myself from an author who then enjoyed such prestige among critics that no one would have been able to imagine the disfavor, unjust in part, that he was to be subjected to in our day.

It is not sufficient to say, I believe, although I have thought so for a long time, that the point of departure for *Le Palais de sable* is a meditation on the religious dilettantism that I then attributed to Barrès.[2] In light of all that followed, I am today led to think that basically it was about questioning, if not myself, at least the philosophical positions that I adopted at the same time. These are formulated, however, not without some confusion, in the *Fragments philosophiques* which, at the request of Father Blain, I consented to have published some years ago. Isn't that clearly a certain idealist conception of faith which here is found rejected not theoretically but rather in quite a concrete manner? At first Moirans believes he is the master of his thought, he takes pleasure in the solitude he believes to be inviolable. He has only disdain for his wife, a simple believer, for his oldest daughter who plans to get a divorce so as to end a lamentable married life, and finally for his mediocre son. And this means that, for him, they are not really human beings, and hence his harsh attitude towards them. It's not the same for his second daughter Clarisse. Here it is more than just some kind of predilection: he believes he recognizes

1 François de Curel (1854-1928). *Le Repas du lion* was published in 1898, Paris: Stock. *Trans.*

2 Maurice Barrès (1862-1923), French writer and politician known for his nationalism and position against Alfred Dreyfus. *Trans.*

in her the child of his thought. Daniel Halévy was to compare the relationship between Moirans and Clarisse to the bond that unites Wotan and Brunehilde, in Wagner's *Tétraologie* (*Ring Cycle*). A terrible misunderstanding nevertheless exists between father and daughter which will be revealed a little later. Moirans discovers with horrified stupor the plan that Clarisse has given much thought to, that of becoming a Carmelite nun. But she is also surprised to be greeted not only by Moirans' sadness but by his hostility and displeasure when she confides in him. After all, hadn't he always preached to her a respect and love for religion? He had even exalted the beauty of the contemplative life. Were all these words then only lies? In reality Moirans was—or thought he was—sincere, but he had never gone beyond a representation of Christianity, to one that was lived. From the moment that this daughter, who is like the flesh of his flesh, finds herself implicated, everything changes. Today I would say that the play has us see the irruption of the existential. And in this sense I believe I can say that it directly anticipates, and not just in my own theatrical work, the overall development of existential thought itself.

Here we are already extremely far from what is called philosophical theatre whereby ideas truly struggle against other ideas. The revolt of Moirans has nothing to do with a particular ideology. His reaction is that of a man beset by what, according to him, the person for whom he has shown such exclusive affection is on the way to becoming. But how could this person not be affected in some way by the unforeseeable reaction that her desire to become a Carmelite nun has aroused in her father? How could Clarisse not begin to feel some unexpected responsibility? First of all she notices, with a feeling of horror, the comedy for which her father seems to be guilty by publicly defending, in the Parliament, a truth that he no longer believed. Did he not in that way question his own salvation? Should she not first see to it that he has put an end to this hypocrisy? But it is just then that her father forces her hand: he will agree to leave politics if she herself gives up her plan to become a nun. But then, for Clarisse herself, the horizon becomes less clear, she finds herself faced by the unknowable: she asks herself a question that she would not have even thought of before the crisis*: can the cloister become a temptation*? In vain she seeks help from a secular priest who doesn't even understand the meaning of her questioning. But in reality everything happens as though she had been contaminated by the paternal *subjectivism*. It's as though Moirans had taken her away from the blessed world of belief where being and thought are but one. She finds herself in turn carried away into the fearful universe where dialectics reigns and where, inevitably, doubt ends up winning.

But how deluded can Moirans be? He imagines that Clarisse, freed from what he calls her wild dreams, is going to be able to lead the life of a normal woman by marrying a doctor who has been in love with her for some time but who has not even declared his love for her. But no, that door is also closed. And Clarisse is condemned to live in an "interval" where there is only room for anguish and nostalgia. But Moirans will have to recognize that he is responsible for such a state of affairs, and this realization crushes him. It makes him reject the kind of aesthetic monadism that he delighted in for so long. Existence itself has burst open the cocoon in which he has tried to live.

The more I think about it today, the more the introductory value of this work appears in all its clarity. One would doubtless be mistaken in wanting to give it anything that could resemble an apologetic character. All that can be said is that, through these people, something is shown. I purposely say *shown*, and not *demonstrated*: what comes out forcefully in the *Palais de sable* is that my situation of being to the world, if it is fully lived—according to a dimension, I would say today, of intersubjectivity without which it would have no bearing, and possibly even no meaning—my situation of being to the world, I repeat, would reject as derisive, perhaps even as *ludic*, any thought which would think only of centering itself upon the idea as idea.

I cannot, I regret, shed any light on what might be the precise origins of this play. My friend Jean-Marie Carré, who was to have a brilliant career as a professor of comparative literature, was surprised, I well remember, about the exactitude with which the provincial milieu was represented in the first act. He asked me, "Where did you get that from?" and I didn't know what to answer. During my stay at Vendôme, I was only in contact with my colleagues and not at all with what could have then been the right-thinking milieu of that town. And the very role of Clarisse? Where did it come from? Perhaps I had already read *L'Annonce faite à Marie* (*The Tidings Brought to Mary*)? In any case, I knew *La Jeune fille Violaine* (The young girl Violaine). Clarisse is, among all the characters of my theatre, one of the only ones and even the only one who can be compared to Claudel's great characters. But it must also be said that, despite everything, nothing is farther from Claudel than what one could call very schematically the concrete dialectic that is at the heart of the play. On the contrary, I see in it the very core of my personal destiny. And it is significant that my first philosophical essay published in the *Revue de métaphysique et de morale*, in 1912, had as its title *Les conditions dialectiques de la philosophie de l'intuition* (The dialectical conditions of a philosophy of intuition.).

If I have talked somewhat at length about this play, unfortunately out of print, and which has never been staged, I have done so because it enlightens more than any other writing of the same period what could have been my state of mind on the eve of World War I. The expression "state of mind" doesn't really satisfy me. The term situation would undoubtedly be preferable, but on the condition of reminding us once and for all that a situation can never be reduced to the awareness that we can have of it at the very moment.

7

As I have always wanted to keep in mind the very reason for undertaking this writing—desiring it to be more of an evaluation than some mere analysis, I feel that I should indicate, in as much as possible, the impact that World War I had on both my thought and my sensibility, one not being able to be separated from the other. This seems all the more necessary since those who only read my philosophical works greatly risk minimizing its impact. On the other hand, it must be clearly perceptible to those who become acquainted with my dramatic work, and here I am thinking not only of the plays written in Sens during the time following the peace treaty but also of the dramatic fragments: *L'Insondable—Un juste*, which have only been published at a relatively recent date.

One might look askance at the fact that I did not fight during the war. Here I feel obliged to explain what I would call the implications of my status as a non-combatant, as it presented itself to my conscience. I didn't want to fight for many reasons.

First of all there could have been a moral reason, that is to say the idea of killing or of shedding blood made me shudder. But there was something else, the fact that I knew my weaknesses. I also knew that my health was poor, and I had the conviction that, were I mobilized, I would soon be sent to some hospital or infirmary. I also wondered whether I would be capable of holding up morally, and it is quite evident that one cannot know in advance what one will be capable of in this or that situation. Later, on two or three occasions, I was able to note that, in circumstances which at a distance would have seemed frightful to me and capable of completely flooring me, I was on the contrary able to suffer the blow. But then I have always had doubts about myself and about my aptitude. Yet what I should immediately add is that to some degree I felt humiliated by my status as a non-combatant, and especially that I greatly respected those who were directly committed to the struggle. Here *Un juste*, to which I referred, says a great deal. It is true that the character Raymond, who has not been drafted, very much resembles what I was.

I was particularly careful, both in correspondence and during the leaves of my friends, about my obligation to say nothing which could possibly discourage them. And I was equally aware what artificiality went along with this attitude. Finally, I found out, quite explicitly, what the unbearable condition of the non-combatant was in itself during a war such as the one we knew. So I felt as though I was being torn apart, and I believe that this feeling lasted until the end of the war.

I should now mention the very special conditions under which I was nevertheless led, in a certain way, to take part in the war. Of course I had the grand desire of making some contribution to the war effort. It so happened that my friend, Xavier Léon, director of the *Revue de métaphysique et de morale*, had conceived of a certain kind of catalogue that, in principle, was meant for the wounded in the hospitals, the aim being to be able to inform methodically the families. In fact, however, under this form, the identification sheets turned out to be useless. They were able to be used later on in another way and indirectly. At the end of August 1914, Xavier Léon left with his family for Aix-en-Provence where he had a house, and he asked me if I wanted to replace him in some way and take care of this service which depended on the French Red Cross (the Union of the Women of France). Naturally I accepted. Thus was I led to direct an information service, but its true objective only became clear after the catastrophic events at the end of August 1914, when disappearances multiplied and innumerable families desperate for information came looking for news of their sons. I will talk later about this service.

But first I have to say what my initial reaction to the event was, I mean, to the declaration of war. I can affirm that these last days of July 1914 and early August have stayed with me in a very earthy manner. These were magnificent, sunny days, and the heat was rather intense. I was returning from Switzerland where I had gone with my friend Jean Wahl. We had made two visits to the upper mountains of the Valais, first in Saint-Luc and then in Saas Fee. I can still see the exact moment when, seated on a rock overlooking the valley, I said to Jean Wahl: "Until now we have been taken up with the Caillaux trial; but this seems much more serious to me!" This was the news of Austria's ultimatum to Serbia. We immediately left to meet my family who were in Flueli-Ranft, above Lake Sarnen, a vacation spot in the canton of Unterwald. I remember the evening walk we took in Brigue where we had to spend the night while waiting to take the train for Loetschberg. We were obsessed by the thought of this horrible event which none of us had been able to believe until then and which was truly *upon* us. I remember, and I must say it without being embarrassed—but I am bound to be sincere—that the idea of disappearing in this war without first being able to express myself, without first being able to reveal what I was carrying in myself, seemed quite unbearable to me. The following day we made a rather long and somewhat tedious trip, and then I met up with my grandmother and my aunt. One of my uncles also joined us and brought news that was even more disturbing, and so we decided to return to Paris. And I can see us arriving in the hectic capital early in the morning. Then the events followed each other. Useless to recall them.

But what I would like to remember is the very special feeling I had at that time. I would say that, in the end, until then, I had no clear awareness of my patriotism. Had I been asked, "Are you patriotic?" I would have answered: "Yes, I think so." But I would not have said so with absolute conviction because something in me leaned towards a certain cosmopolitanism. I had no sympathy for neo-nationalist literature which had flourished in France during the years which preceded the war. Well, suddenly, seeing that Germany was attacking, noticing that France was directly threatened, I had the profound satisfaction of feeling myself in agreement with most of my fellow citizens. I remember having gone down the streets of Paris with a feeling of relief: I no longer felt alone, I no longer felt as though I was imprisoned in what could be perceived as a kind of dilettantism. I felt I was *with* everyone, like everyone; I shared the same hope and also the same fear. But hope certainly dominated my feelings, because I was quite far from imagining what this war could be and, besides, who could have then imagined it? I won't elaborate on the first days. One of my friends, I don't remember exactly which one, led me to the town hall of the sixteenth arrondissement, or district, of Paris where numerous requests were being made by people from the provinces who wanted to return home and who needed to get transportation permits. But I can say that what sustained me during these painful days was the feeling of somehow being liberated from my "self." My "self" stopped wielding the kind of preeminence that, more or less consciously, it had suffered from during the year of inner searching which had preceded the war. And I think I can say that, because of it, I lived what I was to later express when I declared that the self was in the end a kind of covering.

It's as though the cover had disappeared, as though it had been removed.

Yet, very quickly, the first bad news came. It was around August 10 that my father, shocked, told us that the son-in-law of friends of ours, or rather the fiancé of their daughter, had just been killed. This was sometime before Charleroi. Then I began to experience a kind of fear that was to engulf my spirit during these years.

I don't think it useful to go into detail regarding my work with the Red Cross. I will simply say this: for me it was a question, as much as possible, of taking every particular case that was handed to us by an anguished mother, wife, fiancée, or sister and of gathering the necessary evidence that would allow me to shed light upon the disappearance of a soldier. And it was particularly here that the catalogue of the wounded from the hospitals run by the Union of Women of France was useful, because we classed them according to regiments, and that allowed us to say to a given person: "A friend of your son is cared for in this hospital; we can write him in order to find out whether he can give some information regarding your son." Then I obtained precise information about the prisoners, that is to say about the camps where the soldiers who had been captured in this or that fighting had been imprisoned. After quite long delays, it was possible to obtain from these prisoners other information that was then able to complete or confirm what we had gathered through the first procedure. And so forth. I was then able to create for myself (at that time my memory was quite good) a kind of catalogue of the French army. I was able to say: "This regiment was involved in this fight on a given day; many prisoners were taken: most have been sent to this camp, but others were sent to yet another camp." I think that I had been somewhat helped by the intellectual effort I had to put forth to constitute this catalogue of the mind. It could have been extremely dangerous, that is to say that for me it would have been able to convert the war into an abstract schema. But what kept this from happening were the visits I received several times a day and which, almost every time, upset me because I would find myself in the presence of great suffering or anguish. This was a moment when I could welcome these people who came to me in a rather personal and human way such that they wouldn't feel as though they were having to deal with some official at a desk or a window. I believe this was very important because, in the end, it was like the first apprenticeship of intersubjectivity as I was to define it much later on.

At the same time my philosophical reflection centered upon the kind of questioning to which I submitted my visitors. It dealt with the very thought of questioning and more deeply with the conditions by which a questionnaire can be established, and simultaneously the limits within which a response may be obtained. Because of this, a kind of thinking started to take place in my mind—the *Journal métaphysique* gives irrefutable proof of it—that went beyond and which tended towards what no longer clearly belongs to the order of information, towards what is beyond information and also beyond any questioning. It's evident that, in this perspective, the metapsychic facts and thought about these same phenomena were to take on much importance. I think it would be wrong to ignore the very narrow link which for me connected this very sorrowful experience of the questionnaire and search, the metapsychic experience properly called, such as it was to develop for me during some memorable months in the winter of 1916-17.

I just indicated that very little of any of this, except for a trace here and there, will be found in the *Journal métaphysique* as it was published, and one might be surprised not to find these events mentioned in it. But I should add that I kept another diary which I have never thought of publishing but which, on the contrary, did deal with the events and news that came to us from right and left, on the information received, perhaps also on the anticipated actions one could be tempted to undertake. But this diary was situated on a level that was completely different from the *Journal métaphysique*, properly called. For me there could be no question of mixing them up, and I repeat, there was no reason to foresee its publication.

In 1915, the Ministry of Education, knowing I was on leave and that the review board had exempted me from military service, asked me to teach at the Lycée Condorcet.[1] I was given a class of philosophy with an accompanying class in elementary mathematics and, at least for a year, a class in philosophy for the best students in the twelfth grade. In that way my life was fortunately filled with activity; I truly had the impression of helping in some way. At the same time, I was moved when I saw these young men seated before me and thought that they could be called very quickly to leave for some military base and, finally, to the front. I believe that this contributed to our friendly relations, to the fact that I truly cared for them. Perhaps at the same time I also felt a bit embarrassed and humbled, for the reason I have already stated: my condition as a non-combatant. It was something for which I felt I needed to excuse myself. I think that were I to reread the notebooks of my classes for the years 1915-1918, I would have to remark that there is almost no trace of any personal philosophical preoccupations. There was a kind of compartmentalization. I didn't feel myself capable of having my students benefit from the work that was going on in me and that would only manifest itself later.[2]

I am tempted to wonder what could have been the war's influence on my religious development. Certainly I can only express myself conjecturally here, but I think I can say this: I think that superficially the war certainly retarded my entry into Christianity, that is formally entering into this or that church. I was greatly shocked to observe how opposing adversaries each claimed God's support. It seemed to me that—and this is also evidence for me—God could only be above and, I would even say, outside such a conflict. I will return to this later. But, if we consider things a little more deeply, I think that the war made

1 A French secondary school of education on the Right Bank. Marcel Proust figured among its former students. *Trans.*

2 Marcel's World War II Journals are preserved in the Carlton Lake Collection of the Harry Ransom Humanities Research Center, University of Texas at Austin. *Trans.*

me an existential thinker. The war let me get rid of any idealist traces which are still evident in the first part of my *Journal métaphysique*. And because of this we can say that the war helped me examine more directly and immediately what I would have then called, but which I would no longer call, the religious problem properly speaking.

I mentioned the war. A rather persistent question for me was to know whether we had, we and our Allies, the law on our side: in short, whether we could believe, in all truth, that we were committed to a just war. I remember having read, with some anxiety, *Le Livre jaune* (The yellow book) that was published by the Ministry of Foreign Affairs shortly after the outbreak of the war. I would even say that my opinion on this point has changed considerably. It isn't a question of disputing whether aggression was committed by Germany and, perhaps even more so, by Austria. Today I think—and moreover I believe I sensed this towards the end of the war—that the responsibility of Poincaré, at the time of the Peterhof talks, at the end of July 1914, was extremely heavy, because nothing had yet been decided. I believe that if Poincaré had told the Czar that he would not be able to guarantee France's support in case of war, since it was not one of the scenarios foreseen by the Alliance treaty, the Czar would have perhaps hesitated, the Russian mobilization might have been delayed and peace maintained. But my conviction is that Poincaré was, in the end, a man of revenge and that he always considered war to be inevitable. I am afraid that he then thought the circumstances to be, after all, rather favorable. Here I return to certain ideas that Alain expressed with much force. I find myself in agreement with him and also, I must admit, with Fabre-Luce who was to develop these ideas in a book that was the object of heated discussion, *La Victoire* (*The Limitations of Victory*).

Some years ago, I was led to reconsider this situation in a lecture where I put the emphasis on the kairos, that is to say on the role of the determining occasion. For me the decisive example took place in March 1936. That was probably the last time we and the English could have been able to react and should have reacted at any cost against Hitler's campaign. The reoccupation of the Rhine's left bank definitely justified military action, and everything would now have us think that Hitler, had some force been used, would have been undone and that the German staff would have overthrown him. It is in this spirit that I reconsidered the event at the end of July 1914. I must acknowledge that the circumstances in which World War I began are much more mixed up and lend themselves to considerable discussion. All the same, I still think that here the French statesman played a nefarious role. No one would think of contesting Poincaré's patriotism, but I think that he was a blind patriot. I especially believe that he committed a grave error—I would even say, from a Christian point of view, a sin, in thinking that the war was inevitable. Again, on this point, I fully agree with Alain who was, and I am speaking for myself, one of the few French philosophers to have been truly affected by the war. Or so I thought, because the war didn't seem to trouble the others in any profound way.

There is no question of my describing in detail what my reactions could have been as events unfolded. All I can say is that I followed them with an emotion that resembled anguish. I am especially thinking about the disastrous offensives that the French command launched and that, in the end, implied such a tragic ignorance of the horrible conditions characterizing what war had become.

Although I don't want to reproduce here a narrative that can be found elsewhere in my writing, I don't think I can do so without evoking what my metapsychic experiments were in the winter of 1916-1917. These experiments have had a profound influence, and this has not yet been completely recognized, on the development of my thought. I often spent the evening with my friends the Davidses who lived near us on the Rue de Prony. The couple were talented painters; one did my portrait, the other a portrait of my son. They were not innovators but they had, in my opinion, a remarkable technique and a rare sense of interiority. Renée Davids was very much a spiritualist. Her husband was less absolutely so. He was even nervous, impulsive and might contradict himself on this point from one day to another. Both told me things that had interested me: I can't say that these facts left me sceptical but, despite everything, they didn't completely convince me. One day, looking at me as painters might, they told me: "But you yourself certainly have the gift of a medium!" I admit that this idea seemed rather peculiar to me. It seemed to me that a medium would be someone who was purely intuitive, rather primitive, whereas I had the impression of being someone given over to thought and deprived of the talent one finds in primitives. Nevertheless I said that we could try out an experiment. It was carried out, not with a table, but with recourse to the ouija, a little moving plank that had a point one placed on a big sheet of cardboard on which the letters of the alphabet were traced. You would put your hand on the plank, and if one was really a medium, a time would come when the plank "moved," the needle pointing to this or that letter of the alphabet. The beginnings of the experiment were extremely painful: I distrusted myself, and all the time I had the impression that it wasn't the board that was moving, but that it was I who, more or less subconsciously, moved it in a given direction.

Everything changed from the moment that a friend of the Davidses, Madame R., asked us whether we would have a séance concerning her, or rather concerning the disappearance of her husband. It so happened that, in my work of research for the Red Cross, I had inquired about the disappearance of this officer. I had not gotten any precise information; but it seemed to be infinitely probable that he had been killed during the battle of Fossé, in the Ardennes, 30 August 1914. At that time, the French army was retreating very quickly. It seemed quite reasonable to me that there could be no burial and that, consequently, the death had not been officially registered. What struck me was that the phenomenon changed from the moment that the young woman attended the séance. This time, I had no more doubts: it was indeed the plank that moved under my fingers, without my doing anything. It was indisputable. An entity showed itself: by this I mean that the needle pointed to the letters of the alphabet, corresponding to a declaration made by someone who pretended to be him. To have some confirmation, we asked him if he could name one of his children. He couldn't do it. This half surprised me, and I especially thought that even if he had been able to give the name of one of his children, this would not have been any proof of his identity, because the young wife was there and this could have simply been a phenomenon of reading one's thought. What did surprise us was that the person who was revealing himself seemed to have been completely modified by his passage into the beyond. We were looking for an historian who belonged to a Jewish family that no longer had the faith, but here we were in the presence of someone who was quite religious and dogmatic, strongly expressing himself with conviction and radically contrasting with what could have been his manner of expression during his lifetime. There was nothing decisive in all of this. But the first positive phenomenon was this: when the wife had absented herself, her father took her place and the entity seemed to address the absent wife with singular tenderness, and suddenly the ouija wrote the name of the Greek muse Clio. The entity evidently spoke to her by calling her Clio. We could not understand this until the wife came back into the room. We told her what had just happened. She shivered and told us, "But I do understand quite well why he called me Clio. During a visit to the *Terme* museum in Rome with him and with my brother, they both stopped to look at a statue of Clio, saying, 'It's extraordinary how this statue resembles you!'" That was an extremely interesting phenomenon because it implied at least a mode of communication that was very difficult to grasp, to conceptualize, between what we probably call, quite improperly, the unconscious of the wife and us. I do say "and us," because Madame Davids and I both had a hand on the ouija board. Perhaps sometimes I was the only one, but most of the time there were two of us. We then tried to learn under what conditions he had disappeared, what had happened to him in the battle of Fossé. We were told, contrary to what I had supposed, that he had not been killed on the battle field, but that he had been able to find refuge with some farmers who had hidden him with two men whose names he gave us, one called Leriche and the other Nano. "And then," he told us, "we were denounced. I was taken to prison." I'll return to this later.

But who were Leriche and Nano? I examined my catalogue. Madame R. did the same: we found no trace of Leriche. But fortunately, as head of the Red Cross service, I had access to the general catalogue at the École Militaire which listed the losses of the French army. I went there one morning and, with my heart beating, I asked to consult the catalogue of names for the 46th infantry, the regiment of the missing officer. I calculated that this catalogue contained about eight thousand names. The 46th infantry was a regiment of the Parisian region which had been particularly affected. I found a card with the name of Leriche, missing in the battle of Fossé. I can say that this was one of the emotional moments of my life, because now it was absolutely impossible to talk about any coincidence without being absurd, and on the other hand the practice of having an explanation through a reading of thought or through some other phenomenon of this sort was evidently not possible: there can be no communication of this kind with a card catalogue. So it seemed that what we had was irrefutable proof of the possibility of coming into contact with a person who has remained conscious and capable of informing us, at least partially, about what had happened to him. As for Nano, I believed until the end of the war that this was a simple error, because the information we received about him was later contradicted in the course of an inquiry we made in the area around Paris, in the region he was supposed to be from. But one morning, not long after the Armistice, my eyes fell upon a request for information which was published in the newspaper *Le Parisien libéré*. A certain Madame Annot, who thus had the same name, although it was written with one of its letters inverted, was trying to find out what had become of her husband who had belonged to the 89th infantry (a regiment forming a brigade with the 46th) and who had disappeared at the battle of Fossé.[3] So here we had at least a partial confirmation.

I now come back to what we later found out. And this seems to be pure invention. The statesman, who was the father of the officer, had been one of the most ardent supporters for requiring service in the military for a period of three years, during the time which had preceded World War I. I mention that he was Jewish. In short, he was someone for whom the Germans could only feel marked hostility. We had been told that, at Montmédy, the missing officer had been taken by boat down stream by a certain German major, whose name was given, and that the major had made the boat shake so that the officer was drowned. This seems to me contrary not only to all verisimilitude but even to every possibility, because, according to what I was able to find out, the Montmédy stream, the Chiers, is not navigable. On the other hand, we tried to have the German Red Cross confirm the name of this major, and here again we obtained no result. But what is peculiar is that the force of conviction which came from the narrative was such that the wife, who was a noble person, intervened when we

3 In the name Annot, the "t" is not pronounced. *Trans.*

were told that the major would pay for this through his son, who would be killed on the Russian front. And I will always see this woman protesting, "I cannot permit an innocent son to be held responsible for a crime committed by his father." An answer was given to this in the rigorous and dogmatic tone I evoked earlier, "You know nothing about divine economy." Shortly thereafter the wife left with her children and her mother for the seacoast. But after the offensive of 27 May 1918, I was to learn later that, since they feared the worst, Madame R. and her mother were somehow irresistibly called to invoke the ouija board. They then learned in no uncertain terms that, in a few days, the Allied offensive would begin and that, for the Germans, this would be the beginning of the end.

So I remained alone. Then a rather peculiar phenomenon occured, one whose importance, I believe, cannot be underestimated. The Leriche case had given me such assurance and confidence that I wondered whether I had not been somehow providentially chosen to take some proof of an afterlife to the countless anxious people who consulted me everyday. Then everything happened as though an intelligent power was trying to punish me for such presumption. The phenomenon clearly began to disintegrate. The ouija seemed to put us in touch with a home for the crazy where absurd affirmations followed one another. We were placed in contact with extremely problematic entities ... one of them them gave information about itself that an inquiry proved to be inexact. I went from one extreme to another and, although I had first been quite confident, I came in some way to despair. And then, in my opinion, the most extraordinary phenomenon of the entire story occurred. Its purpose was truly to reassure and show me that I was not wrong to believe in the truth of the phenomenon but that, at the same time, I should be on guard against an exaggerated confidence in the very possibilities that I had been granted. The entity presented itself as someone called Domerat. It claimed to have been the student of the mathematician Hadamard, and this assertion was refuted by the inquiry that I was able to make of him, since his sister was one of our close friends. This Domerat reassured us that he knew what was going to happen. It was in late spring 1917. We had two major concerns: the battle which was being pursued on the Chemin des Dames, on the one hand, and what, on the other, was going on in Russia. On these two points nothing significant or interesting was revealed to us but only what I would have been able to say myself. But we hadn't asked about the Italian front. Well this is what was said about it: "One more time the Italians will try to retake the offensive in the direction of Trieste, they will be pushed back and then the Austrians will take the offensive, the Isonzo will be crossed and there will be 100,000 prisoners (in reality there were more), Udine will be taken." "What," I then cried out, "Venice will be threatened!" "No," I was told, "the Austrian advance will be stopped before Treviso."

Consequently the battle of the Isonzo was predicted to me, to me personally three months before the event—and that is something I can swear to. I had the opportunity to mention it to some Italians and to ask them: "Do you believe it was rationally possible to say something like that?" The answer was negative. It was impossible: we were truly in the order of pure prophesy. When, some weeks later, I went to tell the whole story to Bergson, he was keenly interested: but the fact of the prediction embarrassed him a lot because it challenged everything that he had written on duration and unpredictablility. To which I answered: "What can I say, a theory cannot stand up against an experience! And that experience seems to me to have such a compelling value that we should start with it ...." I'll return to this in a moment. What impressed him, on the other hand, was to learn that my *feeling* was modified according to whether this or that entity became incarnate in the board. I told him—because this had been quite a definite experience—that when it was a question of a young person, fully committed to life, the movement of the board had something rather lively about it (that's the word I used). On the contrary, when it was a question of an older person (we had been in touch with the father of Leriche) the board moved painfully, as though limping along. This impressed him.

Of course one may find in the *Journal métaphysique*, in the second part, the essence of the thought that this experience wrought in me. I can say that it was decisive because it showed me in an absolutely irrefutable and direct manner the positive character of certain experiences which, for me, had only been objects of speculation until then. I had also refrained from drawing exaggeratedly general conclusions, especially as regards prophecy. And here I cannot keep from making comparisons between what had been given me and what might happen for a novelist. I also remember having spoken about it to Édouard Estaunié, who had a fine mind and whose work is, in my opinion, much too forgotten today. He was most keenly interested in metapsychic facts because he himself had had some experiences. It may be—and it is what Estaunié confirmed for me—that a scene in a novel comes to the inner vision of a novelist before he is capable of accounting for the scene. That's what had happened for him in one of the novels whose title I have forgotten. Later on, he had been led to write everything that turned out to have prepared for this scene which had, once again, come to him, straightaway, and he could not understand why. Since then I have often thought that perhaps it was in the order of the creative imagination that we might best be able to find the analogue of what we call the historical process. It is possibly through comparison with the work of the creative novelist that we should search for and think about the historical event. This has led me, of course, to think a lot about the notion of *scene*, and more directly still about that of situation. Sartre was to tell me quite much later, during one of the very few cordial conversations that I had with him, that it was I, and not Jaspers, who had revealed to him the importance of this notion *situation*.

If today I am tempted to say that World War I made another man of me, it's unquestionably because, on the one hand, it awakened in me a sense of compassion whose roots probably already existed in me but which would not have been so intensely developed had it not been for the tragic events in which I participated. On the other hand, it's also because I was able, on account of the war, to enter into this area of occult reality, to which I think the philosopher of the future should devote an incomparably more minute and strict attention than has been the case until now. Few of the philosophers I have met ever truly had any sense of this reality and especially of the necessity to devote their thought to it. There has been Bergson, there has been, to a certain extent, René Le Senne and also Gaston Berger. During our travels to South America in 1951, Berger and I spoke about these problems, and I felt he was sincerely open to this kind of research. But nearly everywhere else I noticed a sort of ill will, I would even say a willful opaqueness which has always seemed extremely annoying to me and which, as I understand it, is based on fear, but a fear which is not admitted and a fear that takes on, as is often the case, an air of arrogance.

I should add that these facts were important not only for me. My wife, to whom I was to mention them some years later, always told me that they had contributed to awakening in her an awareness of the invisible world and, in that way, I would say, a religious meaning which risked becoming atrophied at the time we met each other. I remain convinced that, within certain limits, metapsychic study can constitute a kind of propaedeutic in relation to faith properly so called. This does not mean that we should confuse one with the other: that would be a very serious mistake, absolutely inexcusable, but there does exist a connection that should definitely claim the attention of the philosopher.

I feel that my story has been told too frequently and, I would even say, overly repeated, and so there lingers over it an odor that is somewhat offensive. I find in it the odor that characterizes stagnant water whose harmful nature I have so often pointed out. However, it is impossible for me to make, in any manner, an abstraction from what was, doubtless, a decisive event. Of course I am quite far from questioning all that was disconcerting in this experience, and I even think that the disconcerting character should be emphasized. After all, it seems to me understandable that such experiences are formed according to an unforeseeable plan and without any conformity to what we would like this plan to be. What seems quite clear to me, and which too many people persist in misunderstanding, is that these experiences cannot be, properly speaking, usable, in the sense that scientific experiments produced in a laboratory are. The idea that one can here proceed to an experiment in the precise sense of the word hardly seems reasonable to me. I don't ignore the persevering effort of such men as Rhine Warcolier and many others to accomplish experimentation in this area, and I don't ignore the interest of the poor results that have been arrived at. But I do remain persuaded that, in the end, they will only be able to reach what I would call the border, the quite superficial border of phenomena. These, considered in their essence, certainly appear to me to be irreducible to every attempt at reproduction in response to a well determined intention. In other words, I strongly doubt that a metapsychic science can in any way be constituted. We are in an essentially *intermediary* realm between art and science properly called, where certain categories intervene that we do have, we must admit, the greatest difficulty in determining as we should.

When my friend Pietro Prini wrote his book on my thought considered as *Méthodologie de l'Invérifiable* (Methodology of the unverifiable), he correctly noticed, I think, what was most important and perhaps, after all, most new in my undertaking: a methodology of the Unverifiable, one could say a methodology of the Unforeseeable, a methodology such that this Unforeseeable remains itself—quite far from finding itself—in some way reduced to what is not itself. And after all, if we think about the most personal features of our life, that is to say—and I have always emphasized it—about the encounters with all that they might reveal, we observe that here also we are in the Unforeseeable and that this Unforeseeableness must in any case be expressly recognized.

Going through my *Journal métaphysique*, I notice that in 1915, that is to say long before the experience related above, I wrote a note that basically anticipates, rather curiously, all that was to become clearer to me later on, thanks to these experiences. Unfortunately, I cannot remember what the context was for writing this note.

> *15 October 1915*
>
> The possibility of divination is bound up with the nature (not the degree) of the interest which attaches thought to its ideal object. But on the other hand, as is plain, an objective dynamic of interest is in itself impossible. Interest needs to be *real*—and this cannot be expressed in the language of quantity. To express it better, the mind needs to participate totally in the interest (mere curiosity remains *isolated* in the midst of pre-occupations that it does not suppress). The essential point is thus the relation of the idea in tension to the mind itself.
>
> *Journal métaphysique*[4]

4 The translation for this passage is taken from Gabriel Marcel, *Metaphysical Journal.* Translated by Bernard Wall. London: Rockliff Publishing, 1952, pp. 129-130. *Trans.*

These few lines show rather well that there was already in me a current of thought that tended toward, must it be said, intuitions, which were to become clear later on in great part thanks to these experiences that were, in themselves, I repeat, unforeseeable in 1915.[5]

If ever, as I wish, anyone should undertake the publication of my works, taking into account their chronology, that is to say including the plays in the weft of the *Journal métaphysique* properly called—in addition to this volume I am also talking about the first part of *Être et avoir* (*Being and Having*) and about *Présence et Immortalité* (*Presence and Immortality*)—one will be led to note that on the dramatic level the prolongation or explanation of what had only been felt in light of the metapsychic experience was realized. Here, of course, I am referring to the last scene of *Quatuor en fa dièse* and to the last scene of *L'Iconoclaste*. I clearly remember that, in their first version, these two plays were composed during the war. The question asked at the end of *Quatuor* (Quartet): "Myself, yourself, where does a personality begin?" only takes on its full and radical meaning in light of the experiences I have evoked, and I think that here one of the fundamental assurances which have governed my entire work was then constituted. It appeared radically absurd to imagine, in the manner of the monadists, that human beings could be considered as kinds of distinct unities and not communicate among themselves. What is perhaps still more absurd is what would seem to follow from a literal and perhaps even misunderstood Freudianism, that is the idea that each of these unities possess, I would say, a sort of unconscious suburb which would essentially belong to it and which would be distinct from the neighboring suburb. Regarding this, it is quite important that several psychoanalysts, such as Ehrenwald and Eisenbudd, have been clearly led to bring forward telepathic connections during their experiments. This was related to me in the most formal manner during the Congress of Parapsychology held in Utrecht in 1953. I don't mean to say that one is necessarily led by that to the notion of collective unconscious, such as we find in Jung. Here I would express my-

[5] I would like to say, however, that my entry for 1915 certainly refers to what my friends the Davidses had related about their friend Commander Caslant who practiced not only astrology but divinations whose origins are to be found more or less in Chinese techniques.

self less categorically and with more reservation. I would simply say that there is an emergence of personal awareness from a certain element upon which it is difficult to shed any light but which, in all cases, appears, upon reflection, as not belonging of itself, as a kind of dependency, to the person in question. I believe that this is extremely important and that it is here that we find the foundation of intersubjectivity such as I was led to evoke much later, because I only used this term at a relatively recent date, in any case after World War II.

8

One shouldn't think that this kind of enlightening assurance, which for me derives from my experiences of 1916-17, constantly comforted me during the period which followed. This would be quite inaccurate. Anxiety, which may indeed be one of my traits, remained with me until the end of the war. Unfortunately, it was to resurface after the Treaty of Versailles was signed.

Now I want to talk about the tragic event which followed the disastrous offensive of 16 April 1917: I want to talk about the mutinies. Of course, we were only partly informed about what was going on; but all the same what was communicated was enough to make us worry a great deal. In addition, it so happened that one of my best friends from the Sorbonne—why not name him—Michel Alexandre, whom I have already mentioned, took part in the writing of defeatist tracts that were sent to the front during this period and that probably contributed to demoralizing the unfortunate soldiers, some of whom were to end up on trial. I was shocked by the news when it reached me. I could hardly conceive that a man such as Michel Alexandre had assumed responsibility for an action which could result in having French soldiers shot. I never had a conversation with him about this. We didn't meet during the period which followed. I was to see him again later, in 1940, and also shortly after the war. A problem arose for me: how is it conceivable that a generous man, deeply concerned about justice, could assume such a responsibility? This question, which I found difficult to answer, is the basis for the one-act play *Un juste*, which was not published until 1965. The decisive scene brings together Raymond, a sickly young man who, because of his health, is on inactive duty, and his friend Bernard, an officer in the infantry who is returning from the front, from a particularly dangerous sector, for a leave of forty-eight hours and who is convinced that he will be killed once back at the front. For him it is a question of handing on to Raymond something more than just a message, a kind of appeal. He is deeply convinced of the absurdity and foolishness of the war. He foresees that, even should it lead to what is called a victory, it will be ephemeral. The winner will turn out to be unjust and thus pave the way to a new conflict. And under these conditions, he calls upon Raymond to undertake, with others, initiatives that could shorten this absurd and murderous fighting. It is certain that I was impressed by the conversation that I had, during his leaves, with yet another friend who was also close to Michel Alexandre. This was another young philosopher, Marc Boasson,[1] who was to be killed at Mont Kemmel on 30 April 1918. He never indicated a defeatist attitude in any conversation he had with me. But he was very worried, and he quite nobly refused to be named an officer because he wanted to be as close to his men as possible and not risk having to send them off on some bloody mission.

What was then my own thought? It is very hard for me to say. And here I most clearly see what was necessarily dramatic, I should rather say dramatical, in my awareness itself. I felt myself divided, irreparably divided. On the one hand, I wanted in spite of everything to still believe that a victory worthy of this name was possible, and I especially refused absolutely to say or write anything that could possibly risk discouraging the soldiers. I was quite aware of my situation as a non-combatant, my feeling about it was so strong that my desire could only be an absolutely permanent one. Yet, on the other hand, there was also in me someone who deeply sympathized with the suffering of those who had revolted, of those who had foolishly tried to put an end to the struggle. I recognize that between these two antagonistic positions, there was no reconciliation, no possible synthesis in the Hegelian sense. There was only one tension, and I think that this already appeared as one of the signs of what was to be my

[1] After the war I published with Librairie Plon the admirable letters of Marc Boasson to his wife which appeared under the title *Au soir d'un monde* (In the world's evening).

thought as it was elaborated later on. I am referring to the refusal of an illusory synthesis, this concern about maintaining a tension which could only, in certain cases that were truly unforeseeable, be resolved in an illumination come from some point much higher than man. Did I quite sense at the time about which I am talking what I now see rather clearly? I can't affirm it. I find it very difficult to reconstitute in an absolutely rigorous manner what my states of consciousness could have then been. I believe I adhered too strictly, too exactly, to what happened on a daily basis for there not to be some refusal in me to anticipate. Certainly the refusal to anticipate, which I experienced these last months and years, was at the origin of *Le Mort de demain* that I wrote in 1920 in Sens.

9

My engagement to Jacqueline Boegner was concluded about the time of the Armistice of November 1918, and I then knew a period of at least relative euphoria which was not, however, to last very long. Certainly the relief that the end of the fighting brought us was immense. But until the end of the battles, we received news concerning soldiers, struck down at the very moment the nightmare was coming to an end. I remember the emotion we felt when, from the first floor of the Ministry of the Navy, we viewed what was called the victory parade. Only music, and I am particularly thinking of Beethoven, is capable of translating this conjunction of sorrow and joy, which doesn't allow for translation in a conceptual language. It was to be the same experience several months later, at the time the peace treaty was signed, when we went to the Place de l'Étoile where in the crowd I was to meet again an old friend I had not seen since the beginning of the war and who was to play a major role later on in our lives.

It is certain that, for some months, under the influence of the reading I had done of Royce, at least the indirect inspiration for Wilson, I was able to believe that a new era was beginning for humanity. But very quickly, this hope was to dissipate, and I have always noted with increasing anxiety, from 1921 on, all the events that seemed to announce, in the not too distant future, a sinister renewal of this horrible struggle.

I don't think it necessary here to expatiate on what my marriage was like. There is a certain indiscretion which makes me shudder. But what I insist on mentioning is that the appearance of Jacqueline Boegner in my life was most certainly at the origin of a kind of inner renewal which was to be translated very quickly in my works, and I think especially here in my theatre and in the plays which I alluded to at the beginning of this journal. I must add that, contrary to what most often happens, it wasn't only she who entered my life, it was her entire family. Besides, if I had thought of her as a possible companion, it was above all because her brother, Henri Boegner, had been a very beloved friend. We were different, our interests were different, but there was in him, even in his physique, something which had deeply and, I would even say passionately, touched me. It was in February 1912, at the time of the death of Alfred Boegner, director of the house of Evangelical Missions, that I first entered the family circle of Henri Boegner whom I had known for two or three years. What was bizarre was that the very person who welcomed me, during this visit to express my condolences, was Geneviève Boegner, the only surviving member of the family and one who has been more closely a part of my life these last two years.

What led me to the Boegner family was the incredibly spontaneous and free character of a Protestantism which, had it been presented to me under its most rigid forms, would have most definitely estranged me from Christianity. My mother-in-law was one of the most spontaneous beings I have ever had the opportunity to meet. A most affectionate relationship developed between the two of us very quickly. And yet I felt the presence of someone who was absent, as though he were living. This was Edmond Boegner whom, unfortunately, I did not know. I had only had a glimpse of him through an open door, at the beginning of the war. An auxiliary doctor, he was killed at Bois des Corbeaux on 16 March 1916. Everything indicates that a brotherly bond would have been created between us. He adored music. He was an exceptionally modest and spirited person. And I was never able to get over not having known him on earth. But how can I not admit that I still hope to meet him in another way and in a dimension which is not that of our earthly world.

Our marriage was immediately placed under the sign of music, for it was music which brought Jacqueline and me together. She was one of the best students of Vincent d'Indy. After excellent studies in piano, she took up learning the organ and, in addition, she taught harmony at the Schola Cantorum. I had the joy of introducing her to certain works, mostly French, and I saw to what extent she gave herself to those which were quite dear to me. In particular, I am thinking about the last works of Gabriel Fauré. For me that was the irrefutable and evident sign of a relationship which could only be strengthened with the passing of time.

I am reluctant to talk about the first months of 1919. We took a trip to Italy immediately after our marriage. Then we had our first visit to Alsace. And yet I still feel here the need to say how happy I was to be admitted into this vast family community which came together again so happily in July 1919. I found myself among the Alsatians who were forced to remain in Alsace under German domination, and all those who, like my wife and her relatives, had again become French people living in France. I have spoken enough about how I suffered as an only child, but now I was welcomed into a grand family where it seemed to me it was good to get to know and greet everyone. In addition I experienced a magnificent moment in my life which has contributed to this sort of renewal that the war had already prepared.

At one time I thought of asking for a position as lecturer in a foreign county. I remember having considered Prague which, not long ago, was to take on such a central place in my thought. And then, for some unknown reason, I gave up the idea of going abroad. I believe that the thought of our two families influenced my decision not to leave, and I asked for a teaching assignment in France. There was a question of my being sent to Chartres. But finally, I was assigned to Sens. I won't return to what I said at the beginning of this work, about the years spent in Sens. They were particularly productive ones. I can say that I experienced a kind of revitalization of every creative power that might have existed in me. Yet I must also admit that, as for teaching, this stay in Sens was something of a disappointment. My classes were quite small. I took as much interest as possible in my pupils who were, despite everything, rather mediocre. I had no illusions about what I thought I could really teach them. In 1922, I decided to ask for a leave and to return to Paris.

For me it was especially a question of having gotten over the anxious struggle I had suffered on account of my first contacts with Parisian theatrical life. Three of my plays had been staged while I was still teaching in Sens: *Le Coeur des autres*, at the Théâtre Montmartre, under the auspices of the group "Le Canard sauvage;" *La Grâce*, at the Théâtre des Mathurins, by the company La Grimace; and *Le Regard neuf* at the Ambigu (Cercle des Escholiers). Reviews by the critics had been altogether favorable. I had every reason to hope that other plays would be staged, and I felt the need to be present. Certainly, at this time of my life, I was mainly taken up with the theatre. Of course, this doesn't mean that I, in any way, abandoned philosophy. The second part of the *Journal métaphysique*, many notes of which were written in Sens, makes that abundantly clear. It is true nevertheless that, at the time, I didn't feel the need to clarify the connection which linked these two activities together. I am also convinced that, given my particular situation at the time, it was better for them to remain without any apparent connection. I remember feeling liberated in dedicating myself to the characters who came to my inner vision: the Jordans (*Le Regard neuf*), Jeanne Framont and her family (*Le Mort de demain*), Rose and Daniel Meyrieux (*Le Coeur des autres*).

As I indicated at the beginning of this work, we experienced a sense of plenitude in this house on the Rue Chambonas, and thinking about it today moves me still. Music and reading aloud were a most important part of our existence, and I also remember the long walks in the countryside and particularly the hamlet of Clérimois, from which one could contemplate an immense horizon to the east. And from this vast landscape a question arose for me: what would our life be later, would it be spent in Paris or much farther? Would my career be that of a playwright? Would I give up teaching? So many questions that I anxiously asked.

And then, for the two of us, yes, I think I can say so, there was as intensely for me as for my wife the question of a child. We decided without waiting any longer to adopt one. My wife would have certainly preferred that it be a new born babe; I felt differently. I wished, perhaps selfishly, that we be spared the difficulties that usually accompany the first months, even the first years, and I especially desired to find myself in the presence of a child who was sufficiently developed so that we could immediately see what his or her personality would be. I won't go into detail about the steps we took to adopt Jean-Marie. I'll limit myself to recalling a summer day of 1922 when we went to a house in Boulogne where he was to be given to us. He had just celebrated his sixth birthday. We had been told that he was a timid child, who would perhaps not let himself be known too easily. How moved we were in seeing him run towards us and throw himself into our arms, as though he had truly been waiting for us. This was a moment of grace which I still keenly feel today. Here adoption took on its full meaning. Were we the ones who were choosing? Were we not rather chosen?

At the time we were afraid of the still distant future when he would ask us about his origins, when we would have to tell him something about the drama which had surrounded his birth. Our fears were groundless. He never asked us, and I dare say that he was more essentially our child than if there had been a simple bond of nature between us.

We had just moved to Paris, beyond the Lion de Belfort in an apartment where I never truly felt at home. But the presence of the child seemed to cast light upon and magnetize this banal dwelling at the corner of the Rue Tombe-Issoire and Rue Émile-Dubois.

I think I can say that this adoption was one of the most significant actions of my life, one of those I never regretted. It was certainly the basis for the text I was to compose twenty years later, *Le Voeu créateur comme essence de la paternité* (The creative vow as essence of fatherhood). This lived experience allowed me to dissociate radically paternity considered in its essence and procreation understood biologically. It needn't be said, moreover, that I kept myself from proceeding to a rash induction and from claiming that every adoption carries with it the happy consequences as it did in our case. In *Le Coeur des autres*, which anticipated what actually happened, had I not presented the conflict which unfolds between the father and the adopted son? It is true that in the play, the case is very different, since Jean is the natural son of Daniel. What life has revealed to me is that, in perhaps privileged conditions, adoption can assume the character of a kind of spiritual grafting. In fact, in 1943 our adoptive son married our niece, the daughter of Henri Boegner, and so the children who were to be born from this marriage would thus find themselves related to us, at least to my wife, by blood. This story, that I don't have to relate in detail here, and which for me witnesses to the very mysterious coming together of nature, freedom and grace, is perhaps revelatory of what we call history.

Worried about finding work that would be remunerated in Paris, I contacted two publishing houses, Plon and Grasset, who both accepted to take me on as a reader. I thus had the opportunity to read a very large number of manuscripts and sometimes the happiness to welcome a writer at the beginning of his career. That was the case when Georges Bernanos had sent *Sous le soleil de Satan* (*Under the Sun of Satan*) to Plon. Since the readers' reports were contradictory, I was chosen to step in as a judge and, since I recognized the extraordinary originality of the work, I declared that there could be no doubt as to the timeliness for publishing it. The book appeared in the collection Roseau d'Or, directed by Jacques Maritain, and I do think that the latter would have published the work in any case.

Thanks to the intervention of my friend Roger Lévy—at least this is what I think I remember—Louise Weiss, who was then in charge of *L'Europe nouvelle*, assigned me the theatre column of this weekly that played such an important role in the area of politics until the early thirties.

Finally, somewhere around 1920 or 1921, I again contacted Jacques Rivière who had formerly been my fellow student at the Sorbonne and who now directed *La Nouvelle Revue française*. I ended up contributing a rather large number of critical notes to this review, which, at that time, enjoyed a very fine reputation. I attended, rather regularly, the receptions that Jacques and Isabelle Rivière gave on Sundays at their home on Rue Boulard where one could meet almost all the major writers of the new generation. Here I made the acquaintance of Charles Du Bos, who was to become for me the best of friends.

If I were to reread the critical notes I mentioned above, I am almost certain that I would be embarrassed, and perhaps even irritated, by the somewhat artificial and rigid tone that I thought I had to adopt in order to show myself worthy of the publishing house that had taken me in.

I would have the same reaction were I to reread some one hundred pages of the novel I tried to write during that very same period. I had given it the title *L'Invocation à la nuit* (The invocation to night).

Fortunately, I realized just in time both the artificial character and the exhibitionist desires which this attempt at writing a novel showed. Far from persevering, I recognized that I was not a novelist and that the most elementary wisdom would be to abandon expressing myself in an area not my own.

Regarding this, I remember that a friend of my father, the sister of the ambassador Paléologue, who did me the favor of putting me in contact with the excellent critic Henry Bidou, asked me several times why I didn't write novels instead of plays. The psychological weight which characterized my works probably seemed to him disproportionate in relation to the requirements of the stage. But, in fact, had I written novels, either these would have been presented as confessions and I would probably not have overcome the obstacle that every self-criticism goes up against, or the dialogue would have taken on too much importance, as with Miss Compton-Burnett. But to me that particular form of the novel always seemed to belong to a bastard genre. A fact that has always bothered me, and one I must acknowledge, is that my theatre has always been more read than it has been staged. I can still hear Edmond Jaloux, at the time *Le Dard* was being played, telling me in the hallway of the Théâtre des Arts, "It's as good as when one reads it." I retorted, "It's much better," and he refused to admit it. I think, however, that I was right. Later on I will talk about the very particular conditions in which the play was staged in 1937.

A cooperative of playwrights was formed in 1925, with the highly qualified Henry Bidou as an advisor. It was under its auspices that *La Chapelle ardente* was staged at the Théâtre du Vieux-Colombier. The play was also billed with *Simili* (Simili), by Claude-Roger Marx, who was above all an art critic. The play was somewhat poorly served by actors who were rather badly chosen for their parts and whom the director Gaston Baty had also somewhat led into error. This was at least the case for Jeanne Lion, who interpreted the role of Aline. A few months later she told me with heartfelt sincerity, "I realize that I betrayed your play and I hope you forgive me for it." In a general way, one must admit that no one was less qualified than Gaston Baty to stage one of my plays. Had he not told me, after a reading I had done for him of *L'Iconoclaste*, "For me you are truly the enemy, because you create so *well* the very theatre I want to do away with."? Did he not insist, despite my objections, on placing a Jansenist crucifix on the set of *La Chapelle ardente*, even though, from what can be seen, religion had no role in the life of the Fortier family?[1]

What is certain is that during these long years I was not successful in getting my plays performed in Paris, and this situation created a state of tension in me, I would even say infinitely painful frustration. I nevertheless continued to work for the theatre. But *L'Attelage* (The yoke) written in 1926, and *L'Horizon*[2] (The horizon) have never been performed.

I have always had trouble understanding the nature of the resistance I had ro face when dealing with theatre directors. This can probably be explained, at least partly, by the fact that I was known as a philosopher and that, contrary to all truth, my theatre was judged to be philosophical and, as such, hardly accessible to the public. More deeply still, I think that my plays troubled some, to the extent that they resisted classification.

Should I have been resigned to this state of affairs? I'm not sure. I strongly felt that some injustice had been done, and I know quite well that my sentiments were also shared by Henry Bidou. I had the conviction, and still do believe, that a dramatic work worthy of the name must live on the stage, that it must be incarnate, even though I think that, were it only read, it should keep a part of its power and, I dare say, of its radiance.

I note, moreover, that the actors who interpreted my plays never questioned for a moment their essentially theatrical nature.

I don't want to forget, however, that my activity as a reader and critic interested me very deeply. It's true that, in some way, it could have had the drawback of keeping me from my most personal vocation. It's not

1 The Jansenist crucifix represents the body of Christ with arms nailed closer together on the cross, thus symbolizing that few will enter the Kingdom of Heaven. *Trans.*

2 *L'Horizon* (out of print today) was published by the Éditions Spes in 1945. [*L'Horizon* was reprinted with *L'Iconoclaste, commentaires par l'Abbé Marcel Belay* and followed by Gabriel Marcel's essay "L'audace en métaphysique" (Courage in metaphysics), in a volume entitled *Percées vers un ailleurs. Sélections.* (Breakthrough toward a beyond. Selections), Librairie Arthème Fayard, Paris, 1973. *Trans.*]

by chance that, for some years, my essentially philosophical work was somewhat abandoned.

I no longer remember exactly under what conditions I gave Jean Paulhan certain texts of what I then called the *Journal métaphysique*. I would be singularly ungrateful if I didn't recognize that he rendered me the greatest favor in deciding to publish it among other titles in the series Bibliothèque des Idées published by *La Nouvelle Revue française*. I don't recall any hesitation on my part when he approached me about this. It was, however, an extremely important decision. For many years, and even up to a time that I can't quite pinpoint, I had considered this *Journal* as a simple preparation and was hoping one day to compose a work that would present, to some degree, the character of a treatise. By allowing the *Journal* to be published, I gave it a new character. I was admitting that it could somehow stand on its own and that perhaps my style of thought excluded the possibility of any type of dogmatic finish that I had envisaged for so long.

It is also possible, even though I can't quite affirm it, that the influence of Charles Du Bos was at work on me in some fashion at this time; for no one was more on guard than he against dogmatism in philosophy and more capable of appreciating the witness value, if I may say so, of a *Journal* such as mine. He professed a certain distrust towards philosophers in general—except for Plato, Plotinus and Bergson—with a global judgment against metaphysicians, a judgment—of course—that I could not share.

It is, I think, quite significant that our meeting took place on Rue Boulard, listening to the music of Ernest Chausson.[3] At Pontigny, Charles Du Bos had come upon my play the *Quatuor en fa dièse* and upon the musical epigraph which is none other than the admirable second theme of the sextet. Until then I had only read a few articles by Du Bos that were published in the review *Critique des idées et des livres* and which had, I must admit, struck me by a certain preciosity and even a somewhat apparent mannerism. Yet, rather quickly, I came to recognize that I was quite superficial in my judgment and that I was in the presence of a person gifted with a sensibility and analytical powers that very few share. Although we were different from each other, we were to enter into an intimate friendship that was to become

[3] French composer (1855-1899). *Trans.*

ever deeper. I will even say that if Charles Du Bos had not confided in me when he returned to the Catholic faith, it is highly probable that, under the circumstances I will talk about later on, my attitude would have been different.

For a long time I faithfully attended the lectures that Charles Du Bos gave successively at the home of the Duchess de Trévise, Quai Voltaire, then at the home of Mme Ridel, and finally in the apartment of the Rue des Réservoirs, in Versailles, where he mainly gave his course on Goethe. It is unfortunate that the author of *Approximations* (Approximations) could only speak in salons about writers for whom he had such affection. It may well be that his reputation suffered from a worldliness which, while it may have been somehow in keeping with his tendencies, was also a profound limitation that was in no way desired but assumed. It would have been good for him to have had seminars such as those, for example, that I myself gave in several American universities. Our university system, infinitely too rigid, didn't provide him with this chance, because the only official diploma he had was a licentiate.[4]

It may come as a surprise to see me taking time to remember this companion of my better years. But I would be sinning against an essential truth, it seems to me, if I didn't render homage to a person who gave me so much and to whom I feel so bound well beyond the limits of this existence.

I shall always regret that he did not complete the beautiful study he had undertaken on my thought, the first part of which was published in the *Le Roseau d'or*. With Malraux and others, he had been one of the first to recognize the importance of the *Journal métaphysique*. Later on I would show him all my writings, including my plays, which he appreciated perhaps all the more since, in general, he hardly enjoyed the theatre. In my works, he found something that was missing, and

[4] Paul de Man, in his edition of *Madame Bovary* (New York: Norton, 1965), included an essay by Du Bos on Flaubert's novel that originally appeared in *Approximations*, I: "On the 'Innner Environment' in the Work of Flaubert" ("Sur le milieu intérieur dans Flaubert"). In 1938 Du Bos became a member of St. Mary's College, Notre Dame, Indiana. The public lectures he gave that year, and wrote, in English were published under the title *What Is Literature?* New York: Sheed & Ward, 1940. In 1947, Sartre will publish his own *Qu'est-ce que la littérature* (*What is Literature*?) *Trans.*

this he deplored, in the theatre of contemporary playwrights, with the exception of Giraudoux and, of course, Claudel.

What adds to my debt is that, at his home, I met important people whom I would otherwise never have had the chance to meet, be it Scheler, Jakob Wassermann or Rainer Maria Rilke who, one particular evening, at the Du Bos residence on Rue Budé, gave us quite a moving account of his visit to Iasnaïa Poliana.[5]

The cosmopolitanism of Du Bos directly responded to my ever present aspirations. I was also very grateful to my friend when, in 1927, he asked me to take on the direction of the series Auteurs étrangers that until then he had directed for Plon. With Plon he had published the *Correspondance de Goethe et Schiller* (*Correspondence Between Schiller and Goethe*) and also what was to be the first translation of the complete works of Chekhov, that of Denis Roche, which was unfortunately mediocre. Some fine foreign novels had been published in this series, such as *Légende* (*Legend*) by Clemence Dane and *Nocturne* (*Nocturne*) by Frank Swinnerton.

With the complete approval of the publishers, I decided to give a somewhat different character to the series. The title and subtitle that were chosen —"Feux croisés—Terres et âmes étrangères" (Cross fire—Foreign lands and souls) indicated rather well my desire to reveal to the French public works as meaningful as possible that presented attitudes quite different from our own and that should be presented in a way that would allow us to assimilate them.

And so began for me an activity to which I gave myself with a kind of passion.

I think it quite important to emphasize this, since this aspect of my life has nearly always been neglected by those who have tried to take my work into account. Nevertheless, there is doubtless here an illustration of that desire for intersubjectivity that has always been mine.

Of course I was to notice quickly the nearly insurmountable obstacles that beset the translator, and it happened to me more than once to associate myself directly with the rewriting that was necessary

[5] Jakob Wassermann (1873-1934), German writer of Jewish origins, author of *Caspar Hauser*. Max Scheler (1874-1928), German philosopher. *Trans.*

for a translation that was done too hastily, at the expense of a text that should have been transposed without altering it.

How well I remember browsing in English bookstores where I was able to put my hand on this or that work that had just been published. These visits to bookstores had somewhat the look of a hunt to them, especially if I found something before another French publisher.

For example, as I had read with impassioned interest *Point Counter Point* by Aldous Huxley, then almost unknown in France, I wrote the author to ask whether he could not give us the rights for such a beautiful and rich novel. Some days later, he phoned me, we set up a time to meet and I received the rights. This was the beginning of a friendship which lasted until the death of Aldous Huxley. Through him I made the acquaintance of D.H. Lawrence, of whom I was to later publish an important *Choix de lettres* (Selected Letters). This extraordinary writer, then nearly diaphanous and near the end of his life, recalled with overwhelming affection at the home of Daniel Halévy, Quai de l'Horloge, in front of a group of friends I had joined, this New Mexico where he had found the fatherland of his torn heart.

I haven't yet mentioned Daniel Halévy. Even though he spoke very little about himself, I shall always remember him with affection and gratitude despite the fact that we were not quite on the same intimate terms as I was with Charles Du Bos. In his beautiful home on the Ile de la Cité, he knew how to create a hospitable atmosphere, and with a dignity devoid of all affectation he presided over discussions that he knew how to direct without impinging upon their spontaneity.

It was he who, in his fine series of the Cahiers Verts, successively published two of my plays: *Le Coeur des autres* and *Un homme de Dieu*. I don't know if one has sufficiently recognized the admirable insight he demonstrated by encouraging the beginnings of those writers who were to mark literature between the two World Wars, be it Mauriac or Montherlant, Giraudoux or Malraux, without forgetting André Chamson, Jean Guéhenno, Louis Guilloux, and so many others. It was also at his home that I made the acquaintance of Robert Garric with whom, especially after World War II, I was to be later united by the bonds of a perfect friendship.

With a gripping sadness I remember today, in this autumn of 1970, the hospitality I received at homes on the Quai de l'Horloge, Rue

Budé or Rue des Réservoirs where one could find, not only in Paris but, I would dare venture, even in Europe, the essence of what was then most lucid, sensitive, and vibrant. Am I giving in to an illusion—often decried—as to think that all this has vanished and that nothing has really been able to take its place? No, truthfully, I don't think this is an illusion.

These days I have written an "Open Letter" as a response to an article of Denis de Rougemont that appeared in *Les Nouvelles littéraires* whereby the author tried to refute the pessimism of Valéry. I underscored the weakness of the arguments the author called upon to justify his persistent confidence. And, giving in to the irrepressible pressure of my deepest feeling, I wrote, "European civilization died on 1 August 1914." I had never said this nor even quite thought it, and yet this fact suddenly appeared to me with all the tragedy of its evidence. Remembering the brilliance of our literature between the two World Wars, today I find that this was a phenomenon quite comparable to the strange light in which a landscape at times bathes after a sunset.

But can I sincerely affirm that, at the time I am referring to, I was aware of the reprieve granted to a world that was disappearing? It hardly seems possible to give this question a simple or categorical answer. Certainly, I was aware of living in a broken world: the play which bears this title testifies to that; but how could I have not also hoped for the worst to be avoided.

Le Monde cassé and the lecture entitled *Position et approches concrètes du mystère ontologique* (*Concrete Approaches to Investigating the Ontological Mystery*), that I published in an appendix of this play, are situated at the beginning of the thirties, that is to say at the beginning of the period which immediately follows my conversion to Catholicism in 1929; and here I feel obliged to reflect on it.

My father had died in 1926, after a long and painful illness. I was very sad to see him retreat into a distressing silence. This man who had been so active was now reduced to doing nothing. It was more and more difficult to distract him and, although he was a tireless reader, he was now too prostrate to give himself over to what had been the heart of his life. The continuous efforts on the part of my aunt to get him out of this kind of sleepiness were not successful. As she was extremely scrupulous, she was later to heap upon herself the most unjustifiable reproaches just as—I believe I have already said this—she did after the death of my grandmother in 1919. My wife and I both suffered from our powerlessness.

Without being able to decide whether this was coincidental or not, my health weakened, and for several months I experienced intense fevers for which no explanation could be found. I got well later under conditions that were just as incomprehensible, and finally I returned to good health.

The publication of the *Journal métaphysique*, I have said, gave me the encouragement I greatly needed. I insist on this, because I probably could not have decided to enter the Church if this decision had appeared as though linked to some state of trouble or disequilibrium.

It was after the publication of a short article I wrote concerning *Souffrance et Bonheur du chrétien* (Suffering and happiness of the Christian) (was it in *La Nouvelle Revue française* or in *Europe nouvelle*?), that François Mauriac wrote me, not only to thank me, but to invite me to abandon this kind of state of uncertainty in which I had confined myself until then. It would be false to say that this invitation overwhelmed me. On the contrary I remember that, as I read the letter and during the minutes that followed, I experienced a kind of peace which would have been at once Life and Light. Never had I felt more free while having to decide by myself and for myself while being fully aware. It seemed to me that here Mauriac simply played the role of a mediator between myself and an invisible power which, certainly, was not unknown to me but, on the contrary, I would say, using the words of Saint Augustine, more interior than myself. On several occasions, in my writings and in my lectures, I had taken a stance in favor of believers, I had placed myself on their side without, however, recognizing that I was one of them. In other words, I was proclaiming the eminent value of faith, I was denouncing as scandalous the claim of those who dared attack it from the outside, but it was a faith that I had in all conscience believed incapable of calling my own.

I therefore judged this situation to be untenable, and from a logical point of view, it was definitely that. On the level of existence, it had nevertheless been able to prolong itself for many years and nothing after all could better show the duality of the rational and the existential. But in the new light that this letter had just realized, not in me nor around me, but as it were beyond this very distinction of the outside and the inside, I suddenly discovered that it was necessary for me to make my actions conform to my thoughts, in short that I should make a commitment. These words *I should* designated nothing which might resemble a constraint or even perhaps an obligation in the strict sense of these words. To tell the truth, I was perhaps not at all clear about its meaning, but it was more like new evidence that I greeted than something I underwent. Yet a question immediately arouse; in fact, Protestantism, especially as I experienced it in the family I had joined through marriage, had appeared to me until then much more accessible, closer than Catholicism. I especially kept up a correspondence with my brother-in-law Louis Dallière, pastor at Charmes, in the Ardèche, which testified to the existence of a veritable spiritual relationship between us. As for my wife, the situation was slightly different. Though she belonged to the Reformed Church, I knew that her association with it did not exclude certain doubts, and Gregorian chant or even the Roman liturgy exercised an attraction on her that was more and more irresistible. Some years before her death, she was to join me in the bosom of the Roman Catholic Church.

Under these conditions, should not the commitment I had decided upon be carried out to benefit Protestantism? What is strange is that my answer to this question was categorical and negative. It clearly seemed to me that to choose Protestantism was to remain in an ambiguous position which I definitely intended to leave: in my view liberal Protestantism was only an ethic that disregarded what appeared to me to be most fundamental in life or in Christian affirmation. Was not Protestantism in solidarity with an idealism that I had broken away from? But, on the other hand, the little I knew of Barth bothered me and seemed to me to imply a refusal that was opposed to the philosophical reflection that it would be impossible for me to do without.

Did not Catholicism alone concentrate in itself the fullness of the Christian message? Was there another way for me to commit myself to it other than by explicitly embracing the Catholic faith?

I therefore let it be understood, regarding this question, that the influence of Charles Du Bos was very likely decisive. The word influence is even too vague. Rather would I say that his example was enough to persuade me. Here I had the irrefutable proof that a free spirit and one which had particularly received and assimilated the most precious strains of Nietzschean thought was able to find in Catholicism what could satisfy his highest aspirations.

So it was then quite natural for me to call upon the man who had been a spiritual director for Charles Du Bos and whose merits he had praised, Fr. Jean-Pierre Alterman. The fact that he was born into a Jewish family was in his favor and won me over in some way.

Everything therefore seemed to happen as though I simply had to occupy a place which had already been reserved for me in a spiritual family that was quite ready to welcome me.

Under these circumstances, the attitude of my in-laws was admirable. Any form of sectarianism was foreign to it. What was most important, in the view of my wife or her sisters, was that I was taking my place among Christians.

My aunt's feeling was certainly quite different. She would probably have been happy to see me rally to the side of Protestantism, but her prejudices against the Roman Catholic Church were such that she could only suffer from a decision she judged to be incomprehensible. On the contrary, my decision gave great joy to my aunt Mme Jules Marcel, who was a Catholic. If I mention her reaction, it is because during a visit I made to her, she told me that my mother, some days before dying, had been to see a priest of Saint Augustine parish and perhaps had even been baptized.

It could have been that my conversion was like an answer from Heaven to a prayer that she made without knowing that some days later she would leave this earth. Shaken up by what she had shared with me, I walked through Paris, given over to a kind of ecstasy.

I never received, it is true, any confirmation of this news. It doubtlessly strengthened me at a decisive moment. Oh that I might, in the life to come—the thought of which enlivens my daily existence every single day— receive the supreme assurance which will come as though to validate my decision of 1929.

But when I recall the weeks that followed and during which Fr. Alterman worked to prepare me for baptism and first communion, I realize that these preliminary preparations were certainly too short.

One might think that, philosophically, I was ready to get down to work. But that wasn't the case concerning the psychological data, probably even concerning the social givens of the situation. In all, I had remained until then outside the Roman Catholic Church, and I don't think I am exaggerating if I say that it had always inspired a certain distrust in me because of its dogmatism and its claim to alone hold Christian truth in its integrity. Can I say in all sincerity that this distrust has forever disappeared? I don't believe so, and it so happened, during my discussions with Fr. Alterman, that I let him see clearly my thought in this regard. One day I surprised myself when I told him: "In the end, we don't know at all what God thinks of the Protestant Reformation." He imprudently cried out, " Well I do know," not without at once trying afterwards to take back such a thoughtless statement. Nevertheless, that very evening, I wrote him a very respectful letter in which I told him that to me it seemed preferable to put off our conversations, at least for awhile. And it is to his great credit that he didn't have it in for me. Many years later, after the death of my wife, he paid me a visit that I cannot think of without being moved.

When I think about what my Catholicism has been, I notice that it has always been buoyed up by an assurance that was, if I may put it that way, accompanied by a certain reserve: on the one hand I understood in principle that catholic meant universal; but on the other hand, I could not hide the fact that insistence on universality found itself constantly attacked even within the Church and probably rather often at the top of the hierarchy.

With such a perspective, I couldn't, of course, admit that the Church had the right to take as its own a particular doctrine such as Thomism. Yet I put forth some effort to become acquainted with the doctrine in question, but I had to admit rather quickly that it remained foreign to me. During an entire winter in Versailles, Charles Du Bos and I had regular conversations with Jacques Maritain during which the latter tried with a touching firmness to introduce us into the heart of a system to which he had totally given himself. Unfortunately, his efforts were hardly crowned with success. I especially remember that he tried in vain to have us confirm the conception of evil as a *privation*, which is developed in the *Summa*. We did come, it is true, to some kind of compromise when Jacques Maritain accepted, it seems to me, rather favorably my suggestion to speak, not of privation, but of *lesion*. But I think that this agreement was founded upon an equivocation, as is often the case. In my mind, the word *lesion* clearly referred to an attack upon a certain vital or living order, without in any way being able to define this attack as a privation.

When, some years later, I read the long book of Jacques Maritain on *Les Degrés du savoir* (The degrees of knowledge), that I was to review for the *Revue des jeunes*, I didn't fail to indicate the malaise I felt in the presence of a language that was so foreign to modern philosophy. In my article, I even asked the question as to whether, from the apologetic point of view, this recourse to medieval terminology didn't risk setting up an obstacle for readers who would see in it the sign of some incompatibility between the Christian theological given and the mentality of the men of our time. Out of courtesy, I had sent the text of my article to Jacques Maritain, but I must say that he took it quite badly and asked me not to publish it. Unfortunately I acquiesced, but his attitude confirmed me in the judgment that I tended to have about neo-Thomism.

Nevertheless, I will add that I probably should have studied more than I did the thought of Saint Thomas and especially come to know the work of Father Maréchal. Here, as in other cases, I sinned by a certain impatience and even, I would add, by a kind of laziness which, looking back, seems to me rather unpardonable. I would also reproach myself for having voluntarily left aside all the problems related to exegesis. I had the feeling that I risked getting bogged down without coming to some positive conclusion. But I would also say that this decision was in some way commanded by fear: I was afraid that an attentive reading of contemporary exegetes might awaken certain doubts in me. I preferred "to keep my distance," that is to say stay with my own positions as regards both the unverifiable and creative fidelity, and so from this perspective feel myself dispensed from an inquiry that, it seemed to me, could only be interminable, fastidious and finally disappointing. In all it was convenient for me to fall back on the example of my Christian friends and to find some reassurance in thinking that they were more knowledgeable about work in exegesis than I was and this had not troubled them in their faith.

In the course of this retrospective examination, I feel myself obliged, if not to condemn my attitude of that time, to underline at least what could be criticized about it. I am, nevertheless, far from seeing clearly what I should have done, and this in light of the present situation, a kind of displacement that threatens Roman Catholicism. Nevertheless, I am able to affirm not only that I had then acted in good faith, but even that I have never given in to any impulse arising from anxiety or from anything which might resemble it. I was, on the contrary, quite serene. Had it been otherwise, I have already said this, I am quite sure that I would not have become a convert.

The notes recorded in *Être et avoir* speak directly and irrefutably about the joy I experienced during the month of March, 1929, following the decision I had taken. I can add nothing today to what I then wrote; any paraphrase would here be useless and even suspect. On the other hand, I will keep from undertaking some kind of self-critique, now in fashion, and from tagging as illusion the kind of elation I then enjoyed. May I even say that all this belongs to the past? That would be an ambiguous assertion and could lend itself to an interpretation whose inexactitude seems evident to me. Taking as my own, as so often happens, the words of Antoine Sorgue in act 3 of *L'Emissaire*, I should say "that it is also true that I still am and that I no longer am the man of that time"; and should I not recognize that as always this kind of contradiction is the driving force for an existence worthy of the name?

In a quite similar manner, I should say that I could express myself in a contradictory fashion about the effect my conversion was able to have on the development of my philosophical thought. I should probably appeal to the term illumination if I want to present clearly the subtle change that an attentive reader will not fail to notice if he compares texts written before my conversion and those written after it. I use the word "illumination" in its German meaning *Erhellung* which one frequently finds in the work of Jaspers and which should be distinguished from *Erläuterung*, which designates clarification.

I now note that Jaspers's *Système de philosophie* (*Philosophy*), which I read not very long after its publication in Germany, if it did not influence me, properly speaking, it nevertheless contributed notably to reinforce certain strains, as my study on *Les Situations limites* (Ultimate situations) shows and which was first published in *Les Recherches philosophiques* (1932-1933) before being taken up again in *Du refus à l'invocation* (*Creative Fidelity*). Of the three volumes of his *Système* (*Philosophy*), it was by far the second one consecrated to Existence that made the strongest impression upon me. The first had left me a little indifferent, and the third volume, with its *Théorie du chiffre* (Theory of ciphers), has always seemed questionable to me. I was to meet Jaspers only once in Basel, two or three years, I think, after World War II, and this conversation which dealt mostly with political problems disappointed me. It's as though the awareness Jaspers had of his reputation, his value, and the weight of his writings, somehow came between us. At least this was my sentiment, something I later never had the opportunity to either confirm or rectify.

10

When I recall the beginning of the 1930's, I again encounter the feeling of mounting anxiety that the news of what was happening in Germany caused me. I believe I already said that my fears as to the nationalist awakening in Germany were calmed only for a little while. I don't recall too well what my attitude had been at the time of the Ruhr's reoccupation. However I don't think I am mistaken in saying that it was contradictory. Something in me approved the determination with which Poincaré gave himself to assuring or reinforcing the security of France in the presence of Germany. But I couldn't quite hide the opposite effect that these efforts could not fail to have on the advocates of revenge who were already making their position known beyond the Rhine. I remember, to say the least, that when Wladimir d'Ormesson published his little book *Confiance en l'Allemagne?* (Confidence in Germany?) in the Documents bleus series *of La Nouvelle Revue française*, I found that the relative optimism, every proof of which he wanted to signal, was hardly justified. I also remember my disappointment in 1932 when André Tardieu, in Geneva, kept from making public the overwhelming information that he had been able to gather about the clandestine rearmament of Germany.

About the same time I had a brief conversation with Henri Lichtenberger, a professor at the Sorbonne and a specialist on Goethe and Wagner. He had just returned from Germany. I asked him whether he was not terribly worried. He said he was not; his friends had reassured him, telling him that what was going on beyond the Rhine was only concerned with interior politics. I was not only stupefied but amazed to observe the degree of ignorance that my interlocutor showed, and today I still wonder how he could have been so blinded. What a terrible awakening was in store for him!

I insist all the more on emphasizing the anxiety that never left me during those years, something that my publications probably scarcely reveal; and yet I am certain that this anxiety was much like the continuo of my existence until the war broke out. This can be understood all the more since, without having fought, I had become keenly aware, during the war, of the nameless sorrows, individualized to infinity, that this conflict entailed and about which intellectuals all too often had but a purely abstract idea. But at the same time, the pacifism that these same intellectuals so often subscribed to appeared to me to be illusory and dangerous. I well recognized that predatory forces would be able to exploit it for their profit, as Wilhelm Forster was to show in a lecture which I attended in 1937, if I am not mistaken, at someone's home in Passy.[1] Emmanuel Mounier was also there, but one sensed that he was clammed up and obstinate; he didn't want it to be true.

The previous year I had gone to Budapest where I had been invited to give some lectures, the day after Hitler's forces reoccupied the left bank of the Rhine. The journalists were waiting for me on the platform of the train station, and they asked me what the reaction was in Paris. I was in no position to answer their question, but I believed it all right to say that the French government was not taken by surprise and was being calm. The few days I spent in the Hungarian capital were ruined by the mortal worry which had come over me. If the French government decided to mobilize, would I not risk finding myself cut off from France and reduced to waiting for what followed in a city which, if not quite the enemy, was at least neutral and practically under German control. I fear that I experienced a rather cowardly relief in learning that the indignant words pronounced by Albert Sarraut had had no effect. But, almost immediately after, I understood that the opportunity for reacting had been missed in an unpardonable way, perhaps the last before the worst. That is what a French general was to tell me some months later in the living room of

1 Passy is a neighborhood in the sixteenth arrondissement in Paris, situated on the Right Bank. *Trans.*

Madame Dietz, and his judgment straightaway seemed to call for no response.

In the period that followed, the elections that brought the Popular Front to power were held. I can still see us, my wife, my aunt and myself, at the Place de l'Opéra, where we had gone to hear the election results. They seemed immediately catastrophic to me, at a time when all energy should have been put forth for the defense of the country, against the criminal enterprise that was developing beyond the Rhine. I couldn't forgive Léon Blum for having declared some years earlier, as though enjoying the favor of an oracle, that Hitler would never come to power.

Here as before, if I examine my conscience, I must recognize that then I was only imperfectly aware of the event. Certainly the future was to show to what extent my worries were founded, but on another level and in the long run, one could also understand, not only that certain reforms introduced by the Popular Front, such as the institution of paid vacations, answered a need of elementary justice, but also that a parliament and government, let's say of the right, would never have taken such initiatives. Historically speaking, the tragedy of the situations resided in the fact that these initiatives came too late at a time when, on the national level, they could be judged inopportune. But, in retrospect, wasn't it appropriate to incriminate the governments which had not been able to adopt at the right time measures which seemed necessary?

In light of all that we have seen since then, I cannot keep from reproaching myself for the bourgeois reaction that was nevertheless mine, particularly when the factories were taken over. In the end it was as though I had replaced my father who, even as far back as the time of his adolescence, had seen the excesses of the Commune and contracted the fear of disorder. Wasn't it this same fear that had kept him from becoming a Dreyfusard? But I have already mentioned this. My case was probably different. With me there were more contradictions, because in some ways I was a romantic and at no moment would I have been able to admit that the thought of public order should prevail over justice or truth. I cannot insist too much in saying that these contradictions could not merge into a dialectical synthesis of the

Hegelian type; they couldn't even be, properly speaking, resolved but only surpassed through the unity of drama. In me, from the beginning, the man of contradictions and the playwright were but one. And the philosopher? ... one might ask and I do ask myself. It seems to me that his principal task was for him to be aware of these contradictions, but at the same time to resist the temptation of emptying them at the level of language and simply be satisfied with a simple appearance. As I was to say much later, during my talk in Frankfurt, in 1964, vigilance appeared to me, at the very time I am speaking about, as the fundamental virtue of philosophy. Yet I have not wavered on this point and even today, despite the distressing and apparent diminution of my creative faculties, I try to be watchful.

This disposition was already clearly apparent in the lecture I gave in 1932 to the Société de philosophie de Marseille, the title of which was *Position et approches concrètes du mystère ontologique*, about which men as enlightened as Father de Lubac think, and rightfully so, that it contains my essential contribution to contemporary thought.[2]

In *Être et avoir* you can find the notes that I wrote during the weeks that preceded my trip to Marseilles. I fondly remember the long walks through Paris during which this lecture developed. With a profound joy I could see thoughts becoming organized in me that, until then, had only appeared in a scattered fashion. This was particularly the case for the distinction between *problem* and *mystery*, which, much later, after I had received some recognition, was to be reproduced so often, in such schematic conditions that it thus risked having no meaning. One can never be too much on guard against a "portable" philosophy. Here I remember the unfortunate Georges Duhamel who told me one day, it must have been around 1948: "What you existentialists lack is a slogan, like the Cartesian cogito." The cogito treated like a slogan! Poor Descartes! And especially poor Duhamel![3]

With the distance I now have today, I must acknowledge the central place that the Marseilles lecture occupies in my philosophical work. It also seems rather curious to me that, from that time on, I was quite

2 Henri de Lubac (1896-1991), French Jesuit, theologian, writer and founder of the series *Sources chrétiennes*, which made patristic and medieval texts available to scholars. *Trans.*

3 Georges Duhamel (1884-1966), winner of the 1919 Goncourt Prize for *Civilisation*. (Civilization) *(1914-1917)*. Paris: Mercure de France, 1918. *Trans.*

aware of living in what I called "a broken world." At first the expression shocked people. Since then it has been taken up by men who have probably never seen me. But what I must especially emphasize is that, contrary to all those who before me had approached speculation on being from purely abstract premises, I felt that this speculation—I would more willingly say research—only took on value and meaning from a kind of observation that accounted for the very situation of the world in which I found myself engaged. In that way I placed myself on what was not yet commonly called existential ground. For me, then, it was not a question of elaborating a treatise but of pursuing a meditation, and this word would in the end take on the meaning close to the one Descartes had given it and, in our own time, Husserl. I must underline, however, that in my case the subject was no longer that of the Cartesian or Husserlian cogito. It was a living and concrete subject that did not see, in the end, any reason to question its own existence and intended to stay away from a "hyperbolic" doubt. This subject, about which I should not speak in the third person, appeared to itself as one among others, and refused to be granted a transcendental or ontological privilege. What I had done was finally to get rid of the idealist postulates that, in the first part of the *Journal métaphysique*, I had often rather awkwardly criticized.

I don't think I'm mistaken when I say that it was then, during the first months of 1932, that I became fully aware of my own thought and of the path that was mine to follow. As I said earlier—but the point is too important not to return to it—I have some problems in discerning the role that the event of 1929 played in this kind of maturation. Earlier I spoke about a new illumination. Yes, that is probably it, but can I say in all certainty what its source was? This word is in any case more appropriate here than that of "cause" which would be lacking in meaning. Probably my play *Le Monde cassé*, written at the same time, lets one best discern what took place in me at a level that, by itself, philosophical reflection can reach only with difficulty. Of course I am thinking about act 4 and especially about the two final scenes.

The conditions under which the play took shape in me seem rather significant. I knew an intelligent young lady, beautiful and appreciated by all her friends, whose husband, a good yet self-effacing man, none of them seemed to pay attention to. My attention as a dramatist focussed on him: I wondered whether he was not more hurt in his self-love than in his love. And so were born Laurent and Christiane Chesnay. But to this given, that was in effect provided by experience, was added a theme of a very different kind, one whose origin has remained quite mysterious to me. Why had Christiane been able to marry Laurent? Was there not some kind of traumatic experience at the origin of this unfortunate marriage? It seemed to me that Christiane had been passionately in love with a childhood friend and that, just when she was going to decide to admit her love for him, he told her he was getting ready to enter the religious life. From then on the world seemed to lose all meaning for Christiane. Thinking herself certain of never being able to love anyone, she had consented to marry Laurent out of compassion or some sense of charity, something for which, moreover, she would later reproach herself. And it was again out of charity that, once she understood the type of moral ulcer from which her husband was suffering, she would go so far as to have him believe that she was in love with a Russian composer who has spurned her. And now Laurent literally lives with the thought that his wife is humiliated, as he himself has been. But now she also begins to hold him in horror. She then receives the news of the death of the man in Solesmes whom she had previously loved so much. Henceforth, she is alone, distraught and seeks comfort in the arms of an insignificant man whose protestations of love she has never been able to take seriously. Is she going to go away with him as he would like her to? Leave Laurent and their child? But an unforeseen visit keeps her from this path that would lead to her perdition. Geneviève, the sister of the deceased Benedictine, whom she previously met, but who never inspired her with any particular feeling, arrives bearing what will be a message of life for her. From the intimate notes found in the cell of the deceased,it can be ascertained that the monk, under mysterious conditions, had become aware of the love that Christiane had previously had for him and of the incurable wound that his entry into religious life had inflicted upon her, and so he had taken on a responsibility towards her that he could not let himself ignore. For Christiane it was as though she was entering into an unknown world where separation, which was until then in her view the overwhelming law of our existence, suddenly disappears to make way for a light which at first seems unbearable to her. But then it's as though her eyes become used to it and as though some breath from beyond has mercifully touched her. She becomes aware of an order and a communion which is not only that of the saints but also that of sinners, and from then on a new relationship with Laurent can be established. Certainly we can't be sure that this illumination will last, and that both will not again fall into this "broken world" from which grace has removed them. But this is not important: what does count is that both have seen clearly at least for an instant.

I remember that Jacques Chardonne, who personally was rather quite removed from such experiences, wrote me a warm and understanding letter in which he told me he had discovered through my play that the theatre can come to some *illuminating truths*. Some, on the contrary, have reproached me for my ending, accusing me of having resorted to some kind of *deus ex machina*. But I think this implies complete ignorance, not only of the play in particular, but of my work in general. It is certain that, if I had not already, as I said earlier, acquired through my own experience the certainty that there exists a dimension at the heart of which separation disappears, I would not have been able to write the last two scenes of *Le Monde cassé*. I remember that already, earlier on, in the last scene of *Quatuor en fa dièse*, and without any religious reference, this same intuition was affirmed. Yourself? Myself? Where does a personality begin?

Nowhere, I think, does the continuity of my essential thought appear more clearly.

It was a cruel disappointment for me not to have been able to have *Le Monde cassé* staged in France. A very favorable article by Jacques Copeau had held out some hope of that happening. Would he not agree to produce the play at the Théâtre de la Madeleine where he was then based for a little while? But he answered that he was afraid the public would not understand, and instead he chose *Les Chevaliers de la table ronde* (The Knights of the Round Table), one of the weakest plays of Jean Cocteau.

A quarter of a century later, I was to have the satisfaction of seeing *Le Monde cassé* staged in English under favorable conditions at the Gate Theatre in Dublin.

Perhaps the play will one day be performed in France, in a few weeks or months: a professor in Saint-Étienne who has already put on two or three interesting plays, with amateurs, hopes to stage it.[4]

At least I had, at the time I'm talking about, the satisfaction of having Jacques Maritain accept the play for publication in the series Les Iles, where the lecture I gave in Marseilles serves as an epilogue to it and about which I have already spoken. Thus, for the first time, the close bond which has never ceased to connect my theatre and my philosophical writings was clearly established.

This is an opportunity for me to recall the Sunday gatherings at the Maritains in Meudon, where my wife and I sometimes went. In principle I was pleased to feel myself welcomed with kindness into this ultra-Catholic milieu where men of value were welcomed. But it was disagreeable for me to notice that Raïssa Maritain, in particular, betrayed a kind of condescending indulgence towards my wife, who was then still a Protestant. Whatever might have been her merits, Jacques Maritain's wife had, in the extreme, the faults that one sees only too frequently in converts: she was a fanatic. I am not alone in thinking that in the end she had a rather unfortunate influence on her husband.

[4] This performance did take place on 25 May 1971.

11

It was a little later that German philosophers and writers, who had fled Hitlerian persecution, began to visit me. Some among them came to our home several times to discuss their thought, during intimate evening conversations, among friends who could understand them and who were just as indignant on hearing about the atrocities that were already spreading beyond the Rhine. These encounters were quite important to me, if only because they were to lead me to write *Le Dard* in 1936, which I still consider today to be one of my most significant works.

It was my friend Maurice Boucher, professor of German language and literature at the Sorbonne, who had sent me young Paul Krantz, who was to make a name for himself under the pseudonym of Eric Noth. I knew that he had been involved in a criminal affair which had received much attention in the German press but I have only recently learned the details, having read his *Mémoires* (Memoirs) that were published last year in France by Julliard. I liked him at once, and it was he who became the model for the character Werner Schnee. He was at Aix-en-Provence, when I wrote the play very quickly and as though under some irresistible pressure. I shared it with my actress friend Magdeleine Bérubet, who had received much acclaim in *Knock* and had decided to stage an irregular play with some friends who were professional actors.[1] She was enthusiastic about *Le Dard* and she decided to choose it. When Noth returned to Paris, I read him the play and, believing I remembered him to have once acted, I offered him the

1 *Knock, ou le Triomphe de la médecine* (Knock, or the triumph of medicine) (1923) is a play by Jules Romains (1885-1972). *Trans.*

role of Werner. He accepted without the least hesitation even though he had never actually set foot on stage. After the first rehearsal, Magdeleine Bérubet told me that it was "catastrophic"; my friend knew nothing about acting. Yet, what was peculiar, after the second rehearsal, her feeling changed because she told me, "Perhaps we shall make an actor of him after all." In effect he was to incarnate my character in an unforgettable manner. At the dress rehearsal, at his very appearance, towards the end of the first act, the entire theatre burst into applause.

I must also say that, in composing the role of Werner, I had "tried" mentally each line according to the image I had formed of Noth: would he be able to say them? Would they fit in with his own style of expression? As for myself, I was in no way surprised as to the success. Overall it was exceptional and improbable, as I learned from Robert Kemp, who also wrote a very favorable review of it in *Le Temps.*

Only two matinees had been planned for the Théâtre des Arts, the future Théâtre Hébertot, but we were successful in having a regular production, this time at the small Théâtre des Deux Masques which no longer exists today.

The reading of the *Mémoires* (Memoirs) taught me what I ignored: in the end Noth detested his own role because the idealism of Schnee in no way corresponded to his own state of mind and because he dreamed of taking part one day in the armed struggle against the wave of Nazism. In fact, he was never to have this opportunity. After hidding for a while in Provence, he succeeded in reaching the United States where, moreover, he experienced many ups and downs, and today, back in France, he leads a difficult life.

The year 1937, which was for me the year of *Le Dard* , has left me with a singular recollection. For some weeks it was as though a cover of clouds that weighed down on us had lifted. Thanks to the Universal Exposition of 1937, we again began absurdly to hope. After all, the worst was not sure to happen. We spent some happy weeks as a family in Morgat, an area of Brittany for which I have always had a preference. I would work on either *La Soif* (Thirst) or *Colombyre ou le Brasier de la Paix* (*Colombyre or the Torch of Peace*). The relatively successful *Le Dard* had encouraged me. I felt in full possession of my talents as a playwright. *Le Fanal* (*The Lantern*) was accepted for production at the Comédie-Française. At the beginning of August the International Congress of Philosophy was held in Paris at which I gave a lecture on the *Méta-problématique* (Meta-problematical). Here a short debate on death ensued between Léon Brunschvicg and myself which was to leave a deep impression on many attending who had different outlooks. "The death of Gabriel Marcel," Léon Brunschvicg had said, "preoccupies Gabriel Marcel more than the death of Léon Brunschvicg preoccupies Léon Brunschvicg." To which I answered that what preoccupied me was not my own death but that of the loved one. Certainly I was anticipating what I was to feel two and a half years later after the death of my aunt and later still, after that of my wife. But I was truly speaking here about something that was obvious and that my entire work and life bear witness to.

However, I wonder whether these summer months of 1937 did not definitely mark the apex of my life. This was doubtlessly, to say the least, the period of my full development, before the terrible events that were to wound and tear us apart.

Among the works where my development is most clearly seen, an important place must be given to *Le Chemin de crête*, written in 1935, just before *Le Fanal* (*The Lantern*) and *Le Dard*. It is an extremely dark play, and some might be surprised by the evident lack of continuity between it and *Le Monde cassé*. At the origin of the play, there is especially the meeting with a woman whose name I won't reveal but who had fascinated and troubled me by her exceptional gifts. What had particularly struck me was the way—even though the doctors had pronounced her cured after a lengthy sickness—in which she had continued to live as though she were sick, as though she had not been able to bring herself to live among healthy people. I had also known an analogous case some years earlier. The questioning thought on this ambiguity of the relation between a person and his sickness is unquestionably at the origins of *Le Chemin de crête*. However, here this is only one aspect of an infinitely more complex situation. I wouldn't be able to say how it became clear in my mind. What is certain is that, among all my characters, Ariane Leprieur is one of those who have most deeply interested me, one of those who have most categorically removed themselves from what could have been for me a deliberate plan. The proof for this is that, after the third act, I realized that my characters refused the ending that I had originally conceived. They weren't characters in search of an author, as for Pirandello, but characters in revolt against the author. My wife and I were then in Austria, in the region around Salzburg. There I experienced some days of very painful depression. I had just written the first three acts during three successive stays in the Tyrol and in the Dolomites, and it was as though all my effort had come to nought. I shall never forget the moment when, as we were walking along a path some distance from Saint-Wolfgang, I suddenly saw in a flash the only possible ending. It seemed to have come from within me. But who or what imposed it upon me was a difficult question to answer. What is certain is that on the following day, this time without encountering any obstacle, I wrote, without interruption, act 4, which remains, in my view, one of the high points of my entire work. This unforgettable experience illustrates one of the fundamental themes of my thought: the liaison between creation and receptivity, or let us say economically, the ideal of a creative receptivity.

The ultimate destiny of the *Le Chemin de crête* has been remarkable. I had made the acquaintance of Madeleine Ozeray whom I had congratulated for the way in which she had interpreted Péguy's *Jeanne d'Arc* (Joan of Arc), and so I had the idea of taking the play to her. She agreed to stage it at the Théâtre du Parc, in Brussels, where the play was quite successful. When, a little later, in the autumn of 1953, Madeleine Ozeray tried to revive the play at the Théâtre du Vieux-Colombier with a different staging and other actors, it would not enjoy the same success, and this despite the excellent review Robert Kemp had written about it in *Le Monde*.[2] The critic of *Le Figaro*, in particular, who then had considerable influence on the general public, showed that he had totally misunderstood the play. I add that, since I was unfortunately in a serious automobile accident some weeks earlier, I was not able to attend the rehearsals. I had to be carried in on a stretcher the evening of the dress rehearsal, and it was too late to correct any mistakes made during my absence. The poor reception of the play painfully affected me but I will add that it in no way changed my opinion about the work, one of the most rigorous I have written.

[2] Here I want to note that Éléonore Hirt was remarkable in the role of Violette.

Some years later I was to see it again in London, in August of 1958, where it benefited from remarkable acting; I am thinking especially of Hélène Cherry, who played the role of Ariane.

But how good it would be for the play to be staged again in Paris, at a time, unfortunately hypothetical, when the interior life will have found a place in the theatre.[3] The most enlightened critics have understood quite well that there exists between it and *Un homme de Dieu*, certainly not some vague analogy, but a kind of intimate concordance. But I will say that if, in *Un homme de Dieu*, the influence of Ibsen—the Ibsen of *Rosmersholm*, is perhaps still to some degree perceptible, that's not the case for *Le Chemin de crête*. I repeat: here and in the plays of the same period I liberated myself and, I would even add, once and for all.

3 *Le Chemin de crête* (*Ariadne*) was televised on France-Culture, 31 May 1971, and played by the Comédiens-Français who showed themselves to be excellent actors.

12

Perhaps it would be good to remember that my encounter with the Oxford Groups dates from just a few years prior to World War II. It was through my friends the Davidses that I came into contact with the French Group that, under the influence of the Baron and Baroness de Watteville and Pastor Grosjean, tried to have the movement of Franck Buchman established in France. Certainly the three French people I have just mentioned were worthy of sympathy and respect, and the same holds true for many of their friends. But what attracted me in the Groups was no doubt the eminent value that was granted to the fact of encounter, the metaphysical importance of which I had myself emphasized, especially at the lecture in Marseilles. I would even say as much about the witnessing that played such an important role in the Groups. In all I could affirm that for some time I thought I could find in them a clear illustration of this intersubjectivity—I wasn't yet using the term at that time—around which what I hesitate calling my philosophy was increasingly centering itself. And so we have the explanation that for an entire winter I agreed that the meetings of these Groups should take place regularly at my home. My wife was not opposed to this, although, with her usual lucidity, she was probably sensitive well before I was to what was primary and finally irritable about the spirit of the Groups. When I consider these distant times, I remember that I also attached great importance to the meditation the Groups practiced in light of the witnessing that went on. Had I not, indeed, tried to define the basic character of meditation at the Marseilles lecture?

Unfortunately it was soon evident that the practice of meditation risked leading to serious mistakes. During one séance, a woman, worried about conforming to the requirement for absolute honesty that was part of the Groups' code, had the imprudence of publicly admitting that she was being unfaithful to her husband. During the following period of meditation, a "direction" was called for by the participants; they didn't hesitate to see in this an injunction coming from the Holy Spirit; this woman should absolutely admit the fault to her husband. The unfortunate woman conformed to the "given direction," but the result was catastrophic: the husband was only waiting for the occasion to be separated from his wife and quickly seized the one that had just been given him. It was truly difficult to attribute to the Holy Spirit any kind of role in this imbroglio which was worthy of a Broadway playwright. Other examples have led me to question the value that one might accord the directions that were thus obtained. But on the other hand, what I did not agree with was the kind of interdiction that the Groups sought to have weigh upon all reflection, this being looked upon as an affirmation that was finally illicit for the self, for here on the contrary it was good to forget oneself, and in the end give up the use of critical reason regarded as sinful. From the moment that this appeared to me in all its clarity, it became evident for me that I had nothing to do with the Oxford Groups. A disastrous house party at the Trois Épis, which I imprudently attended, had finally enlightened me. Nevertheless, I still kept up friendly relations with several of the people I had met in the Groups. And much later, after the war, when the Groups gave way to Moral Rearmament, noticing that the climate was fortunately different, I accepted to go to Caux, and I even wrote a long introduction to a book whose idea I had suggested. It included a certain number of accounts, at times overwhelming ones, about the interior changes that many men and women, come from every walk of life, have gone through and who have found in Moral Rearmament an active principle of spiritual regeneration. Today I am still in touch with Moral Rearmament, not without expressing at times some criticism on this or that aspect of the events for which it is responsible.

Some have definitely reproached me for the active support I gave the movement. But to me these reproaches don't seem justified. An experience that can't be ignored demonstrates, I repeat, some of the lasting transformations that took place in Caux, in Mackinaw, where I spent some time, in 1959, with people who were distraught or fanatics who found there a new attraction and who were called to live more deeply in their own church a faith which until then remained purely nominal.

This isn't the place to go into detail, but faced with the general disintegration of belief that we encounter around us, it would seem iniquitous, even scandalous, not to be just towards men and women who gave themselves over entirely to a task that was in the end praiseworthy. My criticism has to do especially with the somewhat primary formalism which may be translated by these four criteria: absolute honesty, purity, disinterestedness and love, and because of this, by the somewhat puerile ignorance of concrete situations which cannot be simplified in such a way. Of course, these errors affect nearly always the plays by which Moral Rearmament tries to communicate its doctrine to spectators who are, most often, new to the theatre. I don't need to say to what extent this naive didacticism goes against everything I have tried to create in my work. Nevertheless, I have been able to notice, and not without surprise, that these same plays often moved and even shook up the enlightened spectators who found in them some kind of nourishment. The fact is surprising but should be taken into consideration. It seems to prove to me that simplicity can become like oxygen for minds asphyxiated by the complications of a world that is more and more technical and by a literature that has too often lost contact with the most fundamental human aspirations.

Yet you will tell me that in *Colombyre ou le Brasier de la paix* (*Colombyre or the Torch of Peace*), written in 1937, I presented a grotesque caricature of the mentality of the Oxford Groups. That's perfectly true! And I am far from regretting it. The idea for the play had come to me in the following manner: as usually happens every year, we had gone, my wife and I, to spend some days in Montana, at the home of some good friends. On one outing, we had visited a grand and beautiful chalet which belonged to an Englishman. The idea then came to me that it would be an ideal refuge for citizens belonging to different European countries who, in the event of war, would be trying to escape eventual bombing raids. But some among them, of course, would try to justify what in reality would be a fear full of panic while presenting it as the expression of a militant pacifism. Nothing would be more absurd, of course, than to see in this satire of a lying pacifism anything which might resemble an acceptance of war: I have repeatedly said that I have always held war in horror; but, I repeat, it was necessary for me to frequently say that pacifists have only too often unwillingly played into the hands of the imperialist powers they claimed to oppose.

Colombyre has only been staged in Belgium by students after World War II, but most of the spectators appeared to be quite upset, not understanding terribly well that a philosopher could have written such a clownish and satirical play. Besides, in a more general way, the role of the comical element[1] in my theatre has been neglected, not to say questioned in the name of a certain schematic idea that I have always opposed: that was the case for Jean Paulhan and even, it seems to me, for André Gide. "My God, what a horrible thing," Béatrice cries out, in the third act of *Le Dard*, "does life only have puppets and desperate people?" (*Le Dard*, act 3, scene 5) Some years later, I gave a similar response to Champel (in act 4) of *Mon temps n'est pas le vôtre* (My time is not yours). Certainly, nothing here resembles what we could call an objective judgment on the men of today but rather something like the exclamation which comes to the lips of a playwright confronted by a world that is broken or out of sync, where the reactions of normal people become more and more automatic, where fanaticism seems to gain daily more territory and where those who try to remain themselves feel as though they were being tracked by despair.

Certainly there is a possible recourse that belongs to the order of grace. Christiane, at the end of *Le Monde cassé*, Werner in *Le Dard* or Arnauld in *La Soif* (Thirst) are there as witnesses, but for nothing in the world, and no more after my conversion than during the years which preceded it, would I have wanted to write anything that might resemble an apologetic theatre where faith would appear as a pseudo-solution, as a kind of stopgap. If since my first plays—and including

1 Neither *Le Divertissement posthume*, nor *La Dimension Florestan* (The Florestan dimension), written thirty years later and which is more than a satire of Heiddegerian jargon, could be considered as secondary in my work.

Mon temps n'est pas le vôtre—there is any value to which I wanted to remain faithful, it is what, however imperfectly, the term integrity translates.

I have intimately known, and among those closest to me, too many people who it seems have not been able to adhere to the Christian faith or, in the end, to any other, in order not to imagine with force, and this in a sentiment which somehow goes beyond simple compassion, what the vision of a despairing person can be.

One should not then be surprised to observe that there is an aspect of hopelessness in my theatrical work; for example, I am thinking of *Le Mort de demain*, of *La Chapelle ardente*, and even of *Le Chemin de crête*. I have never been able to admit in any way that a play must necessarily close with an encouraging or optimistic note.

Can one presume that by this refusal, in such works, I have challenged a demand that is after all quite normal on the part of the spectator who desires to return home reassured? But to tell the truth, I don't think that a playwright, worthy of the name, should have to worry about reassuring anyone. Of course, this doesn't mean that in my thought the writer has to ignore what the spectator could think or experience. But what I think I have always seen, and this from the time of *Le Seuil invisible*, is that the writer had to treat the spectator as an awareness to be awakened, or if you will, an awareness to be opened up to a higher degree of lucidity. There could be no question of providing him with some kind of ready made truth that he would have to absorb like a calming drug or tranquilizer. That would be a degrading and degraded vision of theatre, one that has never belonged to the geniuses we venerate. What alone is important is to detach the spectator from his prejudices, from the received opinions that weigh him down and keep him from entering into himself and communing with another. In short, the theater should help renew him interiorly. It is according to this perspective that my entire dramatic work should be considered, and I should add, of course, that it cannot be separated from the on-going work that took place in me all these years. I was in touch with traumatic events of the two World Wars, even more during the Second than the First, and, of course, I also knew the wake of the troubles that followed.

I would hope that this little book, whose weaknesses, alas, I can see so clearly, might at least have the advantage of underlining these connections which have been, until now, nearly always left aside; and I myself admit quite willingly that sometimes I have also been insufficiently aware of them. Clearly this might be a temptation, even if one keeps from every systematic representation, to think that a work is an intelligible totality and removed from time. There are probably examples in the history of literature where such a representation can be justified; but at this time of my life, I must unhesitatingly affirm that, in my own case, I must reject it.

13

For me as for Charles Du Bos, who was to express himself on the matter in moving terms, in a little book called *Commentaires* (Commentaries), the conclusion of the Munich agreements set up a moral problem, one that in the end had no solution.[1] On the one hand the violation of the promises made to Czechoslovakia could only appear as scandalous. But on the other hand, it seemed evident to me that we could not commit ourselves to a war without running the greatest risks. Under these conditions, the relief I felt on learning that the worst had been avoided was accompanied by a feeling of shame as well as by a deep fear regarding the near future. I saw in the Munich agreements the punishment of a truly irreparable mistake that the English and we had committed in 1936 in not reacting militarily to Hitler's reoccupation of the left bank of the Rhine.

I remember with much emotion the admirable letter my aunt had then written President Daladier: she asked him, in the name of the French who had a conscience, to demand of the country every sacrifice so that the respite arranged by such an agreement that was shameful in itself might be used for the defense of the fatherland that was soon to be threatened. Needless to say, she received no answer.

She was to die some months later, and what gives a representative picture of her is that, before falling into a coma, her last sentence was to ask for news about Finland. She was in complete communion with this people committed in a heroic struggle against Soviet imperialism. Her death on 1 January 1940 caused me one of the greatest sufferings

1 Gabriel Marcel wrote a Preface for *Commentaires*. Paris: Desclée de Brouwer, 1946. *Trans.*

of my life. But, ardently patriotic as she had been, would she have been able to suffer the pain of seeing France invaded? And, on the other hand, because of her Jewish origins, would she have escaped persecution? Would she have agreed to leave Paris? I know that these are vain questions but she has haunted me because she has remained incredibly present to me: and this is still true twenty years later. Recalling the extraordinary forgetfulness of self that she showed throughout her life, I have been thinking recently how she had certain traits in common with Simone Weil. With both there seems to have been a certain legitimate love of self that was missing. That's why it was impossible to give her the smallest gift: she didn't realize that through this refusal she disappointed those who would have so wanted to show her a visible sign of their affection. Although she thought herself to be an unbeliever, she had asked that Christian prayers be said at her deathbed, and I can still see myself running to Pastor D.'s home to have him come fulfill this request. Her example has certainly helped convince me that we ourselves do not know what we believe or don't believe. This agnostic was, I am quite sure of it, infinitely more believing than many supposed believers.

I had placed myself at the disposal of the Ministry of National Education and had been consequently appointed to teach at the Lycée Louis-le-Grand. Tormented as I was by the anxiety caused by the very thought of this "drôle de guerre," whose outcome was still impossible to imagine, I experienced some relief in having to fulfill a precise task which in some ways corresponded to my deepest desires. If correcting papers was quite unpleasant for me, I nevertheless liked the contact I had with the students themselves. The general level was mediocre, but several students were amiable and showed a visible interest in philosophy such as I tried to make it come alive for them.

Because of my aunt's death, I inherited a great amount of furniture and a considerable library that I absolutely wanted to conserve. So the moment had come to carry out a plan that we had formed earlier on, my wife, my son, and myself, that of acquiring a home in the country. Our first idea had been to find a place not too far from Paris, but very quickly we had to give up on this; what we were shown was either mediocre or too expensive. A postcard that one of my students had sent me from Meyssac during the Christmas vacation reminded us of the time we had spent some years earlier in Argentat, as well as of an excursion made by car from Brive. And even more into the past, there was the memory of the short stay that my parents had made in the Corrèze Department, at the home of one of my father's friends. I remembered that he had spoken to me about the waterfall in Gimel and the towers of Merle. He had much loved this undulating and forested country. And so we wrote on the off chance to a real estate agency in Brive that sent us some information concerning a little manor that we might possibly like. My wife and I decided to go see it; this was April 1940. Through a coincidence that was to have unforeseeable effects, Daniel-Rops paid us a visit two days before our departure. When he learned that we were going to visit Brive, he told us he would mention it to his friend Edmond Michelet who was yet unknown to us.

The visit to the agency was a cause for disappointment: most of the information that had been given was inexact. Nevertheless we decided to go see this Michelet about whom Daniel-Rops had spoken. He received us with open arms and told us that, as Rops had mentioned our visit, he had freed himself up for two days and was at our disposal with his car. For me this was much the first demonstration of generosity or, as I would say in my own language, of an availability that this admirable man was to give so many examples of later on. He told us that the best thing to do was, to begin with, to go see the property that the agency had mentioned. Of course we were immediately seduced by the façade with its two asymmetrical towers and its windows with transoms. But on the inside everything would have to be redone, and the thought of such work scared me. However, after having seen other properties, all with various drawbacks, we returned to the first, and Edmond Michelet did not hesitate to advise us to buy it. He encouraged us by mentioning that, without our realizing it, we probably had friends in Brive, and I think I can say that his favorable opinion was decisive. However, the decision was only made a little later, after my wife had returned with one of her sisters who was also seduced by Le Peuch.

Meanwhile the lightning German offensive burst forth on 10 May. After a few days it was evident that everything was disastrous.

The contract was signed during the first days of June, but there was no question of moving into the new home. And when we left Paris, three days before the arrival of the Germans, we went to a chateau that one of our friends owned, located near Noirétable, in the Loire valley, where part of our family was waiting for us.

It may surprise some that I have gone into such detail about the house, and this might seem to be insignificant in regard to the interior development that I am trying to retrace. But in light of what was to follow and because of the vital link that was to be created from the reality of these circumstances, between us and this house in the Corrèze, it seemed to me, on the contrary, that all this preparation, apparently contingent, was comparable to the birth of a human being.

And how could I not refer here to the main theme of my work which is that of incarnation, of the incarnate being.

In writing these lines, I also remember the grand apartment of the Plaine-Monceau where I had lived until my marriage, where my grandmother and my father had died, where my aunt had also just died and where my wife, during the first month of 1940, had spent many heartfelt hours going through so many things accumulated since my grandmother had moved there in 1892.

I can see, in thinking about it, that between this rather somber and large apartment that gave onto a small street of the seventeenth arrondissement, and myself, there existed a sorrowful relationship, a kind of indefinable tension which can perhaps be explained by the fact that I had come there on 15 November 1893, some weeks before my birthday, shaken up over the death of my mother.

In the first part of this narrative I have sufficiently explained what my schoolboy anxieties had been and the deep lack of satisfaction felt from the quite abnormal group that the four of us necessarily formed. It is as though I had always vaguely sensed that the fabric of our life on Rue Meissonier was threaded by death. In thinking about it, I wonder if that isn't the profound reason why, at vacation time, I had the feeling of living once again. But this was always at a hotel, thus in uncertain conditions; and something compelling in me desired to take root in a home situated in the country, in harmony with a land, trees and a horizon.

Nevertheless, I still experienced a terrible feeling in noticing that it was the death of my aunt that alone had made the realization of this desire possible. Wasn't this a kind of overwhelming proof of the tragedy that is immanent in human existence and of which the catastrophe of November 1893 had made me prematurely aware?

I can still remember the frightful hours of our exodus from Paris; I can see us piled into our Citröen with a cousin, our Alsatian maid, and her little child. From afar, towards the west, black smoke spotted the horizon. On the eve of our departure or on the preceding day, we had been able to bid our son good-bye. He had returned from Tunisia with his unit. There seemed to be no future; only the present counted and it was unlivable. It took us six hours to get to Arpajon; unverified rumors were spreading; the least breakdown would be mortal for us. In Arpajon, we left the highway and were then surprised to see that the road before us was deserted. I remember rather keenly the night we spent outside under the stars, somewhere between Sully and Sancerre. Anxiety had given way to a particular sentiment which had its share of sweetness: it was as though, deprived of every human security, we were placing our confidence exclusively in the Invisible.

I won't dwell at length on the stay we made with our friend Mme B. in her chateau du Forez, during these weeks of June and July 1940. It was as though we were consumed by anxiety, cut off from the world, every day awaiting news from our loved ones. What I want to recall now is my reaction to the appeal we heard on the radio 18 June. How could we not have been as though galvanized by these prophetic words! They were in such sharp contrast to the declarations of Marshal Pétain which were marked with such weariness and which revealed a feeling of prostration. Nevertheless, I would like to nuance my feelings at that time. I didn't believe it was possible to continue the struggle; I even experienced a certain relief on learning that blood was no longer being shed. Even today I regard as indefensible the thesis according to which the Armistice could have been avoided. But I willingly admitted that it did not mark the end of the conflict and that the possibility for resistance existed elsewhere; with gratitude I welcomed the institution of a Free France that would have a role in the subsequent phases of the struggle.

Meanwhile, very quickly, I perceived in the call of General de Gaulle something that I immediately felt to be a false note. His condemnation of Marshal Pétain seemed shocking to me and capable of dangerously dividing people. I thought, and I still think, that de Gaulle should have kept from passing judgment on a man who had been his leader and to whom he owed respect.

But, on the other hand, I at once showed myself sceptical as to the possibility of this national revolution that Marshal Pétain announced and welcomed. I judged—and on this point my thought has never wavered—that such a revolution would remain impossible as long as the enemy remained on our soil. On the part of the Maréchal and his entourage, there was an illusion that had to be denounced at all costs. I felt that the government, in such horrible conditions, should limit itself to taking care of current business and assuring as much as possible the material survival of the country. That was already a superhuman task.

In the same spirit, I was to send the following year a short article to Emmanuel Mounier for his journal in which I underlined the scandalous character of the condemnation of self which was something of a refrain in the Vichy government.

Of course I am far from claiming that I always saw things clearly. I believed, until about the middle of 1941, in the existence of a certain secret agreement between de Gaulle and Marshal Pétain. That was a mistake born from my own ardent desire to discern a certain order, a certain coming together of good wills in the horrible confusion which reigned before us.

During the summer of 1940, serious worries about the health of my wife were added to the ones that the events taking place caused. The first effects of the illness that was to take her away from me seven years later required a surgical operation that took place in Clermont-Ferrand: the laboratory analyses allowed for no doubt as to the nature of the sickness she suffered from. Daily medical attention was needed for her convalescence that was long and painful; it was out of the question that this could be had at La Merlée. Nor could we consider returning to Paris. My anti-Nazi position was known; I risked being arrested, and, moreover, the thought of finding myself in an occupied Paris was unbearable. So we decided to go to Lyons where we had relatives. My wife was attended to in a clinic while I stayed with a cousin.

I forgot to say that before the operation and at a time when I still did not know that it was inevitable, we had been able to go to the Corrèze region to meet our son who had just been demobilized and show him the house that he didn't yet know and that he immediately fell in love with. It was during the return trip, between Limoges and Clermont-Ferrand, that my wife revealed that, without my knowledge, she had gone to see a surgeon and that the operation would take place in a few days. It was as though the earth had opened up before us, one of the horrible moments of my existence. For me, looking back, this moment accompanies the time when, in May of 1947, after six years of remission, she told me there was a relapse, meaning that the worst was in sight.

Why have I felt the need, in the course of this contemplative narrative, to evoke these circumstances and, I would even say, why must I open up this wound again? But then it has never truly been closed. If I try to state clearly the constant care I have had since I undertook this kind of retrospective pilgrimage, it seems that I have wanted, perhaps even with an anxious vigilance, to exclude every kind of stylization. I have done so in reaction to the fact that, almost always with those who have tried to account for my thought, one notices the tendency, perhaps an almost inevitable one, to place my work out of time. The poignant event I have just recalled, the one at the end of December 1939 when I had understood that my aunt was to die, is for me something other than the heart rending moments that punctuated my life; they continue to vibrate at the very heart of all that I have since written.

In Lyons, during the somber months at the end of 1940, while my wife slowly regained her physical strength and hope slowly returned to me, I was led to renew contact with Marcel Légaut who was soon to establish a Community of work and prayer in the Drôme region as with Gustave Thibon. I was to learn with some surprise that Simone Weil had worked with him and that the least predictable of friendships had been formed between them.

However, my Swiss friends had invited us to come spend a few weeks with them, in the hope that a stay in the mountains would allow my wife to recover her health fully. I had to go to Vichy to obtain the necessary papers, but I only remained a few hours in this place where so many illusions and, at times, so many petty ambitions rubbed shoulders.

I still keenly remember the painful trip we had to make to get to Geneva, then to Montana, where two generous people waited for us and showered much kindness upon us. But after a few days I received a telegram from the Ministry of Education telling me that I was appointed to teach philosophy in hypokhâgne and khâgne in Montpellier.[2] There could be no question of my refusing. But this interruption of a stay, which could have been so beneficial, seemed cruel to us.

However, taking everything into account, this first trimester of 1941 in Montpellier has left me with some rather sweet memories. We had been able to rent two rooms with the widow of a professor of philosophy and succeeded in forming there something like the embryo of a real home. My teaching interested me. I tried to comfort the young students who, one felt, were often shaken up or distraught. I remember, not without some confusion, that I tried to show them my confidence in a double game within the Vichy government. It was only to disappear in me some months later. We made contacts with the university world of Montpellier, in particular with Pierre Humbert, Pierre Chazel, and others. At this time I also met Jean Grenier. I loved Montpellier—especially the Peyrou—and also certain parts of the area where we took walks on Sunday.

But physically, we adapted rather poorly to a style of life made somewhat ascetic by the circumstances. My wife became ill and, in addition, I also contracted laryngitis which forced me to give up teaching. We tried to find for ourselves a life that was, materially speaking, a bit better, at first in a village of the Ain and then with our old friend in the Ardèche and also in the Haute-Loire.

Meanwhile, my son had found a way to spend a few weeks at our home Le Peuch and to start the work necessary to make the house livable. Then some cousins from Paris, taking advantage of a new

[2] After receiving the baccalaureate degree, French students spend two years studying for the competitive exams that allow one to be received into the professional schools run by the State. *Trans.*

decree from the Vichy government about returning to one's native area, found a way to send us our furniture. It thus became possible for us to move into Le Puech, something we did at the beginning of July 1941.

It is certain that after the period of trouble and repeated moving about that we had just gone through, we experienced, my wife and I, a feeling of calm—and I would even say of reassurance—not only at having once again a home which seemed to be stable but also—and this concerns me more particularly—of moving into it the furniture that had been, as it were, the silent witness of my childhood, especially the vast libraries that had held such an important place in the existence of my father. The term "recollection," in its etymological meaning, is the one that best translates my experience at this time.

But, of course, we should not conclude from this that I had ever, even for an instant, detached my mind from what was happening. We had just learned about the German offensive against the U.S.S.R., and I believe I remember that this news helped stir up in me the hope that had never died. I don't think that I ever imagined, at any moment, that the war could end other than with the defeat of Germany; and I even surprise myself retrospectively that I held on to this assurance so stubbornly. Today I would almost be tempted to say that this fact can only be explained on the condition of admitting that at a certain level of myself, of what it would be necessary to perhaps call my supra-conscious, the future had already been given to me.

What helps support this hypothesis for me is the fact that I was able to write, immediately before the war, the first act of *Le Signe de la Croix* (The sign of the cross) and that, some years later, when I composed the following acts, I changed nothing in the first act, written, however, at a time when I was clearly unaware of all the persecutions that were to follow.

I nevertheless note how difficult it is to reconstitute what could have been my exact state of mind during all this time. I can only describe its parts without successfully finding its unity—but, in fact, does this unity exist?

Our home quickly became a place of refuge, at least temporarily, for those relatives who were less fortunate and who lived in Paris or Lyons. My wife, who now seemed to be back on her feet, spent most of her time gathering foodstuffs and making packages. For sure, we benefited from the good will and kindness of the country people. Contrary to what we might have feared, they had welcomed us with kindness. Certainly they were interested in the reports we shared with them, but I don't sense that they ever took advantage of the situation. I am sure that in other provinces we would have come up against an aggressiveness and mistrust that, in Ligneyrac and the surrounding area, we didn't feel in any way whatever. Thus, little by little, this region became our own.

The fact that Edmond Michelet and his family lived nearby assuredly contributed to this slow and healthy assimilation. We knew, or at least we suspected, that our friend was totally committed to the Resistance although we didn't know every detail of his involvement. Should I reproach myself for not having tried to be a part of this network? I can't keep from wondering, but I believe, nevertheless, that my absence was clearly justified, since I knew that I was weak and not able to be fully active. Then there was my nervousness. The words of one of my characters come to me, from *Le Petit Garçon*, if I am not mistaken: "When our acts are not ourselves, we cannot have worse enemies." Today I still believe that an affiliation of this kind would have been one of those acts—although I naturally suffered from feeling relatively inactive while so many of my best compatriots gave themselves generously to the service of a cause that was my own. I said relatively inactive because I did have, rightly or wrongly, the feeling that my writings were, in spite of everything, in some way actions. I am especially thinking about the lecture I gave at the Jesuit Scholasticate of Fourvière in the winter of 1941-1942.[3]

Father de Lubac, whom I had visited in Lyons some months earlier, had asked me to come speak to the Jesuits, something I then found rather intimidating. Without taking the trouble to think about it, I answered, giving in to a kind of irresistible impulse, "Agreed. I will talk about hope."

Of course, this was not an absolutely new theme for me; in *Être et Avoir* and in *Position et approches concrètes du mystère ontologique*, I had already written about this. But this time, because of the countless

[3] This was one of the theologates for the Society of Jesus in France that was situated on the hill of Fourvière in Lyons.

prisoners languishing in the camps, this theme included for me a reality about which I think I can say it was like the trampoline of my thought. In composing this text which was to appear in *Homo viator*, in 1947, I was rightly or wrongly aware of articulating at the level of phenomenological thought what was to become the common *nisus* for all these unfortunate people who awaited the Liberation. In this sense, it didn't seem to me that my work was done in solitude: I was with them. But also with others, because I discovered that there were other prisons besides those which let themselves be known and counted; I especially thought about the sick and beyond them, about all of us, about those among us, at least, who did not let themselves become too comfortable, or, inversely, too consumed by daily worrying, without some kind of call to take them away from the sad daily agony.

But this lecture on Hope that remains, in my view, one of the most significant I have ever written confirms me in the retrospective conviction I formed above: I have never given up hope. However, I should probably add that I always felt open to despair, as though it might ambush me. Even though this observation might be somewhat humbling for me, I must nevertheless recognize that I was completely dependent on the English radio program "The French speak to the French," though I did not approve of the tone. I thought—it was not, unfortunately, completely false—that these programs were like so many shots that I needed, like a diabetic with his insulin. What would I have become without the radio; without this contact maintained in spite of everything with those who beyond the English Channel continuously prepared the final victory. Would I not have then succumbed to this despair against which, day after day, I felt myself protected?

On the evening of 8 November, Edmond Michelet came to tell us about the invasion of North Africa. Thus did hope take on a body and become a reality.

14

11 November 1970

General de Gaulle has died. This news, which completely surprised us, was announced to me yesterday morning by Marie-Madeleine Davy, before we had even heard it on the radio.

It touches me so deeply that I feel I must interrupt this introspection and, first of all, ask myself why, in such an unexpected manner, I react so intensely to this event.

Certainly I haven't forgotten anything about the errors and mistakes committed and the indignation that they so often aroused in me, and today I still think they were not inappropriate. But I also think quite strongly that what is necessary at this time is recognition in the full sense of the word: recognition, but also recognition of an historical grandeur, certainly one without equal in our own time. It is evident to me that those who would question it would thus bring upon themselves a terrible judgment.

This death that occurred at Colombey day before yesterday … two evenings ago, that was not preceded by any agony, by any anxiety, how could we not see Providence at work in it? How could we not also feel that it was like the mysterious recompense for the silent and admirable dignity with which he retired on the very evening of the referendum!

I was in Prague, I was awake and was feverishly waiting to know the outcome of the referendum. During the night the news was given in the Czech language; of course I didn't understand, but the fact that the name Alain Poher had been repeated several times seemed indicative to me, and, some hours later, our ambassador confirmed the news.

Since then, we have only been able to admire the faultless reserve that General de Gaulle observed, demonstrating that he had been a monarch and not a dictator.

Today, on this anniversary of the Armistice of 1918, my sentiment recalls what I felt, what we felt, on 26 August 1944, when from a balcony of the Rue d'Arcole, we attended the arrival of General de Gaulle on the parvis of Notre-Dame Cathedral.

Then all we could feel was gratitude and happiness for again being united in a liberated Paris!

What we must think today, twenty-five years later, is that this gratitude and this joy were not illusory, and that it was indeed a savior whom we then acclaimed.

Once again, this savior, I am careful not to canonize him. But, as is so often the case—and isn't it one of the major themes of my work—it's as though death brought with it a Light of Truth. Of course, this savior was a simple mortal; who could deny that his pride was boundless and that at certain times when clemency was called for, it was, alas, resentment which won out? Who could question the duplicity that he manifested towards the French of Algeria, in May 1958, or the unpardonable manner in which he handed over, following the war in Algeria, the *harkis* to a horrible repression?

I am not drawing up an inventory here. But what I see is that a higher justice, and one that death would have us realize, with piety and recollection, perhaps requires of us a kind of acceptance, however difficult, and that can only be used with some difficulty. De Gaulle was not Joan of Arc; the uniqueness of his destiny, such as it appears to us in the historical overview that we are inevitably undertaking this day, perhaps—and even probably—included an irreducible human impurity, or at least, one which perhaps would only let itself be reduced in an encounter with God and whose secret we haven't the right to know. We may have been shocked, and legitimately so, by his actions or even, at times, by his words, but they were somehow necessary for his grand plan to succeed. I am thinking, for example, about his somewhat unjust condemnation of Pétain and his ministers that he made from the very beginning on the London radio. Perhaps he had to make this declaration for his voice to be heard; any reservation or silence that we thought desirable would probably have reduced his effectiveness.

I have spoken of his encounter with God: what authorizes us Christians to imagine it, I believe, is the devotion he gave to a poor child, preserved through her simplicity from every temptation, and next to whom, through the dispositions of his last will, he expressed the will to be buried, as though under her protection. That is what proves irrefutably that his pride had not entirely consumed him but had left some place for the authentic meaning of a world where every human power is finally confounded.

A while ago, on television, I was looking at the famous people of this world hurrying to the doors of Notre-Dame Cathedral, in order to pay homage, which is perhaps without precedent in its universal character, to the man of 18 June. And I felt myself shaken by the contrast between this apotheosis and the explicit desire to sleep his last sleep, not at the Invalides or at the Pantheon, but in a country cemetery, near a child who had had the best of his affection. I'm tempted to wonder whether this paradox does not shed some unexpected light on his entire personality.

Yesterday on opening the *Mémoires d'espoir* (*Memoirs of Hope, Renewal and Endeavor*), I found a passage where he talks about himself in the third person. This can only irritate a reader who is not warned and even risks provoking some sarcasm. But on second thought, I wonder whether we shouldn't admit that in him, at a time I can't be too sure about but which we should probably place in June 1940, there developed a more and more marked or felt duality between the individual man with his weaknesses and his doubts and the personage who tended to confuse himself with an idea of France to which he had sacrificed everything. Of course, some might think there is a need to call upon a psychiatrist for insight. But I tend to think that such a reductive interpretation supposes an unforgettable and radical ignorance of historical reality. The incredible adventure that he lived could only have succeeded through the power of the prophetic vision that inspired all his actions. In this there is evidence for me that may well not satisfy the moralist, but that the philosophical historian, or perhaps only the philosopher, can in no way rightfully refuse.

And now I come, it seems to me, to the profound reasons why I felt the need to include these thoughts in a book which has no meaning unless it also be regarded as an examination of conscience.

At the beginning of 1958, I had foreseen the future return of de Gaulle, or I had at least judged it probable, and was happy about it. I had voted for him in 1958 without the shadow of a doubt and even later, though with less conviction. But I think that, as I was traumatized by the Algerian affair, I had shown myself unjust, despite everything, and for several years I lost sight of what again astonishes me in these days of November 1970. And so at least I have the sweetness of recalling, not only in thought but in my heart, this dear Edmond Michelet who, alas, departed from us a little more than a month ago. I have never stopped having a boundless admiration for this excellent man. One encountered in him a certain heroic virtue with a generosity that I have rarely seen exemplified elsewhere. But I could not keep from regretting that his Gaullism was unconditional. Of course, if one sticks to the data of pure analysis, I was right. But today I clearly see that the unconditional, which was the very force of Gaullist action, was to evoke, through an immanent logic, an adherence on the part of those it electrified which was just as unconditional.

13 November 1970

Life has begun again, but the feeling I have experienced during this extraordinary day still persists. Yesterday evening, in spite of the rain, hundreds of thousands of Parisians, responding to the general call of the Council of Paris, gathered at the Arc de Triomphe and placed flowers on the tomb of the Unknown Soldier. Thus, within the axis of a fidelity that transcends daily concerns, unity was recreated between the Armistice of 1918 and Gaullist history. History: it was as though quite suddenly its pulse could be heard. But History is not a simple succession: at the heart of History there is something which is beyond History and which gives it its meaning and impact.

Recalling with a mixture of admiration and envy these Companions of the Liberation who came to Colombey from everywhere to pay homage to the one who had been their inspiration and leader, I was somewhat bitterly aware of my insignificance; I can say that this awareness was like the underside or counterpart of a momentum which carried me towards a grandeur that had been finally recovered.

15

On this day, 13 November, you left me twenty-three years ago. I won't try to remember in detail here the suffering of those last weeks, at most I shall evoke that morning of grace when Father Fessard came to give you Extreme Unction. It was not your worst day. We both received communion, and I clearly thought that our marriage in Heaven was taking place. I think I even stated it in exactly those words. It wasn't an illusion, for I truly believe that You have never left me, even if, some moments ago, I used a word that only answers to appearances.

I would like to clarify something that has troubled me since yesterday evening. This is the fact that your sickness and death, which were almost completely like those of your sisters, belong to a world which history does not account for but which develops according to another dimension. I would almost be tempted to call this dimension transversal in relation to the one whose lightning revelation we had yesterday. This other world, whose boundaries I think we shall never be able to determine, clearly has the uniqueness of opening onto an elsewhere—but an elsewhere which, paradoxically, is not situated in any space. This world of suffering is also that of authentic brotherhood, the one in which Antoine Framont[1] can cry out: "To love a being is to say, you, you are not going to die." This is the world in which, ever since 15 November 1893, I tried, at first in a haltering manner, to build some kind of spiritual dwelling where others could find a spiritual haven with me. Once I got past my adolescence, I was more keenly aware of my plan. But such an undertaking, which might

1 *Le Mort de demain.*

seem outlandish, could be meaningful only to the extent that it took into account, as strictly and as rigorously as possible, the obstacles that had to be overcome. And this would all have to be done not only to get one to this humble sanctuary, as though falling upon some country church, but to have one fully take in the atmosphere and to admit it.

I now return to what I wrote yesterday: if General de Gaulle had declared his will to be buried in the Invalides or at the Panthéon, the event would certainly not have affected me in the same manner. I would have thought that, until the end, he had remained a prisoner of pride, and perhaps I would even have to add of lying, because after all, pride is lying in its principle. But the provisions of his last will clearly show, I have said this and repeat it, that something in him triumphed over this temptation and joined this other world, the one where one suffers, where one dies and where the child keeps a mysterious priority over the adult, however burdened he may be with honors.

It seems to me that many of us will keep in ourselves, after this day, something like a polyptych where will be figured Notre-Dame Cathedral, the Élysée Palace, the Étoile and, way at the top, the cemetery of Colombey.

How can I quite explain to myself the connection that I have tried to arrange between this event that is so filled with such historic importance and circumstances of a private nature that seem to interest only me and my family: even though they open onto metaphysical depths, I must acknowledge that I myself remain overcome by surprise and confusedly worried by what I have just written.

How can one not see behind these troubled lines something that approaches a wavering of thought and of the heart? Reflection leads me to recognize that one cannot hold on to the distinction, even to the opposition, that I established the other day between the two worlds. At most one can only speak here about two directions that could in no way be confused.

But, returning to the emotion I felt when faced with the death of de Gaulle and the extraordinary consensus that it elicited for several hours, I cannot keep from relating it to the fact that, for a certain number of years, I have become ever more sensitive to history that is treated in depth. I should probably not say that this sense of the historical depth that I have so admired in the work of Daniel Halévy, and that he has probably also helped to develop in me, was totally non-existent for a long period of my life. That would be more than an exaggeration. I have sufficiently shown, in the course of this examination of my work and my life, how important events were for me and even how they had marked me since World War I. I think it is exact to say that for a very long time I concentrated too much interest on the news and on the historical factors that might immediately enlighten it. That's no longer the case today, and what proves this to me is that, were I able to read a great deal, I feel that my reading would be above all in the area of works on history.

This evolution could already be noticed at Le Peuch, from 1941-1942, because I then read with great interest the *Histoire de la monarchie de Juillet* (History of the July Monarchy) by Thureau-Dangin and the *Histoire du Second Empire* (History of the Second Empire) by Pierre de La Gorce. I found these two monumental works in my father's library that had been moved to our home in the Corrèze, and this reading gave me the feeling that by means of it I was entering into some sort of living communion with my father.[2]

But what strikes me today—and that's why I insist on it—is that this renewed interest for the historical past seems to be rather mysteriously related to the deficiencies that I suffer from today, regarding my sight and my walking. Would it be wrong to say that these same deficiencies tend towards what one should call a kind of undoing of the present? And so it is that a while ago on the radio I listened with great interest to a debate about Charles the Bold, and that I was tempted to order the monumental work that has just been written about him in Belgium.

But I especially think that this rebirth of interest in history is closely related to the reinforcement in me of a disposition that is much more essential and that the term "humanism" rather precisely expresses.

This is the place to recall the shock I felt from the discovery of what the concentration camps had been. By means of the English radio I had already learned, at a time I would not be able to clearly date but which was before 1945, the fate that was reserved for those who had

2 Paul Thureau-Dangin (1837-1913). A French historian, he is remembered particularly for this work.

been deported, and this news had deeply affected me. But I was quite far from suspecting the magnitude of a collective crime that counts among the most horrible in History.

The reading of certain accounts by witnesses lets me understand that, in many cases, the Nazis were not content to torture and kill their victims, but they had even striven to treat them in such a way as to make them an object of disgust for themselves. This is what I have called "techniques of degradation" about which I have written a study and which appeared, unless I am mistaken, in a periodical and then was included in *Les Hommes contre l'humain* (*Man Against Mass Society*).[3] I then became more fully aware than I had probably ever been of the unpardonable sin that the act of deliberately humiliating another being constitutes. Is it necessary to add that later, on many an occasion, especially as regards racial segregation in the United States, in South Africa, etc., I was to be led to feel again, in the same way, my very first indignation.

Without a doubt, that is the origin for the lectures I was to give at Harvard University in 1961 on "La dignité humaine et ses assises existentielles" ("The Existential Background of Human Dignity"). The title was unduly shortened for the French publication.[4]

What I would like to insist on here is that these terrible experiences led me to take up, in an existential mode, one of the fundamental themes of Kantian ethics, that of the eminent value of the person. Nevertheless, I have always refused to be called a personalist, even in the sense that Emmanuel Mounier has given to the word. It is too loaded with neo-critical associations: I am thinking of the book by Renouvier, *Le Personnalisme, suivi d'une étude sur la perception extrème et la force* (Personalism, followed by a study on acute perception and force).[5]

On this point, as on others, I tend to reproach myself for not always having been explicit enough. This is doubtless an unfortunate conse-

[3] The title Marcel preferred for this work was *Humanity Against Mass Society*, but the publishers prevailed despite his preference. *Trans.*

[4] These were the William James Lectures, 1961-1962, published by Harvard University Press in 1963. *Trans.*

[5] Published in Paris by F. Alcan, 1903. Charles Renouvier, French philosopher (1815-1903). *Trans.*

quence of the fact that I have never wanted, not only to create a system, but even to write a treatise in the philosophical sense of the word.

As for what concerns person, I note that it would be inconceivable for a thinker such as Kant to have written plays, and this is bound, in my thought, to a formalism to which I have never adhered. Perhaps I should be more precise. I would not question that, in the perspective of a rational ethics, this formalism presents a value or that it can even be avoided with difficulty. But then I have never been worried about elaborating a rational ethics. My concern has been quite different. I can say that overall what was important for me was, on the level of life, to enter into a fraternal relationship with people known to be different from myself and, on the level of reflective thought, to find out how this fraternal relationship was possible. But in the course of this search, I had to recognize that this relationship remains necessarily mysterious. Yet the meaning of this word mysterious that has been the object of such literary abuse must be remembered: mysterious means non-problematisable. This means that this relationship does not belong to a certain savoir-faire whose ways of being could be defined once and for all. It is here that the exceptional importance of encounter appears in all its light. One must not give in to the temptation to imagine that an account can be had of an encounter from some kind of transposed chemistry-physics such as that, for example, referred to by Goethe in *Les Affinités électives (Elective Affinities).* When I think of the encounters that have been decisive in my life—of the one with Henri Boegner, which is at the origin of my marriage, of that with Charles du Bos, or with Gustave Thibon, I am obliged to notice that the word "affinity" does not quite correspond to anything that I have truly experienced. Were it necessary to clarify absolutely what cannot be an object of clarification, I would say rather that everything seems to have happened as though these encounters had been created from what comes to us as being a future—but doesn't this finality oblige us to break out of the framework of chronological representation that normally holds us prisoner?

After this digression, which has nothing accidental about it, I'm going to return to what I said earlier about the humanism that, since World War II, has become ever more evident in my writings thanks to the countless contacts that I have had in the course of this last quarter of a century with men and women of different countries.

I would certainly not want to try to unduly conceptualize this predisposition that has manifested itself in me, always more strongly. But what I clearly see, first of all, is this: if at the moment of death I had to articulate whatever could resemble an account about men and women, my brothers and my sisters, I would feel obliged to give homage not only with thanks but with a sense of marvel for all that I will have been given to acknowledge in them. Above all I am thinking of the generosity that has been so frequently bestowed upon me. This does not, however, mean that I am, in the least, inclined to see in man, in the manner of Jean-Jacques Rousseau, anything that might resemble an original goodness. This is a mythical view that does not stand up to criticism. But what astonishes me, what confuses me, is precisely the fact that so many virtues which have culminated in charity could have grafted themselves onto a nature that can only appear to uncritical thought as though given over to the most sordid desires. This is enough to say that humanism, as I conceive it, excludes all dogmatic interpretation, that the kindness that it advocates, even if it does not exalt it, does not let itself be separated from a lucidity that must remain indefectible. We have to recognize that kindness and lucidity are rarely encountered together among modern moralists, but certain great minds of the Renaissance—and I am especially thinking of Erasmus—have paved the way for centuries to come and this under conditions that can only win our admiration, when we think of the sociological and historical context in which their life and work developed. This is, indeed, the reason why, among the distinctions I have been honored with over the last quarter of a century, the Erasmus Prize that I received in 1969 is perhaps the one that I most appreciate.

While I write these lines, I am aware of the deep change that has taken place in me since the distant time when I elaborated the principles of what I hesitate to call my philosophy. At that time, I am almost certain of it, the word humanism would not have stirred any echo in me. I would probably have to say that it corresponded to an outmoded mentality, that of retired magistrates who spent their leisure time translating Horace. A writer such as Montaigne, whatever the consideration I might have for his literary talent, had, in my view, made the mistake of ignoring both the heights and the depths through which the philosopher has to pave a difficult path. Today my judgment would be infinitely more qualified, and for this reason: at that time and most likely especially during World War I, but probably again after the end of the conflict, I was far from having measured the frailty of civilization. The profound views that Paul Valéry, for example, was to present in his *Regards sur le monde actuel* (*Reflections on the World Today*), still remained undreampt of for me. Today we see not only a massive refusal of evidence that, at the time of which I am speaking, was only questioned by a small number of minds whose influence was felt only in a few restrained circles, but we are witnessing an even more alarming erosion of the social and ethical fabric that, until only recently, one might think could resist the bad moments of history. This naive faith is no longer encountered, I fear, except in some minds which, if they are not ossified, are at least incapable of accepting the new evidence that everyday experience offers us rather straightforwardly.

This is to say that today, in my view, humanism can only be tragic, and I would like to try, in the course of this kind of examination of conscience, to clarify perhaps more than I have done until now what we should understand by these words.

As Bertrand de Jouvenel was saying just yesterday evening on television, during an interview on the program "Prospective," this year 1970 will have been marked by the insistence with which those who govern us have themselves denounced the threats that today weigh upon our species, in particular from the pollution of our rivers and seas. And we can't be too surprised over the unforgivable lack of concern that has allowed this peril to grow over the course of these last years. I was remarking recently that pollution and, moreover, many other nuisances against which men try today rather vainly to protect themselves, can only appear to be the materialized expression of an infinitely more essential degradation. This has to do with the way in which man, thinking he is able to take charge of his destiny, has cut himself off more and more from what we should perhaps call his ontological roots.

The serious error that men of our time seem to be guilty of, those who have imagined themselves to be the champions of humanism—

I am thinking, for example, of the author of *Thésée (Theseus),*[6] seems to me to have been that of believing that humanism could be constructed out of nothing, or even still out of nothingness understood in the Sartrian manner.

Here we find, when I think about it, the essential agreement between my own views and those of Heidegger, as regards what he has himself called the forgetfulness of being. I would be ready, to tell the truth, to make some reservations as to the interpretation that he has given regarding the history of philosophy, and I particularly have in mind the way in which he has probably increased the importance of the presocratic thinkers: but this, in the present perspective, seems clearly secondary to me. What alone matters is the importance placed on a loss that has occured at the very heart of man today. If my work has any meaning, it seems that we should search for it in the tenacious effort that I have employed in the course of these sixty years to circumscribe, as much as possible, this abyss alongside which so many minds have skirted with such a disconcerting lack of awareness

If the humanism I dare lay claim to is essentially tragic, it's because it finds its force in the anguish that results from the blindness with which men fiercely pursue what they believe to be a conquest—and that is perhaps nothing more than a sack.

Listening to the allocution at the Museum some months ago that was delivered by Professor Dorst, to whom we had awarded the Lecomte du Nouÿ Prize, I remarked that what is in the act of disappearing is the awareness of what Spinoza, after others, called *nature naturante*, and I asked Monsieur Dorst whether he would accept the invitation to talk about this subject at the Academy of Political and Moral Sciences. He accepted my offer with a quickness that rather touched me, and we shall have the pleasure of hearing him in a few weeks at Quai de Conti.[7]

If I remember this meeting, it is because it affords me the opportunity to underline one aspect of my concerns that commentators of my thought have not, it seems to me, sufficiently noted: I want to talk about my love of nature, which has been one of the constants of my

6 Published in 1946 by André Gide (1869-1951). *Trans.*

7 This lecture took place during the month of March 1971. [It was held at the Institut de France situated on the Quai de Conti in Paris. *Trans.*]

life, because I have enduring memories of my childhood travels. For example, I remember the weeks we spent in Brittany, when I was five years old. I can still see the disgusted boredom I felt on the beach at Pornichet. Yet, fortunately, I was moved by the rustic landscapes of Pont-Aven, and later on the rocks of Ploumanach and Trégastel.[8] Or even, the following year, the pleasure with which I explored the cliffs of Taunus during a stay at Homburg with my grandmother.[9] All that is in me like an inalienable treasure.

But, someone will perhaps ask, what connection can you find between this love of nature and the humanism to which you seem to adhere?

I think that, for a very long time, it would have been impossible for me to answer this question. Today I would be inclined to say that the connection can only be found in art, only in the eminent function that here belongs to the artist, and on this point as on so many others, I call upon—no surprise in this—Proust, the Proust of Elstir.

I think however, and regardless of my admiration for the inimitably subtle and delicate analyses, that the horizon of my thought remains quite different from Proust's own, and this to the extent that I have more and more rejected the radical subjectivism of which he has remained, in spite of everything, a prisoner. In the genial work *À la recherche du temps perdu (Remembrance of Things Past)*, one can truly find, as Charles du Bos had quite well discerned, some precious elements that in some way work against the systematic intentions it states. I am not only or mainly speaking about the famous passages on the bell towers of Martinville or about the death of Bergotte but rather about everything in *Combray* and more sporadically in *Le Côté de Guermantes (The Guermantes Way)* that betrays a specifically ontological sense of the loved one—as an example, perhaps above all of the grandmother.

But what moves us so sorrowfully when we read *À la recherche du temps perdu* is the feeling of implacable erosion that life exercises, from the very fact of its unfolding, upon a certain primordial meaning of being and its fullness.

8 Pont Aven and Pornichet are in western Brittany; Ploumanach and Trégastel in northern Brittany along the English Channel. *Trans.*

9 In Germany. *Trans.*

This digression may seem to be unrelated to the main purpose of this book. I believe, however, that one would be wrong to think so: when, as I try to look back, my vision returns to contemporary works that have most deeply marked me, I think I can say Proust's comes to mind first, and above all others. This is probably due to the fact that we have similar origins, since his mother like my own was Jewish and his father was Catholic as was my own. He was born in 1871, as was my aunt, so he was eighteen years older than myself, and nevertheless I have sometimes thought that in a certain way our lives had been contiguous. Something rather curious, I knew his uncle and his aunt Georges-Denis Weil quite well; I still remember a ride I took with them in the gardens of Versailles. Later I was sometimes the guest of Madame Weil, Place Malesherbes, but I don't remember her ever having spoken to me about her nephew. It was, I remember quite well, my cousin Robert Kiefe who first spoke to me about *Du côté de chez Swann*, some days after the publication of the book by Grasset.[10] I immediately acquired a copy. Robert had just come into an inheritance from his father who left him a fortune that was infinitely more considerable than he had ever imagined it to be. As far as I can judge, this circumstance was deadly because it turned him away from a scientific career that could have been wonderful, and, giving in to a snobbery analogous to Proust's, he got in with some young men of the Faubourg Saint-Germain, like Bertrand de Salignac-Fénelon (one of the prototypes for Saint-Loup, or so I think). From then on we saw less of one another. But I must say that this snobbery could have been my own, that the beginnings of it could be found in me. Indeed, I had sensed its first manifestations in Stockholm when I was happy to find myself in the company of children whose fathers were highly placed diplomats. All that had no noticeable result, but what I want to emphasize, without insisting on it too much, is that sociologically, and doubtless even on a more intimate level, I belonged to the family of Proust such as I have never been a part—to take some known examples—of that of Valéry, or of Giraudoux, and even less still of Claudel. When I think about it, I see that what I was missing was a

[10] Proust had had trouble finding a publisher. Finally the publishing house Grasset agreed to publish this first volume of his grand oeuvre. *Trans.*

provincial element. What replaced it, up to a certain point, was the cosmopolitan element, because members of my family, on my mother's side, lived in Frankfurt, and others lived in London; I don't know whether it was the same for Proust.

But what I feel somewhat confusedly is that there was a kind of mysterious relationship between his quest and my own, even though he possessed certain eminent gifts that I completely lacked. On the other hand, on the metaphysical level, and in the world of drama, I had wandered very far afield of his own territory. Nevertheless, he is truly the only one among French writers of this century who seem to me to be an older brother, of course, a distant one.

How could I not also remark that there is no philosopher about whom I could say the same thing? Someone might ask, "What? Not even Bergson?" No, assuredly not Bergson. The admiration I have felt for him and that I still feel for him is of quite another order. First of all, I still see him today as being *un-situated*. At the lycée he had been a friend of my uncle Ernest Meyer, but he never told me anything about Bergson that I have remembered. I never knew anything about the milieu of his origins. He was presented to me like the fruit of some kind of parthenogenesis. But I have truly never sensed in him this sensitivity to human drama in all its forms that *À la recherche du temps perdu* accounts for so movingly in many places.

Certainly, when on two or three occasions, around 1930, or even a little later, I paid him a visit on Boulevard de Beauséjour, I deeply admired the stoicism with which he held up under an atrocious physical trial. I have often said that through his indefectible courage he gave an existential confirmation of what I would prefer not to call his spiritualism, of his faith in the triumph of the spirit. And yet with him I don't seem to have experienced the feeling of intimacy I knew with Charles Du Bos. Doubtlessly here, as with Proust, the mediation of music worked in a decisive fashion.

This is now the time for me to return to the role that music has played in my life and to talk about the conditions under which, between 1945 and 1946, I composed thirty melodies that I should some day publish one way or another, because they form an integral part of my work and because probably, as much as do my plays, and more than my philosophical works, they clearly delineate its direction.

For many years I had the habit of improvising at the piano, often alone but also at times with my wife present. It was in Sorbiers, at the home of my good friend Jeanne Parain, with her and her mother present, that I first improvised in the presence of a third party. The atmosphere must have been favorable. This improvisation, which was too often reduced to an unplanned pastiche, took on a personal character that day, and my friends begged my wife to note and set down any future ones. The tape recorder did not exist then, or in any case was not widely used. It was only later, abroad and on different occasions, that my improvisations were recorded. This was the case in Porto Alegre in Brazil, perhaps in Milan and, it seems to me, in Tokyo. But I haven't the impression that the improvisations that were then recorded were among my best.

Back in the Corrèze, Jacqueline and I went about doing what had been requested of us. At the end of a few days, I began to give shape to the dreams of my youth: to put into music some poems that I particularly liked. In this way I passed through a kind of feverish period of creativity, and I found in my wife the minute and intimate understanding necessary for the transcription of what I was creating. Although she could offer me nothing on the level of creativity properly called, I can affirm that without her these melodies would never have seen the light of day. In all of this there was for us, during the years 1945 and 1946—thus not very long before her death—a sense of cooperation, the results of which we both felt. I have no hesitation in saying that this was a grace for us. More than that, it was like a stamp imposed by some invisible power, one I am incapable of naming, upon the marriage that had been ours since 1919 and that had begun in the church of Saint-Marcel[11] under the musical sign of the *Concerto à deux violons* (*Concerto for two violins*) by Bach.

Much could be said about the choice of the poems that I had made. Of course chance played an important role in my selection. I especially feel that it will appear profoundly meaningful to whoever takes the trouble to think about it. Whether it be a question of the *Complainte du désespéré* (Lamentation of the hopeless person), by Joachim du Bellay, of *Mes mânes à Clytie* (My spirits at Clytie) by André Chénier,

[11] The Temple de Saint-Marcel is a Lutheran church located in the fifth arrondissement of Paris, Rue Pierre-Nicole.

of *Le Lac* (*The Lake*) or of *Le Cimetière marin* (*The Graveyard by the Sea*),[12] of particular poems of the *France malheureuse* (Unfortunate France) by Supervielle, of the two poems of Catherine Pozzi (*Ave* and *Nyx*) or even of the *Vers dorés* (*Gilded Verses*) by Gérard de Nerval—this list is not exhaustive, far from it—all these texts attest to—needless to say—a lyrical movement in me that had been stifled everywhere else. Marcel Delannoy had written me shortly before his death saying that in me he saw a lyrical soul.[13] As I dictate this book, it seems to lose a certain coherence, but I do want it to be receptive to my actual thoughts and questions: it would not have been conceivable for me not to pause a few moments in the presence of these layers of personal music where, at the heart of my interior landscape, is somehow reflected the Heaven in which I believe.

It is a fact, and one that can be explained, that after the death of my wife my improvisations at the piano always became more rare and that I did not attempt to find someone else who might replace her in the indispensable and humble task that she had so marvelously performed. That would have been a kind of usurpation. The failure of the attempt made during her lifetime with Monsieur de Butzow, about which I spoke at the beginning of this book, had moreover shown me that it was hardly possible, even to a qualified musician, to enter fully into the melodious and harmonic world that was mine.

[12] These last named poems are by, respectively, Alphonse de Lamartine (1790-1869) and Paul Valéry (1871-1945). *Trans.*

[13] French composer, (1898-1962). *Trans.*

16

Of course, it is time to answer the question that an impatient reader could hardly have failed to ask: How is it that what first seemed to be a normal autobiography has tended to transform itself more and more into a kind of rhapsody that is difficult to define? What I must first say is that this kind of transmutation was not premeditated, and it is clear to me that the unforeseeable event that was the death of General de Gaulle, following upon—at a very short interval—that of François Mauriac and of Edmond Michelet, determined this kind of crystallization. This is literally true. But I must add that in my narrative I was approaching a long period about which, for reasons that don't appear very clear to myself, I am inclined to talk much less than about those that preceded it.

What may seem to appear strange, I agree, is that this period was the one that could be qualified, more or less, as that of my successes, the one where I acquired the reputation that I have today.

I would like to mention a thought that came to me this morning, when I heard, on France-Culture, a discussion that began last week about the slave trade of the Blacks. Asked about this by Professor J. P. Chrétien, a Guinean, who by the very tone of his comments seemed remarkable to me, and whose religious position I am not familiar with, declared, without the least perceptible bitterness, that the Church, for centuries, never in the least protested against what was, no doubt about it, one of the most monstrous collective crimes of History, comparable, in every point, to the Hitlerian genocide. Between the leaden wagons where the Jews who were destined for the crematorium smothered and the depths of the hold where Blacks coming from

Africa were piled up, I hardly see any difference, and I was thinking that the unforgivable silence Pope Pius XII manifested when the Jews were deported from Rome could only be authorized because of the most sinister precedents.

Certainly we pay homage to the good will that the present Pope shows during his fatiguing travels as well as the eloquence that he uses for a Third World that is more and more narrowly circumscribed by misery and famine. We cannot deny his good will. But would it not have been desirable for the Roman Catholic Church to make *urbi et orbi* an act of contrition, when one thinks about the secular acquiescence that almost had an air of complicity about it?

I am asking the question here without hiding the fact that no answer can be given to it, and my very clear feeling is that, among Catholics, only a few minds, in the first rank of which I place dear Marcel Légaut, can express themselves on this point in any convincing manner, because they in no way minimize the present or past sins of the Church.

17

Why have I felt the need this morning to begin this unexpected parenthesis? Simply because indignation was smothering me and because at my age one doesn't know how much time one has and because certain words, like certain actions, cannot and should not be put off.

These are certainly not, far from it, the only times when I became aware that I could reproach my own Church, and I recall here what I said about my conversion.

But truly to what extent have I the right to say that this Church is mine?

I won't hurry to answer this question, because it is serious, and whatever the time that remains to me to live, I believe that my answer will probably call for a definitive commitment on my part.

One or two years ago, as I was trying to express, to a friend, the sympathy I felt for certain aspects of the Orthodox Church, she awkwardly indicated her wish that I convert to that church, saying that the event would receive much publicity. I answered her quite strongly that there was no question of my doing so, whatever the consternation I felt in the presence of the actual state of the Roman Catholic Church. I am almost certain to have been right to adopt that position. But I must still clarify, as much as possible, the nature of the bond that still keeps me in this Church that I entered a little more than forty years ago.

I would be lying if I didn't acknowledge that, in a general manner, it disappointed me. Today I am very far from being convinced that what I will call its fundamental claim depends upon some solid historical arguments, and I also think that it isn't on the historical level that the problem can and should be asked. What I believe I see is that this claim has too frequently shown itself under the guise of a universal requirement, which still has, for me, all its importance. Here I can only refer myself to the concrete witness that friends have shown me, without whose example I would certainly not have become a Catholic: Louis Massignon, Robert Garric, Charles Du Bos, to name the main ones. I would also have to add, to be completely sincere, that I heard Charles du Bos himself make statements about Protestants that showed how little he knew them. At the present time, I in no way feel separated from those who, within the Reformed Church, have been authentic witnesses of Christ. Above all I am thinking of the admirable Alfred Boegner, the father of my wife, whom I have not, unfortunately, known directly, and it is strange and moving that it was the day after his death that I entered for the first time this family that was to become my own.

So, without the least reserve, I hold onto the thought I formulated a long time ago when I declared: "When we say: we other Catholics, we are outside Catholicism." I would have done better to say *catholicity*, and in my view, that is what matters.

My answer to the agonizing question asked above would therefore consist in saying that the Roman Catholic Church remains my own, to the extent that, in spite of an organization that I tend to reject insofar as it remains administrative, I still see in it, in the person of its purest representatives—let's say, for example, Father de Lubac or Father Bro[1]—an unfailing faith in Christ and in the fundamental truths, the Incarnation being very much the point of "enracinement" or being rooted for me.

After all, it is from this recognition that I feel myself bound to protest against a certain number of innovations that can only be explained by an inadmissible number of ideological encroachments, suspect by definition, upon the area of what I believe I still have the right to call "revealed."

I would even admit that I don't mention the word "revealed" without a certain hesitation, because it risks entailing some associa-

1 Writer and member of the Friars Preachers of St. Dominic. *Trans.*

tions of ideas that should be cautiously handled. I would say quite simply that I don't know whether the Old Testament, which I have always had so much difficulty getting into, can or cannot be called revealed. This is one of the points—quite numerous—that don't seem fully clear to me. I would admit rather willingly that there runs throughout the Old Testament something like a transcendental teaching with some extraordinary luminous moments, especially in the Psalms and in the prophetic books. But I must confess that I am reluctant to accept the idea of a teaching God, capable of becoming angry and of lashing out against those who have poorly understood or rejected his teaching.

I am not going to develop these remarks; they tend especially to underline how much, in such a domain, I am far from having reached any affirmations that fully satisfy me.

On the other hand, when it is a question of the New Testament, the idea of revelation has for my mind an entirely different meaning and value. This is particularly true, and perhaps fundamentally so, for the Resurrection of Christ. In this, for forty years and even more, I have taken as my own the affirmation of Saint Paul: if Christ is not risen, my faith is vain.

No later than yesterday evening, René Légaut was reading pages from a book by his brother concerning the encounter of Jesus with his disciples at Emmaus.[2] I must say that the thought expressed in these pages seems confusing to me and troubles me. A few weeks ago I even had a conversation on this subject with the author that left me unsatisfied. Marcel Légaut underlined what was for him the unbreakable bond between the Resurrection and the Faith of the Apostles, without moreover admitting in the least way possible, it seemed to me, that there it was a question of the phenomenon of autosuggestion. But to me it seemed that he had not taken into account the episode with Saint Thomas, which seems to be of capital importance. Well, as we were saying yesterday, René Légaut and myself, the attitude of St. Thomas is after all that of the scholar of today who demands proofs. Certainly Jesus shows a liking for those disciples who do not experience the need for proofs, and this is understandable. Nevertheless he

2 Marcel Légaut, *Introduction à l'intelligence du christianisme* (Introduction to the understanding of Christianity). Paris: Éditions Aubier, 1970.

consents to respond to this need. In no way does Jesus condemn anyone who experiences it in a difficult moment when an unanswered doubt turns almost inevitably into a negation.

It is true, I agree, that should one ask me: "Do you believe *absolutely* or *totally* in the resurrection of Christ?, " I would have to qualify my answer and grant that there is inevitably still in me a margin of uncertainty, the obscure fear that one day, under conditions that are still not clear for us, some unknown texts will appear to challenge this belief that is my own, that is ours, and to which we adhere almost carnally.

Here I am going to interrupt myself to consider the path I have followed since the distant time when I composed the first *Journal métaphysique* and when my thought centered upon the unverifiable. Was I not then too worried about protecting myself against every risk that every undertaking entails where the need for verification must play a part? Wasn't that in some degree to misunderstand what our humble condition implies?

But even here, I must admit, there is place in me for hesitation, for the kind of dualism that I expressed—with a rigor that I have perhaps never surpassed—in the final scene of *L'Iconoclaste*.

What I am sure of is that the theologians of today who weaken or minimize, though they may not go so far as to deny, belief in the Resurrection of Christ, strongly risk making some telling blows against Christianity that I am not sure it could survive. And that is the reason for the invincible distrust that Bultmann's project to demythologize awakens in me.[3]

Here I foresee an objection: in fact, it's as though one part of myself addressed this objection to the other part. I suggested the possibility of a discovery of an historical nature that could ruin this belief, but because of that, am I not confessing the precariousness of my faith?

Here again it is difficult to formulate the question in a distinct fashion. I don't believe I can dispense myself from saying that as I see it, my stand in favor of Christ presents in a certain way the character of a Wager (that I will not express in quite the same terms as Pascal). I have said *in a certain way*, because if I hold onto what one calls,

[3] Rudolf Karl Bultmann (1884-1976), author of *Jesus Christ and Mythology* (1958). *Trans.*

perhaps rather improperly, values, these appear as though they had nothing at all to do with historical data as such. But then, can I hold onto these values? It seems to me that my entire work is a negative answer to this question, and that I have always disagreed with those who claim that after all it isn't even necessary, in order to be a Christian, to be sure that Jesus really existed. I must say that I have always detested such a position if only because it implies an obvious lack of intellectual integrity.

The truth is that I attach infinitely more importance to the empirical element than do many theologians, who seem only to give it lip service and perhaps simply in order not to scandalize their flocks. Here I am thinking of the truly miraculous cures and of certain apparitions that are difficult to question. It would be dishonest of me to deny that the interest I have shown, since the winter 1916-1917, in parapsychological facts keeps up relationships that are difficult to circumscribe, I agree, but real ones with the authentically religious given.

Of course I am quite far from questioning the difficulties one exposes oneself to by expressing myself as I have just done, but I would never consent to elude these difficulties by professing a *purism* that can only satisfy the most exclusively intellectual parts of our being.

The risks that an attitude such as mine entails are undeniable, and there is hardly any need to mention them. A great deal of precaution is needed to protect oneself against them, but the worry about protecting oneself also carries a risk with it, a very serious one. I am here speaking about human respect, about this fear of the opinion of so-called enlightened people whom we meet today among the great majority of intellectuals. Nothing, or nearly nothing, remains in them of this childlike spirit that will always appear to me as being the very force of the Christian soul, understanding of course that it would in no way degenerate into childishness. And I repeat that such a sliding or drifting away can only be avoided through a vigilance that is strictly maintained.

Some people will naturally be able to accuse me of not having always been faithful to this rule of critical prudence whose value I have always been the first to proclaim. And, of course, it is clearly possible that in certain cases I have shown myself to be credulous. But certainly this cannot be applied either to the personal experiences that I related in the first part of this work or to the thoughtful confidence granted to the communications obtained by Marcelle de Jouvenel.[4] I have never wavered on this point. I have always said and I repeat that it is absurd to attribute these communications to the writer's unconscious, although we know quite well that Roland himself, from childhood, had shown a surprising gift for clairvoyance. I insist all the more on this since certain Catholic figures whom I prefer not to name have still recently had the impudence to claim that Marcelle de Jouvenel had retracted herself and recognized that her communications were false. Of course I am not questioning that some discrimination must be operative in such messages and that almost certainly some incidental elements whose origin can probably be found in the imagination of the writer do introduce themselves. Unfortunately this discrimination which rightfully appears to be necessary is in fact very difficult to accomplish. As is so often the case, criteriological bases are missing, and I don't particularly see that we can here take into account verisimilitude or lack of it in order to make a judgment, because they are defined by these criteria which—everything leads us to think—cannot be applied to this other dimension of reality, where only narrow breaches open up for us and almost immediately close up. One of my regrets is that the Metapsychic Institute is far from being developed as it should; it is directed by my excellent friend Doctor Martiny, a learned and deeply human doctor to whom I owe so much. On the one hand, we don't have enough mediums; on the other, we must deplore the absence of the small group of philosophers who, as I see it, should be interested in unquestionable phenomena such as telepathy, and retain all possible hypotheses. Then they could formulate test-experiments that would eliminate certain hypotheses and retain those that seem to be confirmed by experience. A man such as Gaston Berger, who died so prematurely, was one of those rare persons who would have been able to participate usefully in this group. But, in a general manner, the necessary qualities seem to be lacking. It is

4 See *Le Diapason du ciel* (The diapason of heaven). Éditions La Palatine. [Later referred to in a work co-authored by Gabriel Marcel and Jean Prieur, entitled *Le Siècle à venir, dialogue, avant-propos du R. P. Maurice Becqué, docteur en théologie* (The time to come, a dialogue, Foreword by Father Maurice Becqué, Doctor in Theology), and published by the Fondation Roland de Jouvenel, 1971. *Trans.*]

significant, for example, that one professor at the Sorbonne, whose name I won't reveal, didn't believe in telepathy until most recently when he personally experienced it. Thus innumerable accounts that have been gathered didn't count! That seems unreasonable to me.

I think that all these remarks are important and that I could not keep from presenting them here, however disconcerting they might seem to what one would have called, at another time, Catholics of the strict observance. Given the crisis, that is in every way dangerous and even a cause for anguish, that the Church is undergoing, it is necessary for certain decrepit and traditional positions held on paranormal facts to be finally reconsidered in a seriously critical manner. We must, unfortunately, believe that this won't happen; because the Marxist grip that one notices upon a great part of the clergy cannot be separated from a kind of rationalist renewal of the worst type. I am expressing myself here without mincing my words, as I am wont to do.

I discover that there is in my thought, and even in my daily life, a confidence that is not unshakeable but that is ever more firmly placed in this other reality. Only its presence can assure, in some way, our movement, alas, that is more and more uncertain in the midst of a world that is falling apart.

Can I say in all sincerity that I had foreseen or at least sensed this disintegration? As always the answer to this question must here be very carefully qualified.

It is certain that whoever studies my work—particularly, of course, my dramatic work—cannot fail to notice that it seems to be punctuated with formulas that open up ever more somber perspectives onto the future. I believe I have already said this.

Yes, I think I can say that I was the anguished witness of a dehumanization that was in my view more evident from day to day. This, however, does not mean that I imagined, even from afar, the paroxysm in the aberration that we notice today. It would even be false to say that I was a prey to the kind of moral consumption that would have resulted for me from a continuous pessimism. It seems to me that there were moments when I regained confidence, at least to a certain extent, for example when de Gaulle returned to power in 1958. Here again, I feel that I am repeating myself. I had sensed it from the beginning of that year, but I shall always remember that, when I shared this feeling in the spring with André Siegfried, he raised his arms to the sky and answered: "He won't come back for many months." Some weeks later my expectation became a reality.

But I must go further into the past and find the interrupted thread of my thought.

I remember the years 1943 and 1944. It was in the autumn of 1943 that we returned to Paris, for the marriage of my son with my niece Anne Boegner—an occasion that was cause for great joy. The adoption was completed in some way by an unexpected grafting. This marriage was to lead up to one of the most perfect unions I have ever been able to know. I would have to refer to my notes to live again in detail this last year of the German occupation. However painful daily life was, especially during the last weeks, it became less burdensome and lightened by the certainty that the victory was now a given: this was especially the case, of course, after the Allied invasion of Normandy, although we had the disappointment of seeing that the Germans were fighting to keep their hold on Normandy and that this beautiful province would be a victim of war and devastation. The landing was carried out under conditions that even today, when a film or radio program relives them for us, do not fail to overwhelm me. The news of the invasion was one of the great moments of our existence. It anticipated the sublime moment when, on 26 August 1944, we saw de Gaulle arrive at the parvis of Notre-Dame Cathedral in Paris. I have already recalled this overpowering moment.

Very quickly, alas, we had to face the evidence. This liberation that was welcomed with such an outburst of gratitude carried with it a side that I will always refuse to admit as being inevitable. I am talking about the purges that were carried out. No one could question that a small number of traitors had merited exemplary punishment. Because of the influence of the Communists, a kind of global discredit, a deceit I have never ceased to judge intolerable, was thrown over what the Marxists did not fail to call the ruling classes. Since the very first day I have always protested against the courts of justice where the judges were most often recruited from among the victims, that is to say from among men and women who could not show the required impartiality.[5] But in fact impartiality itself was proscribed: and this was dictated by a way of thinking, said to be *committed*. The existentialists, then in vogue, provoked my indignation by the cynicism with which they challenged the eternal principles of law. And that is how, to mention in passing, the break took place between myself and writers such as Sartre and Simone de Beauvoir. Until then I had kept up rather cordial relations with them. (Here I particularly remember the long conversation I had at my home with Sartre after the publication of *L'Être et le Néant (Being and Nothingness)* and the visit Simone de Beauvoir paid me in response to the letter that I had written her after reading *L'Invitée* (*She Came to Stay*), probably her best work.

It is quite sad to note that the mental confusion to which so many minds succumbed in the years immediately following World War II is far from having disappeared. Today there are more than just traces of it, and I am only too certain that no theatre in France would dare stage *L'Émissaire*, which was performed some years later in Germany, in Essen.

One will never be able to focus enough attention that is both profound and, I would even say, anxious upon the kind of cleavage that then came about in people's thinking, and this to the surprise of our foreign friends. I remember, for example, the severity with which, in Brussels, I heard our courts of justice criticized by men who, far from belonging to the Rex party, had welcomed the liberation of their country as we had that of our own.[6] The trial that Marshal Pétain went through and the conditions of his imprisonment at Isle d'Yeu are still an object of scandal for me. Not that I feel any sympathy for the victim or even some kind of hesitant indulgence. If the Armistice was inevitable, and I am convinced it was, I believe, as I have already said, that it was a dangerous and mad illusion to imagine that a national revolution could come about in a country occupied by the enemy. The

[5] "Four kinds of courts were in charge of this Purge: the High Court of Justice for government minister, the 'courts of justice' that were to apply the penal code, the 'civil chambers' for those who were accused of 'national degradation,' and the military courts." *Memory, the Holocaust, and French Justice. The Bousquet and Touvier Affairs.* Edited by Richard J. Golsan. Translations by Lucy Golsan and Richard J. Golsan. Hanover: Dartmouth College, University Press of New England, 1996. P. 101. *Trans.*

[6] This was the Fascist Party in Belgium whose political journal was the *Rex*. *Trans.*

fact of having signed statutes against the Jews remains in my view inexcusable, and many other unforgivable concessions could be pointed out. I was one of those who, after the landing in North Africa, conceived of the hope that Marshal Pétain would go to Algiers, and it is blatantly evident that, during the last year, the collaboration degenerated more and more into actual treason.[7] Nevertheless, in the case of Pétain, justice was confused with mercy and if de Gaulle had had even a parcel of the grandeur of soul of which Corneille, in *Cinna*, has given us a lasting account, he would have let this elderly man end his days in the seclusion of his Mediterranean retreat. Left to himself, would de Gaulle have understood him? I think that he let himself become intimidated and even controlled by some men in the Resistance who—he had to acknowledge—had suffered and risked infinitely more than he had and who, in this sense, benefited from a priority which it was necessary to recognize. I think that this situation was extremely painful for him. It was, in itself, essentially tragic and had to have the worst consequences for civil peace. I thought about all this, or most of it, at the very time it took place, that is to say in 1946. One can find the account of this state of my mind in the study entitled *Philosophie de l'épuration, contribution à une théorie de l'hypocrisie dans l'ordre politique* (Philosophy of cleansing, contribution to a theory of hypocrisy in the political order). I sent it to a Canadian journal. There was no question of its being published in France at that time.

Nevertheless for some weeks I was on the Commission of the National Committee of Writers that was to judge those French writers who were thought to be suspects, and I tried, much in vain, to have a spirit of fairness and moderation reign among these men, several of whom, mostly Communists, were inclined to be quite merciless. Like Jean Paulhan, at the same time and for the same reasons, I was quick to leave this commission, having become aware of the futility of my efforts. Moreover I was far from excusing everything. For example, I refused to intervene, despite the efforts of his wife, in favor of a quite well-known writer who was then at Drancy.

[7] The Pétain government decreed its first Statut des Juifs on 3 October 1940 and a second one on 2 June 1941. See Susan Zuccotti, *The Holocaust, the French, and the Jews*. New York: Basic Books, 1993. *Trans.*

What I can say in a general manner is that all these circumstances sharpened the demand for justice in me, which I had always possessed but which only then appeared with a sense of rigor that it had perhaps not known to the same degree. Perhaps I was also unjust towards my past, but what I can say is that since that time the problem of justice has come to the forefront for me. I remember a public meeting in favor of Maurras that took place after his trial, which had unfolded under circumstances that could be strongly criticized.[8] My intervention was brief: it began with these words which stirred those attending: "It is as a Dreyfusard that I have agreed to come to speak today in favor of Maurras." But, alas, it seems that there are still some supporters of Maurras who question the innocence of Dreyfus!

This is the place to clarify the meaning I have myself given to the term *engagement* or "commitment" that, since the Liberation, has seen such widespread use.

Certainly I have never admitted that the philosopher can today establish his dwelling in the *templa serena* of which the Latin poet speaks.[9] In other words, in no way do I think he can remain a simple spectator, wherever certain fundamental values are being attacked, and, of course, I have here in mind above all the attachment to justice and truth. But we must distrust these words when they are written with capital letters outside any definite context. I am always more

8 Charles Maurras (1868-1952). Writer, monarchist, supporter of Pétain and strong leader of *L'Action française*, Maurras had his work as well as this rightist group that appealed to the conservative bourgeois element condemned by the Vatican. In the trial that followed the Liberation, Maurras was sentenced to life imprisonment but, for reasons of health, was released in 1952. *Trans.*

9 A reference to *De Rerum Natura* (ii. 1-14) of Lucretius: "sed nil dulcius est, bene quam munita tenere/ edita doctrina sapientum templa serena,/ despicere unde queas alios passimque videre/ errare atque viam palantis quaerere vitae,/ certare ingenio, contendere nobilitate,/ noctes atque dies niti praestante labore/ ad summas emergere opes rerumque potiri." "But nothing is more gladdening than to dwell in the calm high places, firmly embattled on the heights by the teaching of the wise, whence you can look down on others, and see them wandering hither and thither, going astray as they seek the way of life, in strife matching their wits or rival claims of birth, struggling night and day by surpassing effort to rise up to the height of power and gain possession of the world." Respectively: LVCRETI. DE RERVM NATVRA. Libri Sex. Cyrillvs Bailey. Oxonii: E. Typographeo Clarendoniano, 1921; Lucretius On The Nature Of Things, Translated by Cyril Bailey, Fellow of Balliol College. Oxford at the Clarendon Press, 1950, p. 65. *Trans.*

convinced that, wherever justice is trod underfoot, as is the case, for example, at this moment in the trial going on in Burgos, the philosopher is bound to take a position even if he has to abstract from his own personal position. And so when I left for Japan the first time, I said to Jean Wahl that, were a petition to be circulated in favor of the unfortunate Audin, the professor who probably died under torture for having given his support to the F.L.N., I wanted him to sign it for me, although I was far from approving the attitude of this unfortunate man.[10] It is true—and I don't hesitate to admit it—that we writers, who have been so often requested to do so, have probably too often signed our names; I have never had any illusions about the effectiveness of all this. But, in many cases, I did sign a petition, and at times I have even tried to undertake the necessary procedures to repair a flagrant injustice.[11]

In this very general sense I willingly declare myself committed or *engagé*—but on the express condition that this commitment not affect a partisan air, and it is on this point that I have separated myself from the existentialists whom I mentioned earlier on. I particularly disliked any one-way demonstrations as though injustice were not injustice in whatever camp it might show itself.

Having spoken about the existentialists, I am naturally led to remember once again the misunderstanding I suffered from between 1946 and 1949; and, although I have denounced it many times since then, I well fear, because of manuals of philosophy, that I still feel the effects of it today.

It was at the International Congress of Philosophy held in Rome in 1946 that, to my knowledge, the tag "Christian existentialist" was

[10] The F.L.N. is the Front de libération nationale (National Liberation Front) that was formed in Algeria in 1954. It spearheaded the movement towards independence from France. *Trans.*

[11] Gabriel Marcel had written a letter, dated 17 November 1970, to President Georges Pompidou in support of a pardon for Paul Touvier. In 1972 Marcel publicly recognized that he had been duped. See *Memory, the Holocaust, and French Justice. The Bousquet and Touvier Affairs.* Marcel also signed the petition in favor of a pardon for his former student Robert Brasillach that was circulated by Jean Anouilh, Marcel Aymé, and François Mauriac. See Alice Kaplan, *The Collaborator: The Trial and Execution of Robert Brasillach.* Chicago: The University of Chicago Press, 2000. Pp.189ff. *Trans.*

applied to me. This was the time when Sartre became quite well known. I particularly remember the day he gave the now famous lecture: *L'existentialisme est-il un humanisme?* (*Existentialism and humanism*).[12] My wife and I had wanted to attend but there were so many people that it was impossible for us to find a place, and we consoled ourselves, if my memory serves me correctly, by going to see a film by René Clair.

It is well known that the public appreciates certain antitheses that memory easily retains. My name thus found itself associated with that of Sartre and paradoxically I also benefited from the vogue that he was enjoying. In the right-thinking salons, one was only too happy, of course, to be able to oppose the "wrong-thinking" existentialist that was the author of *L'Être et le Néant* with a "right-thinking" existentialist whom one had supposed to be blessed by the Church. A certain confusion was nevertheless felt: for some people the word "existentialism" implied the word *atheist*; so how could one be both an existentialist and a Christian? It was necessary to recall Kierkegaard and even Pascal in order to bring some peace to a "society woman" who was perhaps worried about reassuring her director of conscience. Do I need to say that all this was perfectly inept, and that this situation caused me a growing irritation. I have often related how, returning from Lille where I had given a talk at the university and spoken, not without criticism, about Sartre's thought, I had heard the lady next to me say on the train, "Existentialism, Monsieur, is horrible! I have a friend whose son has become an existentialist. He is living in a kitchen with a black woman!" This image has stayed with me like a kind of label that is characteristic of the idea that one then formed about the major thinkers of existentialism.

I was also reluctant to agree with Daniel-Rops, when, for advertising reasons, he asked me to choose a certain title for the book of essays that was to be published on my thought in the series Présences that he directed for the publishing house Plon. This was *Existentialisme chrétien* (Christian existentialism). I consulted with Louis Lavelle in whom I had every confidence and who was directing, with René Le Senne, the series Philosophie de l'esprit in which *Être et Avoir* and

[12] The lecture was published in 1946 as *L'existentialisme est un humanisme. Trans.*

Homo viator had been published. He told me he understood quite well my hesitation but that, after all, I was beginning to be known, not only in France, but also abroad, as the principal representative of this movement and that, under these conditions, I could well make this concession to the publisher. I did but it wasn't long before I regretted doing so.

I forgot to say that Jean-Paul Sartre was in reality at the origin of all this confusion, because at the conference mentioned above he went on to give a summary classification where I figured with Jaspers under the tag "Christian existentialist," whereas he named himself in the company of Heidegger as being an "existentialist atheist." This classification was taken up by innumerable manuals of philosophy and probably still is, but it is just as indefensible.

When I visited Heidegger for the first time in Fribourg, in 1946, I asked him whether he accepted this appelation. He strongly protested, saying in particular that he was not an atheist, but that his thought was as though suspended between atheism and theism. I would add that I am, without the shadow of a doubt, infinitely closer to Heidegger than Sartre has ever been but that, on the other hand, it seems to me at least doubtful that one can place Jaspers among Christian thinkers. Thus, all this doesn't make sense. I don't believe, moreover, that I ever spontaneously used the term existentialism—which seems to me in itself to invite criticism. If there is, as I think there is, a philosophy of existence, I don't believe it can become an *ism* without betraying itself. This is particularly clear as regards myself; I have already said it, and I can never repeat it without too much emphasis, that it is above all in my theatrical work that the existential character is present, and it is certainly not due to chance that I have never written a treatise of the genre like *L'Être et le Néant*, where my thought would have taken on a body through transmissible formula. I have always found these formulas to be not only questionable but capable of misleading the reader: they lose the force of their meaning when they are taken out of context. (For example this is the case of my distinction between problem and mystery which, before the structuralist invasion, figured for some time in the manuals of philosophy that were used to prepare for the baccalaureate exams. It's enough to make one shudder.)

So it was in this indirect way that I came to be famous, the importance of which I don't want to exaggerate, but it was to be translated by more and more frequent requests from foreign countries. I am especially thinking here of the invitation that I received in 1948 to come give the Gifford Lectures in Aberdeen, which so many top rate philosophers had delivered before me.

It was during the first days of November 1947, in the course of a short stay in England, that the decisive meeting which preceded this invitation took place, immediately before the death of my wife. But nothing had yet been decided, and she died without receiving the news that would have given her great joy.

At least she had been able, in the course of 1947, to accompany me to Holland where I had been invited to give several lectures (Utrecht, Amsterdam, The Hague, Nijmegen). She felt quite good, nothing indicated the terrible relapse that was going to come about two months later. During these several days, which I fondly remember, I had, it seems to me, for the first and last time the opportunity to feel the happiness that her presence brought me, during these lecture tours that were later to become so numerous, but without my ever receiving the comfort that she alone could assure.

And yet I have no doubt that in some mysterious manner, bereft of all possible representation, she has been there, these last twenty years, assisting me and granting me the strength that I would have so needed during these tiring lecture tours. In this book where I am attempting to say, probably vainly, what is essential, how could I not turn towards her as though to place the seal of my indefectible gratitude upon this entire itinerant part of my life which, without her, I am convinced of it, would not have been able to take shape.

For a short period (1949-1953), I was able to believe that I would finally have my chance in the theatre.

Madame Jeanne Laurent, the director in charge of the central regional theatres that were created shortly after the war, advised André Clavé to ask me for a play for the Centre dramatique de l'Est. After some moments of hesitation, I gave him *Un homme de Dieu*, which had not yet been staged, although on at least two different occasions, some twenty years earlier, this play had almost been performed. The first performance took place in Colmar. To spare me the sadness of finding myself alone in such an important circumstance, my dear friend Jeanne Parain-Vial joined me in the old Alsatian city that I have always cherished. The play was clearly successful in Alsace and, the following summer, the Centre dramatique de l'Est traveled to Paris to give some performances of the work at the Théâtre du Montparnasse. In the autumn, the Théâtre de l'Oeuvre took it over, with a somewhat different cast, and the play was on the billboards for several months. It was then staged in German, a little later, in Münster, in Westphalia, where it was quite well received and then staged in several German theatres. I was to see it later in England. It was staged in Italy, etc .... Without doubt it is the play that has been most widely produced, but this in no way means that in my view it is the most meaningful one.

A little time after its publication in the *Cahiers Verts* in 1925, I had shown it to André François-Poncet, the future ambassador, who was then director of the École des Beaux-Arts. He had told me that it was a play in the manner of Ibsen, and I agree that in the background of the work one can perhaps find a distant influence of *Rosmersholm*. All the same, this reference to Ibsen indicates a very superficial view. It is hardly less so than that of my critics who, when it was staged at the Théâtre du Montparnasse, thought of Paul Hervieu. In thinking about the play, I had to recognize the underlying existence of a problematic that owes nothing to the author of the *Revenants* (Ghosts) and still less, of course, to the one of *La Course du flambeau* (The running of the torch). This problematic was quite well understood by Jeanne Delhomme who made a very interesting contribution to the book *Existentialisme chrétien*, and who was a little later to help me appreciably in the preparation of the Gifford Lectures. She was perhaps the first to underline the role of interrogative thought in *Un homme de Dieu*, and more generally in nearly all my plays. In that I can say that she quite well silenced those who believed they saw in me an author of philosophical plays whereas, ever since *Le Seuil invisible*, I had stated my dislike for this kind of theatre. Nevertheless, particularly among Catholics, there were people who imagined that in *Un homme de Dieu* I had developed an argument in favor of priestly celibacy. Such an interpretation is all the more absurd because when I wrote the play in Sens I was not even thinking about the possibility of ever becoming a Catholic. Here as elsewhere chronology has an importance that should not be underestimated. As for the rest, it was hardly less unreasonable to see in *Un homme de Dieu* an attack against Protestantism. That was, however, the reason Pierre Fresnay gave for not playing the role of Claude Lemoyne in which he would have been admirable. He told me he wasn't a believer but that, having been reared by Protestants, he thought he would be doing something wrong by being in the play. He didn't expect that some years later at Cobourg in Germany the play would be produced before a gathering of Protestant theologians, in the course of a Protestant Week of Theatre, and that it would not provoke any objection from them.

On the other hand, I have been able to observe that here some liberal Protestants had welcomed it unfavorably—probably because the play implies, in spite of everything, the condemnation of a certain moralism and of the blindness that too often accompanies it.

The problematic that I was recalling above is not only that of pardon. What I think I see plainly today, without—it seems to me—having been clearly aware of it in the beginning, is the error that consists in thinking that one can, after an interval of twenty years, question oneself in a worthy manner as to the motives of an action that has only had its meaning and importance in the present. I have often said that I judged Edmée, the wife of the minister, much more severely than the minister himself, because it is she who, in an essentially egocentric movement, influences the unfortunate Claude Lemoyne to undergo a destructive and retrospective examination of conscience.

I cannot help but feel irritated by the fact that those who speak to me about my theatrical work nearly always refer to *Un homme de Dieu*. It's because this play, that I certainly don't disclaim, far from it, does not figure among those where I believe I have given my best, the essential part of myself: *Le Chemin de crête, Les Coeurs avides* (Eager hearts) or *Le Dard*, *L'Émissaire*, or *Le Signe de la Croix*, or the last to date, *Mon temps n'est pas le vôtre*. What is missing in *Un homme de Dieu* is a certain musical quality that, I dare say, is perceptible in the better scenes, those that came to me as if I were a medium—as indeed, I believe I was—as clearly but even more deeply than in my metapsychic experiences during World War I. Here I am especially thinking about the last acts of *L'Émissaire* and *Le Signe de la Croix*: these two plays, which I had started writing much earlier, were waiting to be finished. It was on the eve of my departure for Beirut where I was going as a member of the French delegation to the Unesco conference that, in an incredible burst of creativity, I wrote these last scenes where, I repeat, the best of my thought is concentrated. Here I note that in the third act of *L'Émissaire*, which I had begun some three years earlier in the Corrèze, one can find the explanation for the attitude that Ferrier adopts when he returns from the deportation. What is most strange is that I didn't have this explanation when I wrote the first act. I didn't literally know why Ferrier, now back home with his family, seemed to want to envelop himself in silence, the secret of which they vainly tried to pierce. But when I wrote the last act in 1948, this explanation suddenly came to me. Might one say that, three years earlier, it was already in my subconscious? I agree, but I should immediately add that I hesitate even more to talk about my subconscious, as though it let itself be circumscribed, as though it were some kind of dark compartment of my being. I have already said this, and I am convinced that we should refute this kind of representation.

Similar remarks could be made about *Le Signe de la Croix*. I had written the first act some months after or perhaps even before the beginning of World War II, but the play had remained unfinished, as though I was waiting for the events that were nevertheless unpredictable which would give this act its entire meaning. I wrote the second act during the war, still without clearly knowing the ending. This only came to me in 1948, but I didn't have to change anything that I had previously written. I should add that several years later I felt the need to add an epilogue to the play, the usefulness of which has even been questioned by some who are near to me, whereas others judged it indispensable. The work was to be staged in Nantes by an amateur group of actors, and it was such a success that a dozen performances were given when only two or three had been planned. Theatrical readings of the play were given in Paris, at the Galerie Devèche and later at Maisons-Lafitte, during which the admirable Madame Berthe Bovy played the role of Tante Léna.[13] I forgot to say that Hébertot had decided to produce the play but that he then became afraid after

[13] Situated near the Étoile in Paris, the Galerie Devèche provided a space for lectures, the reading of plays, and artistic expositions. *Trans.*

reading two or three inept articles where I was accused of antisemitism. So he refused to produce the work without, however, compensating me for what was probably rightfully due me.

If I am not mistaken, it was during the summer of 1950 that I received an anonymous message: "The Russians are coming, you are on the lists, take the necessary precautions." It was probably only a joke, and I don't know who wrote it. Though I did shudder after reading the message, I immediately decided to ignore it.

It is probable, though I can't quite exactly affirm it, that the decision Étienne Gilson made some months later to move to Canada set off in me the interior movement that had begun with the message and that led to the creation of *Rome n'est plus dans Rome* (Rome is no longer in Rome). Jacques Hébertot, favorably impressed by the success of *Un homme de Dieu*, had requested a play from me. So I offered him *Rome n'est plus dans Rome*, and he accepted it.[14] The play was on the marquees in Paris for three months and then went on tour throughout France, Belgium and the Netherlands. The critics had not altogether understood it: here I am thinking not only of Jean-Jacques Gautier but also of Robert Kemp and Émile Henriot who didn't understand the link between the religious problem and the political problem in the important scene of act 2 between Pascal and his nephew Marc-André.

My situation as a playwright might then have seemed to be established but, as I said earlier, it was to be seriously compromised in 1953 through the failure of *Le Chemin de crête* at the Théâtre du Vieux-Colombier.

Robert Kemp dedicated a long, welcoming and comprehensive article to it in *Le Monde* but this did not at all compensate for the horrible effect of the review that appeared in *Le Figaro*, which manifested, on the contrary, a total lack of understanding. The play was on the billboards for only a month. However, the success that was due to radio and television seemed to increase. Every day some spectators left the theatre with an air of enthusiasm. I won't linger on the motives for which *Le Chemin de crête* was prematurely closed down. All that is painful and, after all, is of little interest here. Because

[14] It was later that I presented *Le Signe de la Croix* to him and that he changed his mind about my first offer.

it did not have a successful run, everything happened as though I had lost what I had gained through *Un homme de Dieu* and *Rome n'est plus dans Rome.* I could not get *Les Coeurs avides*, which had been well received in Brussels, to be performed in Paris at any of the major theatres. I had to be satisfied with a few performances by amateur actors, in Marseilles and in Paris.

Later on, some of my plays were to be performed sporadically abroad, mostly in Germany but also in Great Britain (*Le Chemin de crête* in London in 1958, *Le Monde cassé* in Dublin in 1959). But no common measure exists between the rather limited success of these performances and my reputation as a philosopher crowned by the translations of my plays and by the numerous lectures I undertook each year until about 1968.

An imbalance that was perhaps inevitable thus came about, but I see more and more clearly that it became quite seriously prejudicial to a profound understanding of my work.

Of course I have not failed to underline, especially in my lectures at Harvard on human dignity in 1961, the essential connection that links my philosophical work to my theatre. It is probably generally admitted today, but this kind of recognition in the abstract is here quite insufficient. It would have been necessary, even indispensable, for my theatre to benefit from the ease with which Sartre had his plays produced. In a certain way I would even say I would have needed it more than he because, except for one or two exceptions, his plays illustrate a philosophical work which stands on its own and about which, on the level of thought, one cannot say that they add anything that might modify its interpretation. That is quite different from my own case, because my work is much less systematic and more existential than that of the author of *Huis clos* (*No Exit).* Here the remarks of Jeanne Delhomme about the role of interrogative thought in my work take on all their poignancy. There is no questioning and there is nothing interrogative in the plays of Sartre. There is perhaps one exception to this: *Les Mains sales* (*Dirty Hands*), by far the best of his plays, in my opinion, but which Sartre forbade to be performed in Vienna, probably because he feared it would be interpreted in an anticommunist way. This is enough to indicate the nature of the difference that separates us—a difference that is never clearly presented whenever one talks about Christian and atheistic existentialism. In reality, it is the very essence of thought that is in question.

18

15 December 1970

Today all our thoughts are turned towards Madrid. The verdict that should close the trial of Burgos is not yet known as I write this, but we have learned that rights of individuals were abolished for six months and that the police had free reign. This is enough to make one tremble. With what fraternal feeling I think of the three hundred Catalan intellectuals who have taken refuge at Montserrat and of the courageous monks who rule over this Abbey. I had visited it with my son in 1933, and the memory of this apocalyptic landscape remains engraved in me.

I now realize that I haven't said anything about my attitude during the Spanish Civil War. One should not think that I was insensitive to it. Horrified by the crimes committed by Franco's supporters and by the Republicans, I had adhered with Maritain and Mauriac to the Third Party headed by Mendizabal. Of course this Third Party proved to be strangely unproductive. But today I can't truly reproach myself for having supported it. I remember, of course, that I had met one or two Spanish Republicans who had won me over, especially Semprun, the father of the well-known writer. But these men, who were certainly just, only occupied a rather marginal place in their party, and we cannot forget the crimes of which it has become guilty. Here as elsewhere, I maintain my position: no fraudulent turning about; let us not credit some with the errors and even the crimes of others.

Today we all fear that Spain will know once more the horrors of their Civil War. But this time I won't hesitate to side with the Basques and the Catalans, that is to say with those who are persecuted.

Some days ago we saw a program on television that was partly dedicated to the position of the Church in Spain. Should we truly believe that the majority of priests in this country are on the side of the opposition? It was certainly painful to hear some declare that, for them,there is no difference between politics and religion and that the essential role of the priest is to open the eyes of the workers to the exploitation from which they suffer. Such declarations manifest the most distressing mental confusion. But what should we think about those who side with Franco? Can one position have us excuse the other?

Why have I felt the need today to include this parenthesis in a development that seems unrelated? But after all I do admit that what I am trying to bring out in such a groping way in this book is the magnetization of my life and of my work, a mutual attraction, because I see more and more clearly that they cannot be separated from each other. Well, I think I can say that concern for justice does influence my attitudes more and more when confronted by certain events. But what does one not have to face? These days I have been able to observe how difficult it is not to stumble upon a path that is so arduous and poorly laid out. I had been asked to receive an individual who had belonged to the Nazi paramilitary force and who was condemned to death in his absence but who was able to escape the death penalty. On this point, there is now prescription, but he would like to be exempt, by means of a pardon, from the accompanying sentences that are still in force. He presented me with a more than watered down version of what his activities had been during the Occupation. I was weak enough to believe him and to write a letter to the president of the French Republic in which I pleaded his case. I was to learn later that he had told me only lies and that he had committed a series of unspeakable crimes. It goes without saying that I demanded that my letter be returned to me before it reached its destination and that I told the interested party about it. But I must acknowledge that, thinking that I had acted out of fairness, I made myself, without suspecting it, an accomplice of hideous crimes. So we should be very prudent when zealously, but perhaps thoughtlessly, we run to help supposed victims. To understand my conduct, I must allude to this pathology of good will that I recalled, some time ago, concerning Paul Ricoeur, prisoner of the attitude that was imprudently adopted in the spring of 1968. How dangerous and difficult all that is! Of course, it is quite tempting to find refuge through silence. But Simone de Beauvoir was right on this point when she wrote *Les Bouches inutiles* (*Who Shall Die?*): abstention is still action—the lowest level of action.

But I must add that the ever more demanding concern for justice that inhabits me is at times accompanied by an equally distinct awareness of the difficulties, even of the contradictions, that beset the institutionalization of justice. It seems more and more to imply an egalitarianism that I could never support.[1] How could I not repeat here what I have often said in my lectures? Contrary to what the formula consecrated by the French Revolution may imply, Equality and Fraternity are in truth oriented in the opposite direction of each other. Equality is essentially egocentric: *I am your equal*. It is made up of claims and, as Scheler has so keenly seen, of resentment. Fraternity, on the contrary, is hetero-centric: *you are my brother*, and because you are my brother, I am capable, not only of recognizing your superiority but of rejoicing over it.

It is certainly possible that, because of the number that seems to appear more and more like the enemy of any true wisdom, egalitarianism will win out everywhere, but this can only be at the expense of essential values. Nothing could ever convince me that a cleaning woman should earn as much as a professor.

So the idea of social justice that in fact basks in such confusion presents itself to me as not being reductive to the ideological simplifications with which so many thinkers are content to find sustenance. This is the same as saying that in my view a civilization worthy of the name certainly implies the safeguard of a certain aristocracy, but it goes without saying that it cannot be assimilated to a class, and we must also recognize that it is in a plutocratic world, alas, such as our own that it has the least chance of being established.

I sometimes think, mainly because of demographics, that socialism has perhaps become inevitable. But we know only too well to what

[1] On second thought, this assertion appears to me to be equivocal and questionable.

extent this term is, as it is the case for democracy, loaded with fearful ambiguities. It is too evident that if we have to choose between Marx and Proudhon, I will unhesitatingly choose the latter, but it has not yet been shown that a regime according to the thought of Proudhon can be realized. The incredible success that Marxist ideology has had still remains to be explained. Even here, moreover, we know quite well that ambiguity and equivocation abound. What we should notice in any case—and this is a remark of immense importance—is what a Rumanian had me observe the day before yesterday, namely, that intellectuals believe in Marxism to the extent that they have not concretely experienced it, the opposite being equally true.

This book should certainly not end up being a diary. Nevertheless I feel a growing need to refer to more and more alarming events that have occurred these past days. The verdict of Burgos is not yet known and it doesn't seem that Franco can remain deaf to the solemn appeal made to him by Pope Paul VI. But the crisis that has begun seems too serious and too vast to be resolved through the commutation of an eventual sentence.

Today, moreover, the news that comes from Poland is what concerns us most. After the riots of Gdánsk and Gdynia, the trouble seems to be spreading to other parts of the country. The Kremlin is reacting. Should the situation get worse still, a military intervention on the part of the Soviets could be expected. Other facts, in themselves less serious, such as the persistence of social troubles in Italy, would give one the impression that the situation is evolving in a dangerous direction. Certainly, to an objective onlooker, France may appear today to be benefiting from privileged conditions. Nevertheless, there is a certain lack of satisfaction that is more and more general and also equally perceptible, in spite of the soothing assurances that the government gives.

19

As my main concern in this somewhat hybrid book is to be true, I feel rather obliged to say this: the day before yesterday, after a full day, and *though I can't speak of premonition*, I had the impression that I was going to die in a few days, and the feeling of panic that suddenly took hold of me indicated to what extent I delude myself when I think I am ready and, finally, detached. Here, as elsewhere, that is to say wherever the self is in question, everything is in some way at once true. The strange term that is "incohesion" is the one that best suits a situation about which we could say that it challenges the principle of contradiction, without in any way corresponding to what the Hegelian thematic implies.

When I think about it, I do notice that very early on I had become aware of this incohesion but I did not articulate this awareness as I have been able, of course, to do so today. As I think about it, it is probable that if I have emphasized ambiguity and ambivalence in my work, and primarily in my theatre, it was in order to explain and, in so doing, transform up to a certain point, this primitive feeling, this *Ur-Gefühl*. It seems to me that it is probably on this point that commentators of my work have been up to now the most at fault. This is especially translated by the fact that they have accorded, so to speak, no place to the comical in the general economy of my work. It doubtlessly plays, however, a very important role, and it is not insignificant that each day, or nearly so, some phrase of a dialogue for a burlesque character comes to mind and which very often has to do with words or names. There is thus a zone where, and this would come as a surprise, ... I communicate with Ionesco. Robert Kemp had alluded to it, at the

Galerie Devèche, if I am not mistaken, in talking about *Mon temps n'est pas le vôtre*. Yet there is still an abyss between us, and that's all I shall say about it here.

The events taking place in Poland continue to develop: Gomulka has been sent away, as has the minister of economics, which says much about what has occurred in the port cities of the Baltic. On the other hand, one wonders whether this change in government will not somehow influence the famous opening up to the East. Ulbricht is showing himself to be more and more difficult, and nothing seems to indicate a modification in the status of Berlin which alone would make the ratification of the two treaties by the Bundestag possible.

This is not, as one might think, a parenthesis bereft of all meaning or of any connection to the deep sense of this writing. It is a fact that the problem of relationships—of our relationships—with the countries of Eastern Europe is of growing importance to me.

This is probably the place to remember the meeting with Siegfried Foëlz, which will have been one of the most moving and valuable of my life. About five years ago, or perhaps even more, he wrote me for the first time from Dresden. This Catholic priest, this Oratorian told me that, in order to pay back the debt he had towards my writings, he was making every effort to publish, in Eastern Germany—in Leipzig, with Sankt Benno Verlag—a selection of texts that might make my thought known in a region which was not acquainted with it. I answered him by return mail to tell him how much I had been moved by his letter: for me Dresden, which I had never yet visited, had always basked in a special prestige and, on the other hand, I had never ceased to think that this city's destruction by Anglo-American aviation was one of the most characteristic crimes of war.

Since then we have kept up a regular correspondence. Contrary to what was expected, he succeeded in overcoming censorship and in having two small books published in a handsome format where my texts were preceded by a long and excellent introduction that he wrote. I told myself that I would do everything to get to Dresden, to express my gratitude personally, and especially to meet the man in whom I recognized an authentic spiritual son. But I probably would never have been able to realize this desire had it not been for the good will of two American students, Stephen Jolin and Peter McCormick who, knowing my wish, placed themselves at my disposal and touchingly offered to drive me to East Germany. It was in the last days of April 1969 that this lightning trip took place; I shall never forget it. I won't retrace its stages but only recall the hours spent waiting near Hof at the line of demarcation. We were about the only ones to cross over that day. While we were waiting, I wondered with exasperation what exactly was this telephone inquiry that the customs officers in their Russian military uniforms were making since they had taken our papers and were submitting them to one only knows what kind of investigation. Were we finally going to be told to return home? We weren't, and at nightfall we disappeared into this gray and ostensibly dehumanized world that contrasted in such an almost overwhelming manner with the Frankish world that we had just left. It was night time when we arrived in Dresden, a city that was almost unrecognizable where immense vacant areas of land are interspersed with large sinister apartment buildings, quite similar to those one finds everywhere, from Paris to New York, or from Buenos Aires to Hong Kong. We had some trouble finding the Hotel Astoria where our rooms were being held and where Siegfried Foëlz was waiting for us.

At my request, he had sent me a small picture. I already knew that he was a young man, with a handsome contemplative face, but, afraid of being disappointed despite everything, I couldn't imagine to what extent this meeting would overwhelm me.

If I have dedicated this book to him, it is not only to express my gratitude and affection openly but to say that I regard him as one of the most intimately qualified inheritors of my thought, one of those in whom it is called, it seems to me, to endure and be renewed in the most efficacious, perhaps the most creative, manner and that precisely because it is happening in a country that is suffering martyrdom. That my thought could have been able to present this decisive significance to a man who has lived the very extremes of suffering and upheaval is a kind of distinction that no official recognition can begin to approach.

This sentiment was to become clearer, first of all, during the very intimate conversation I had with him the following day at Pirna, the little town near Dresden, where he had recently been living, and even more during the Mass that he celebrated for us alone in the small church there. At that moment I was fully aware that this encounter marked one of the high points of my life. For me it clearly showed that the discovery of my work had been decisive for him at a particularly critical moment of his existence.

I would like to avoid any misunderstanding about the meaning and importance that this encounter had for me. More than any other—and naturally I recall here the countless letters received from and sent by people I never knew—it confirmed me in the idea that I had not thought in vain. By this I especially mean that I did not avoid those problems which exist, certainly not for all men, but at least for those who have come to a certain sense of awareness—with all the uncertainty, and I am even able to say all the anxiety that this inevitably entails. It was truly as though I had been allowed to perceive not only a certain light but suddenly to have the assurance that this light was the one that the Other was seeing, the brother who was at once distant and yet so close.

All this will probably be clearer for the reader if I add that I have always felt myself given over to a global questioning of my philosophical work, and this happened most often at times when discouragement had overwhelmed me.

But I should probably assert this while remembering what I said earlier about the feeling of incohesion that is in me like an initial given. I wonder whether the meaning of my life has not resided above all in this relentless effort to free myself of this incohesion in order to come to some assurance that would have a universal value, and that could not be reduced to the ready-to-use formulas that sustain the ideologue.

I should not forget to mention my visit to the Pinakothek of Dresden that I had made in the company of Siegfried Foëlz and of two eminent people of the city, the director of the museum and an admirable woman who had looked over the restoration of the Hofkirche. That morning the weather was magnificent. From the windows of the Pinakothek, we could look down over the Zwinger, miraculously restored. We could see children playing in the narrow streets: a bit of sweetness and of joy was again blossoming in the heart of the tormented city. And then in the rooms of the Pinakothek, the perdurability of art was affirmed beyond every madness and crime. A blessed moment.

Taking advantage of the relative closeness of the two cities, we had decided to spend thirty-six hours in Prague, which I did not yet know and of which I had often dreamed. Siegfried Foëlz accompanied us as far as the border. We were able to dine together, and I shook his hand with the fear that our "au revoir" was, alas, an "adieu."

In Paris we had been able to obtain a Czechkoslovakian visa, and there was no problem in crossing the border. It was a Sunday, the weather was radiant, one could have thought we were traveling in a happy country. The Soviet occupiers and others were invisible. But I knew how things were. A Czech living in France, whom I had met just a few weeks before, had been able to put me in touch with some friends in Prague and let me know, right before our departure, that I was invited to give a lecture at the university. This unexpected news caused me to be rather moved. I clearly knew what retrenchment was going on in the Czech capital and I am convinced, in view of later events, that I took advantage of the last possible moments to address a relatively important public in Prague.

Since I noticed that the French language had lost considerable terrain since the "l'entre deux guerres,"[1] I decided to speak in German and relied upon the memory of the lecture I had given, in this language, in Vienna, in September 1968. I spoke about the stages of my spiritual development, but recalling the impressions felt in East Germany, I did not hesitate to underline my position strongly in the presence of this muzzled country. I was aware of the anxious attention of my listeners but, unfortunately, it was not possible for me to speak on an individual basis with this or that person as I would have wanted to do.

This visit to one of the most beautiful European cities, which was so marked by history, was much too brief. I was to remember it most profoundly.

[1] This term is used by the French to refer to the years between World War I and World War II. *Trans.*

Husák, back from Moscow, had just given a press conference to talk about his conversations with the men in the Kremlin, and we had been able to see, in the courtyards and in the hallways of the chateau, the anxious and silent crowd that was waiting to learn its fate.

It was the only time in my life when I had been able to come into immediate contact with the immense drama that so occupied my thought.

The experience of that moment was probably not unrelated to the decision I was to make, some months later, to dedicate a part of the money received from the Erasmus Prize, which I had been awarded in Rotterdam at the end of October 1969, to some travel scholarships to be given to intellectuals from Eastern European countries who shared a respect for essential values with us.

With us, I wrote, but who is this *us*? With this pronoun it is unfortunately no longer possible to understand the group of intellectuals of the West; a disastrous cleavage has taken place among us for a certain number of years under conditions that future historians will have to try to understand.

But as for what concerns me, I have been able to observe with Toma Pavel, Janos Pilinsky, Radovan Grgec, and even quite recently with Tépéneag and Michel Sora, a community of thought and, as it were, of interior vision whose equal I would not be able to find among the countless teachers of this country who blindly pursue their work of destruction.

In this sense, and however paradoxical it may seem to appear, I, who unfortunately don't know the Russian language and, generally speaking, Slavic languages, I do feel myself more and more drawn towards this world of the East, such as it has revealed itself to me for more than half a century through the work of great novelists and more immediately still in that of a Moussorgsky.

20

23 December 1970

Although I am making every effort for the last part of this writing not to become a simple diary, there are some circumstances that I have to mention when they come to mind because they are situated in a kind of magnetic field that stretches around my life and that gives it meaning.

Here I am particularly thinking about the death of my cousin, Pastor Marc Boegner, and the admirable funeral service that took place yesterday at the Oratory.

He had officiated at our wedding, 24 April 1919, in the Temple de Saint-Marcel. Since then, a very strong bond of friendship formed between us, in spite of the pain he felt, I well fear, in reading *Un homme de Dieu*. I had been very happy to meet him again at the Academy of Political and Moral Sciences, of which he was one of the best presidents. The extraordinary tenacity with which he dedicated himself not only to his pastoral role but also to the service of a thought that was truly ecumenical, won for him the admiration and gratitude of all. And how can I forget the courage with which, during the Occupation, he adopted a position against the laws condemning the Jews, and later against the scandals of the cleansing that followed World War II! I don't hesitate saying that, among my colleagues of the Academy of Political and Moral Sciences, he was the most justly and universally respected. And while I write these lines, the term that comes back to me is "companions of eternity," a term that W. E. Hocking and I used at the time of our first and unforgettable encounter during his time of retreat in New Hampshire. This visit took place during my first and quite short trip to the United States, the one that had taken me to Mackinaw, on the little island of Lake Huron which is the veritable center of Moral Rearmament. I'll come back to this visit a little later on. But now I want to recall the dear and noble face of Hocking. His receptive and generous philosophy was an outgrowth of the encounter between Husserlian philosophy and the speculation of a Whitehead. For me, he continues to be one of the very rare, exceptional incarnations of the modern thinker at a time when, so often, professors of philosophy either pursue their task with the blind tenacity of a mole or, alas, in the manner of Sartre, change themselves to end up as demagogues. I truly don't know what Hocking would think about the last developments of American politics or, rather, I have an inkling. I am certain that the absurd war in Vietnam, whose outcome no one can any longer see, would cause him the deepest suffering as would indeed other tragedies to which our friends on the other side of the Atlantic are prey: racial conflict, the scandal of generalized pollution, the terrible increase of drug addiction, etc. It's as though he were at my side as I write these lines, but I am almost certain that he would encourage me not to abandon hope, because an invincible faith in man dwelled in him, surely not in the positivist sense but in man being rooted in God.

But what I would like to add is that Hocking was not the only one to give me the best idea of what a certain elite might be in the United States. How could I not mention here the name of my very good friend Henry Bugbee? I had come into contact with him during the summer of 1954-1955, after I read an article he had sent me and which I had liked. It was then that he sent me a kind of metaphysical journal which was both quite lucid and profound and which he later published under the title *The Inward Morning.*[1] I wrote him expressing my desire to make his acquaintance. He received a small scholarship which allowed him to come spend a month in France and to participate in the colloquium that was held at the chateau of Cerisy-la-Salle, in La Manche,[2] on the work of Martin Heidegger, who had come to France

[1] Henry Greenwood Bugbee, *The Inward Morning; a philosophical exploration in journal form. With an introduction by Gabriel Marcel.* State College, PA. Bald Eagle Press, 1958. *Trans.*

[2] The administrative department or region of France that is situated in north western France, along the English Channel, which bears the same name in French. *Trans.*

for the first time for this event. It was here that our lasting friendship began. He was later to spend a year near Paris wth his wife. Still later he welcomed me in Missoula, Montana, where he was a professor and, finally, in 1966, he accompanied me during a short and marvelous trip to the Northwestern states: Idaho, Washington, and Oregon. What I have always admired in Henry Bugbee was a kind of preserved freshness that combined speculation with a vitality that was elsewhere so frequently missing. This scrupulous and precise thinker is also a man of nature, interested in fishing for trout for weeks on end in the streams of the Rocky Mountains. I don't think I ever spent a time in my life that was so uplifting as when I was with him among these grandiose spots where a kind of unadulterated virginity of the countryside exercises a regenerative action upon the soul. Rather than in the metropolitan areas, it was there, in his presence, as before with Hocking in the solitude of Madison, that I was able to sense America in its force and grandeur. Of course, I was not insensitive to the apocalyptic beauty of New York, especially from the other bank of the Hudson where one can contemplate the city. But how would I not feel, there as in Chicago or in other large urban centers, the terrifying threat that besets everything that, for us men of the Old World, bestows value and meaning to life.

Nevertheless, after the four or five trips I was able to make to the United States from 1959 to 1966, and especially in thinking about the impact that the reading of Royce, Hocking, and even up to a certain point William James had upon me before and during World War I, I believe I can say that one of the poles of the magnetic field I mentioned was and remains, in spite of everything, America. And I don't think that it is due to chance that my thought has spread more rapidly in the United States than in certain countries of Europe. That was especially the case, of course, following the lectures I was invited to give at Harvard during the autumn of 1961.

As I had arrived in Boston rather late, I was somewhat worried. I was then welcomed at the airport by the young philosopher Hubert Dreyfus, whose acquaintance I had made in Paris, some weeks earlier, and who arranged everything to facilitate my adaptation to a university milieu that was entirely new to me. I must acknowledge that the contacts with the professors of philosophy at Harvard, nearly all neo-positivists, were reduced to simple polite exchanges. But in the course of a few seminars that I gave, besides my regular courses, I made a strong impression upon a certain number of students, and later on I was to experience the same thing at a number of other universities, particularly in Cleveland, Pittsburgh, San Francisco, and so forth.

Is the interest I have shown for Moral Rearmament for some fifteen years due to the disposition I recalled above when talking about Hocking, Henry Bugbee and, in general, a certain American elite? Certainly not. I must say, on the contrary, that the American character of Moral Rearmament has often called forth a feeling in me that is close to irritation. Here I am especially talking about a tendency to simplify and to schematize which expresses itself, for example, in the famous criteria I alluded to in talking about the Oxford Groups. But what struck me and what I also insist on underlining is the extraordinary good will—I use the word here with a meaning that is rather close to its Kantian use—which I recognized in a large number of people who were directly connected to Moral Rearmament, as I have already said. And what I must add is that here it is not simply a question of individual cases but of a spiritual milieu that is so efficacious that one has frequently seen people be completely renewed from the moment they entered it. What I am talking about are the authentic conversions that showed their mettle in such a way that those who were converted became in turn radiant. Perhaps it would be better to say irradiant. This is a fact of such importance that from the moment I noticed it—the first time was in Tokyo, in 1957—I no longer thought I had the right to keep my distance even if, in some respects, I thought myself obliged out of a sense of honesty to show some reservation. This principally had to do with certain exterior manifestations that I hardly liked: I am here talking about certain plays and films that seemed to me much too simplistic and also about certain meetings at Caux where accounts were given that necessarily reminded me of what I had least liked in the Oxford Groups. But if I refer to certain recent facts, it is not impossible that the leaders of Moral Rearmament can find some response among students who are sincerely motivated by the desire to transform a society whose faults they are well aware of but who are less and less convinced about the foundation of the discordant interpretations that Marxism or its substitutes offer them.

Here my reaction is quite close to what it is concerning parapsychology: here and there I don't claim, I affirm that we are in the presence of a core of realities that are too frequently covered over by doubtful accretions, or even at times by abusive superstructures but which, as such, requires from us the most demanding and serious attention.

I believe that I must insist on this all the more since these are points for which my attitude has been criticized. Étienne Borne, though a Catholic philosopher who has generally shown sympathy for my work, has wrongly reproached me for the interest I have in research in the area of metapsychics.[3] Here, it would be dishonest and unworthy to compromise by cowardly acknowledging that I was perhaps victimized. Once again, maybe I was here or there mistaken as to the interpretation of a given fact, but not in the general direction that my research took.

Likewise, as for what concerns Moral Rearmament, I can only reaffirm here my feelings of esteem and gratitude for the good men about whom it can be said that they are the salt of the earth.

The time has also come, I think, to acknowledge the positive value of the movement and not to consider it as a kind of smuggler or poacher. It is particularly important for the Church, which had earlier shown itself to be here so narrow and unjust, to recognize the service rendered by Moral Rearmament. The statements made some months ago in Rome by Cardinal Ottaviani to my friend Michel Sentis also eloquently show that justice is on the way.

[3] Etienne Borne is the author of *Le problème du mal. Essai sur l'athéisme contemporain.* (The problem of evil. Essay on contemporary atheism.) Paris: Presses Universitaires de France, 1958. *Trans.*

21

29 December 1970

Justice.

The scandalous verdict of Burgos has been known since yesterday evening. We don't yet know whether Franco will pardon at least some of those condemned to death. The fact that three among them have been condemned twice seems to indicate that the judges wanted to be protected against any move toward clemency and make sure that those three would be executed. One senses that Franco is overwhelmed on the Right and that the possibility of civil war is being created in this troubled country.

The news from Russia isn't any better. Even if we suppose that the two people condemned to death in Leningrad will not be executed, everything indicates that new trials are being prepared for the Jews of Russia who try to leave for Israel. But at Tel-Aviv, the reaction is extremely violent, and one cannot keep from fearing that the Russians will resort to military intervention as a response to this reaction. This could be the most serious threat to peace in a number of years.

I feel that the cold weather which is now raging and which has already claimed numerous victims is like the symbol of the horrible inhumanity which is asserting itself more and more.

In the last analysis, that is the true problem and the only one, and nothing irritates me more than the kind of blind outlook whose results are told us from time to time and which ignores what is essential since it only deals with technical data.

Yesterday I sent a short article to the *Tribuna Medica* of Madrid for a special edition on pollution, where I try to show that it is the sign of an infinitely more disturbing disorder. It is the meaning of *nature naturante* which is being lost, and at the same time man is taking abusive powers over nature which will then result in the development of a mortal encapsulation. I am using here, though giving it a new meaning, Jaspers' term: *Das Umgreifende*.

Six French Nobel laureates have just launched a protest, this time directed against the judges of Burgos and against those of Leningrad; this is good news. What appears to be clear is that a totalitarian regime, no matter which one, engenders the same monstrous consequences; this proves rather well that, in substance, Marxism is perfectly unable to handle effectively the instincts that are so rooted in our species and that, we have every reason to believe, only grace can vanquish.

31 December 1970

Yesterday we learned that the six people condemned in Burgos were pardoned, and it seems that clemency has also prevailed in Russia for the unfortunate Jews of Leningrad. We may think that, for once, the pressure exerted by the universal conscience was indeed effective. So much the better. But I think that we would be wrong to come to any optimistic conclusions from this. All that we can say is that the year 1970 is finishing up less badly than we might have feared even yesterday morning. But in no way have I the impression that the prognosis for 1971 is really reassuring. I am especially thinking about the situation in the Middle East which only seems to be getting worse, in spite of the renewal of the Jarring negotiations: they risked being unproductive right from the start.

5 January 1971

The Christmas season, always so painful for me because of the memories and especially the separations that come with it, has fortunately ended. I have the impression, and it is rather physical, of again pursuing a path that is almost straight.

The time has come to write the last part of this book after a very long parenthesis, whose only purpose was to underline the fact that, contrary to certain other philosophers, I remain closely dependent upon the event. It is impossible for me to disengage myself from it: the truth is that I could not tolerate being without news of what is happening in the world.

But perhaps I should also say that I have felt the need to put off mentioning everything that could resemble a narrative of this twenty-year period during which dramatic criticism, on the one hand, and lecture tours on the other, not only in Europe but in North and South America and in Japan, not to mention Lebanon and Morocco, have somewhat drained my energy.

There can be no question of my giving a detailed account. I would like to indicate some salient features, but I recognize that this summary, reduced to what is essential, risks leaving out some significant experiences that have been able to contribute, even if I have not been fully aware of it, to the orientation of my vision.

As of 1946 I started going back to Germany where, for reasons that are too evident, I had not wanted to set foot for twenty years. In Fribourg I had had my first meeting with Heidegger and had then been able to remark, as I have already mentioned, the serious mistake Sartre had made in classifying him among atheistic existentialists. Fribourg was to become for many years one of my main points of support beyond the Rhine, and this thanks to the understanding and friendship that Father Ruf, chaplain of the Catholic students, has always shown me.[1] Cologne, on the other side of the Rhineland, was also to welcome me on several occasions, and I now remember with gratitude the noble face of Father Nyssen. But this in no way means that I was "confiscated" by the Catholics, something that would have been radically contrary to my deepest leanings. And so some years later I was to be invited to Cobourg where a Protestant Week of

1 Six of Gabriel Marcel's Freiburg im Bresgau lectures were published in a book entitled: *Auf der Suche nach Wahrheit un Gerichtigkeit*, ed. Wolfgang Ruf, Freiburg im Bresgau, Verlag Knecht, 1964. The volume was published as *Searchings*, New York, Newman Press, 1967; lectures it includes: In Search of Truth and Justice; Science and Wisdom; The Sacral in the Era of Technology; Death and Immortality; Martin Buber's Philosophical Anthropology; My Dramatic Works as Viewed by the Philosopher. *Trans.*

Theatre had been organized at which, as I have already said, an excellent performance of *Un homme de Dieu* was given.

In fact I was in turn invited to nearly all the large cities of West Germany, from Kiel to Munich, and particularly, of course, to university cities such as Marburg and Göttingen, Bonn, Heidelberg and Tübingen. My lectures were given in German, but the translations were not my own; I limited myself to looking them over and to correcting this or that point. I would read, but very freely, as I wanted at all cost to avoid giving the impression of being monotonous, the pitfall of reading. I had specified, in the beginning, that I was ready to answer any questions, even any objections that my talk might suggest among the listeners. In the very large conference rooms, this exchange of views was often difficult, and I had to call upon another person to repeat the questions that I had poorly heard. But quite often, we would meet in a smaller room and even sometimes in a cafe where true conversation could ensue.

One shouldn't think that I have ever lost sight of the recent past; on the contrary I have always kept in mind the horrors that took place in Germany. Nearly always the people who had invited me and those who took care of me in the cities where I was to speak brought reassuring information about what their attitude had been regarding Hitlerism. Of course, I may have been taken advantage of at times, but in no case would I have been inclined to show the least indulgence, if I had had proof that my interlocutors had participated in crimes, the thought of which makes me shudder. That is what this little anecdote proves: at the time of my visit to Bayreuth, where I had gone to give a paper, a lady invited me to have tea in her home, telling me that she was a philosopher and had just published a book on metaphysics. I spent an hour with her, and knowing that I was going to Bamberg, she sent greetings to Dr. Pfeil whom I was going to meet there and who was to introduce me at the lecture. I did as I was asked, but Professor Pfeil did not hide from me the fact that the person in question had been a Nazi. I could not keep myself from writing a short indignant letter to the one who had taken advantage of my confidence, saying that it was impossible for me to conceive how someone who called herself a philosopher had been able to adhere to Nazism and make herself an accomplice of the worst acts that history has ever recorded. She took this quite badly and had the impudence to write me that she had not known of the crimes I alluded to, without which ....

As I write these lines, a question comes to mind that the reader has perhaps already asked. When I had visited Heidegger, I certainly already knew that he had, at least for some time, *mitgemacht* (that is to say, participated). I am using the German word, because it allows for a certain indetermination that the too precise term complicity excludes. Because of this there can be no doubt that I experienced a certain uneasiness, and if I did overcome it, it is because I knew that after a certain time he had distanced himself from Nazism. This uneasiness was all the more felt when I found myself in the presence of his wife who was, I have every right to think, one of his bad genies.

Today, I ask myself, "Should I have for this reason refrained from visiting the author of *Sein und Zeit* (*Being and Time*)?" Quite frankly, I don't think so. The best thing would doubtlessly have been to have had the courage to ask the question directly as Lucien Goldmann was to do later on, at the time of the colloquium held in Cerisy which was marked by the first visit of Heidegger to France. I must also admit that the answer of the philosopher lacked clarity, and I am one of those who believe that he should have publicly acknowledged the grave mistake that he had become guilty of. Well, to my knowledge, he never made this act of contrition. I cannot keep from thinking that it was his pride that kept him from doing so, even though pride is, without the shadow of a doubt, that interior disposition which the philosopher must constantly fight against. But despite this, and with all due respect to Vladimir Jankélévitch, French philosophers had the duty to come into contact with the most original thinker that Germany has given birth to since Nietzsche. Such a position will perhaps be judged contradictory by some, but it is one of those to which life condemns us, by reason of the very ambiguity that affects it in its very principle.

On the other hand, I would like to say that in awarding me the Goethe Prize in Hamburg, in 1956, and the Peace Prize in Frankfurt, in 1964, the Germans had the merit of accentuating the struggle for humanity that has ever become more important for me since the horrible drama of 1939-1945. [2]

It is also in the same spirit that I was awarded the Erasmus Prize in 1969, as I have already said. I well remember the welcome I received in Rotterdam on this occasion as well as the wonderful words of Prince Bernhard of the Netherlands. This was doubtless, along with the one in Frankfurt, in 1964, the most beautiful of all the ceremonies that honored me. But I must add that on such occasions my thoughts turned with the most fervent gratitude towards my own relatives and friends as well as towards those who had given me so much, and to whom I realized deeply was due something of the homage that I had received. Their absence at such moments would have been literally intolerable if I had not kept the mysterious assurance that in a certain manner that cannot be represented or conceptualized, they were there with me, nearer to me than myself.

It was the same kind of emotion that I felt in Salzburg, when I was invited to deliver the opening talk of the festival at the end of July 1965. This Mozart who had been the first composer chronologically to speak to me, so much so that at the age of 5 I had asked to keep near me the score of *Don Juan*, I was invited now, less to celebrate than to invoke this Mozart, in the very place where he had opened himself to the light. And on this same occasion I was able to pay tribute to and acknowledge the noble and pure poet Hugo von Hofmannsthal whose *Ballade de la vie extérieure* (Ballad of the Exterior Life), I had put into music some years before.

Here I was in the heart of the Austria I had dreamt so much about in my adolescent years, when, before World War I, I dedicated two of my very first articles, one to the theatre of Arthur Schnitzler,[3] the other to the *Italienisches Liederbuch* of Hugo Wolf, in the review *Sim*. Remembering these beginnings today, I don't find them to be meaningless. Schnitzler is certainly one of the foreign writers who influenced my theatrical work: I am thinking of plays such as *Zwischenspiel (Intermezzo)* and *Der einsame Weg* (*The Lonely Way*); in these plays I find a twilight quality that has moved me. As for Hugo Wolf, I think

2 Clippings of newspaper photos and articles about Gabriel Marcel's visit to receive the Peace Prize in Germany are preserved in the Carlton Lake Collection, Harry Ransom Humanities Research Center, University of Texas at Austin. *Trans.*

3 In *La Grande Revue*.

of him today as when I discovered him, that he is basically one of the most profoundly genial composers of his time. Recently as I again listened to some of the most tragic pieces of the *Spanisches Liederbuch*, marvelously sung by Fischer-Diskau, I again had the certainty that never had a more profound and authentic song been sung.

It is doubtless through these two creators that Vienna has exercised such a power of enchantment over me, well before the brief stay that my wife and I made there in 1935. Of course, I did not know the city during the grand period, but it is nonetheless, among the European capitals, the one which, with Rome, has generated in me the most intense feeling of presence. I remember the emotion which came over me, when I returned there in 1946, when the wounds caused by the aftermath of World War II were still bloody. While walking through the wounded city, I could not keep from thinking that we Westerners were indeed to blame for an unforgivable fault in destroying the Austro-Hungarian empire which, in spite of everything, remained, in the heart of Europe, a center of civilization and, I would even say, of spiritual hospitality. Still, one could not then see what would become of these *disjecta membra* and particularly of unfortunate Czechoslovakia.

One of my regrets is to have never been performed in Vienna, except for two small theatres which didn't have the means, I fear, of interpreting me in an adequate manner. On several occasions I was promised that one of my plays would be performed in the Burgtheater, but this promise was never kept—without my ever understanding the nature of the obstacle that had arisen.

I have often returned to Vienna since 1946. I gave a lecture there on *La Musique dans ma vie* (Music in my life), which has never been published.[4] It is also meaningful that here I also wrote, in German, *Mon testament philosophique* (My philosophical testament) in the context of the 1968 International Congress of Philosophy. It was also in Vienna that the translations of the *Journal métaphysique* and the *Mystère de l'être* were published by Herold Verlag around 1950. Today they are out of print; I don't believe the publisher is planning

[4] This was later published as "La Musique dans ma vie et mon oeuvre" (Music in my life and work) in *Présence de Gabriel Marcel* (Presence of Gabriel Marcel), Cahier 2-3, Paris: Aubier-Flammarion, 1980. *Trans.*

another edition. I will probably have to think of finding another publisher, preferably in Germany, to oversee it, but I hardly have the strength to undertake any steps in this regard.

It seems to me somewhat useless to dwell on the lectures I gave in Great Britain and in Italy, as well as those in the Netherlands. I have already alluded to the trip of 1947, the memory of which is still with me, but I was to return to Holland on several occasions, particularly for the performances of *Rome n'est plus dans Rome*, in 1952, and for the Congress of Parapsychology that was held the following year in Utrecht. The lecture tour I made in Italy in 1952, for the Alliance française, took me to Sicily. I fondly remember Monreale, Agrigente, and Taormina, and I recall, with gratitude, the welcome I was given in Palermo by the Marquis Fatta, a remarkable historian and a specialist of Saint-Simon.

These are only indications, something like spots of color on a palette that has many others. But nearly all these trips were disappointing to some degree, in the sense that I did not belong to myself, that there was not much time for myself, because of the schedule that had been set up for my lectures. There was one happy exception when, in 1962, the Minister of National Education in Greece invited me to a conference on dramatic art in Athens. I traveled with Henri Gouhier who, like me, was going to Greece for the first time. The Congress was not really that interesting, but I did meet Roger Planchon and François Billetdoux, and I was happy to note that, contrary to my expectations, the Acropolis in no way disappointed me. Here again, a strange conjunction came about between the present and a distant past that one might have thought buried. Had I not imagined at my desk in the lycée, in my junior or senior year, that I would one day be a Hellenic scholar? This Greece experienced by the school boy on reading Homer and Plato was now stretched out before me in all its splendor. And, of course, there were Delphi and two plays by Euripides at Epidaurus.

I still hope to return to Greece, to renew and deepen this rejuvenating experience. But, even if this hope cannot be realized, the light of these days in 1962 will remain with me until the end.

I would be tempted to use the same words to evoke certain other predestined places I was able to visit on two occasions. It would certainly have been good to spend more time in these cities in order to assimilate the essence which, more than any idea formed after reading, contributes to the edification of our interior being: Fez in Morocco, even more than Marrakech. In Spain, there was, above all, Granada, but also certain little squares in Seville and Cordoba. I appreciated Andalousia more than Castilla, even though in Avila and Salamanca, in Segovia and, of course, in Toledo, I had the feeling of opening myself to a world that was quite different from the one I had known until then. Since I discovered Spain well after Italy, it has remained for me more intact and mysterious; it attracts and repels me at the same time. If, unfortunately, my ability to read was not as affected as it is, I would be tempted to lose myself in the Spanish language, which I know so imperfectly, but which has for me such extraordinary depth. Although I may not give clear reasons for this, I can say that it is through music that I am able to compare Spain, which I have visited, and Russia, which I have not. Russia has perhaps become closer to me than any other European land. For many reasons, but especially because I don't know the Russian language, I am not thinking of visiting this country, but I realize that an affinity exists between it and me. This awareness has also been kindled and clarified by many encounters and even friendships that have enriched me. How could I not here remember Doucia Ergaz, the incredibly intelligent and feeling novelist of the *Faveurs du Ciel* (Favors of heaven) and her so sorrowful fate?

But the picky censor that I always carry within me calls out to me: "Why," he asks me, "this much too rapid remembrance, which becomes reduced at the very mention of certain names of people and places?" While I call out these names, still others come to me—the names of some cities that have affected me like certain people. Should I not rather say that they were like people with whom I was attuned: Coimbra or Dubrovnik. *You were with me*: as for so many books or musical works that we had the happiness of discovering together, we deciphered them, these cities, in a kind of happy exaltation, and it was the same for so many landscapes, contemplated for a long time. Today I would tell my censor that I have the feeling of a debt that I must at least acknowledge even though, alas, I haven't the means to pay it, as this would be the case were I a painter or even a poet. And now, when I remember these travels, I sense that a call was given me that I didn't know how to answer, because pure thought, on the one hand, and dramatic imagination, on the other, had drained all my creative faculties. Perhaps I should add that, had I gone further into musical composition than I did, probably there, and only there, I would have been able to respond in some manner, though of course indistinctly, to the places I visited and loved so tenderly. At this late hour of my life, I still poignantly feel that there was in my experience something of a lacuna that I have not been able to fill. What, at least, I feel obliged to affirm is the ardent love that in every period of my life I would have vowed to sensed beauty. I also needed to share with someone close to me what I had been given to experience, as though this gift only became effective in and through this sharing. In this respect, as in many others, I discovered myself to be radically different from my father who was able to travel alone without ever experiencing solitude as a lack. In the museums or churches of Europe that he untiringly visited, in the presence of the work he admired, he was all right being alone, between it and him there was realized an exchange that lasted for some time because of his marvelous memory. This intersubjectivity that has become for me always more clearly the essential category of my experience seems to me to have been hidden from him by the sovereign presence of the object. In the end, I think that people did not interest him in themselves, but only through the ideas for which, as it were, they were the vehicles; whereas for me, very early on, the person encountered presented himself as being worthy of attention. This was perhaps also the case because—as being—he became for me a possible individual.

This opposition is, however, too schematic. How can I forget his ardent love of music? Although his writings dealt almost exclusively with painters, he granted primacy to music. And the way in which, as an experienced and sensitive singer, he interpreted certain melodies of Schubert or of Schumann, his favorite composer, sufficiently testified—I am quite aware of it today—to his participation in a trans-objective world that remained for him an un-thought, even an unthinkable, immediacy. But it is through this immediacy that I join him today in a movement that I shall dare call *fraternal.*

22

3 February

Suddenly I remember that my aunt would have been a hundred years old today: she was born in Brussels on 3 February 1871, but immediately, a voice with a peremptory accent can be heard: "This conditional past has no meaning." The truth is that it is enough for me to close my eyes to see her again and, a strange thing, each of the thousand expressions of this mobile face among others remains in me—I don't dare say still. For here mobility remains as such. It is the triumph of the "Thou."

Yesterday I received an invitation from the University of Chile at Valpariso to come give some lectures on the idea that we have to formulate about a just society. This invitation interests me all the more because, since the last elections, Chile has become a socialist state. I would certainly have accepted, if unfortunately I had not learned since my return from Tokyo in 1966 that the Boeing is very dangerous for one with weak eyesight and that this last trip from Tokyo to Paris is doubtless at the root of the little retinal hemorrhages I experienced. Were I to experience them, I would risk losing the little sight I do have which allows me to still enjoy landscapes.

But this is the place to recall quickly those faraway trips and to underline what has remained with me.

In 1951 I was invited to attend the International Congress of Philosophy in Lima, and I was fortunate enough to have Gaston Berger as a traveling companion for the trip. I have always felt a sense of communion with him regarding ideas on many essential points.

On this trip, I visited most of the countries in South America. Without a shadow of a doubt, I was most strongly impressed by Upper Peru, on the excursion made in the company of Ambassador Gilbert, over one of the highest peaks of the Cordillera at Huancayo, and especially by the trip made some days later to Cuzco and Machupicchu. I am still moved when I think about the ancient Inca city, the valley of the Urubamba, dominated by the glaciers of the Cordillera, and the sublime landscapes of Machupicchu. How could I express today the kind of exaltation experienced in the presence of a world I had not expected to find. I felt as though I had been swallowed up by this nature that was nearly absolutely virgin and yet somewhat mysteriously pregnant with the shadows of a former civilization.

A doctor I met in Lima had offered to take me with him to spend a few days with a tribe in Amazonia. He had lived there for two years and was so fond of the Indians that he acquired some land and went there regularly every year to stay in touch with a population that had won over his heart. How I would have wanted to be able to accept this invitation! But as always, I was the prisoner of a program, of a schedule. I was expected in Santiago where, once again, it was impossible for me to accept another invitation extended me by a philosopher of La Paz.

If I recall, if I relive—as I write—the emotion I experienced during these days in Lima, it is because there, as in Japan, some years later, I clearly felt that an incoercible movement was encouraging me to go beyond the too narrow limits of the world which I had known. And suddenly, I observed that this dream of exploration that I had formed at the time of my early childhood translated a disposition that was probably an essential part of my being but one that life had not allowed me to realize or, rather, it was as though this necessity to explore had transposed itself onto quite a different register.

I cannot forget the warm welcome I received in Chile and in Brazil. Rightly or wrongly, Santiago seemed to me to be the South American city where I would be able to acclimatize myself the most easily because of its latitude and especially because of the absence of any social conflict.

In Rio, I was fortunate to meet up with Robert Garric who, as he had taught in Brazil at different times, had numerous friends there to whom he introduced me. French culture, and this is saying too little, the French spirit in its most authentic manifestation, will never have had a more brilliant missionary. I will never be able to say how much his death in 1967 left me impoverished and wounded.

My two trips to Japan, in 1957 and 1966, doubtlessly marked me even more strongly than the two months spent in Latin America. It was Professor Kojima who had come to ask me, in 1956, whether I would accept the invitation that the Association of Professors, whose president he was, was planning on extending to me. I accepted without the least hesitation, and I cannot sufficiently express my gratitude for the care he showed me at every moment during my two trips. He had organized them while taking into account the demands of the two large newspapers of Tokyo that had financed them. My only regret was to have spent too much time in Tokyo where one breathes the air of an authentic Japan in only a few preserved areas. I remember the feeling of deliverance I felt on leaving this huge metropolis for the first time in the little luxury train that took me to Hakone with the background music ... of César Franck! Nevertheless, it was during my second stay that I had the most beautiful view of Fuji, not from Hakone, but from a hotel, whose name I can't remember, that overlooked one of the lakes and that faces the sacred mountain. We had arrived in weather that was more than gloomy: we could see nothing and suddenly, at the end of dinner, Fuji showed itself to us in a splendor that I had never expected.

Yet what generally touched me most deeply in Japan was a harmony between art and nature where I believe I can see the essence of shintoism and which struck my sensibility above all in Kyoto on the one hand, and especially in the marvelous gardens of the Suga-Quin, and of course in the sacred grove that surrounds the temple of Ysé. Nor have I forgotten the isles which dot the sea around Sendai, nor the crossing of the Inland Sea.

My Japanese friends had had the excellent idea of having one of their compatriots, who spoke French perfectly, accompany me during these different trips: Mademoiselle Akiku Arishima, a fervent Catholic who allowed me to recognize to what depths Christianity penetrated a small fraction of the Japanese elite. I don't believe, however, that one should expect there to be a large number of converts. But I do think that, in such a domain, one should be on guard against the importance one might give to statistics.

Of course, I am careful not to ignore the superficial nature of the experience I owe to these trips. But what I have to note, with a sense of gratitude, is that the lectures I have been able to give in these different lands have left a trace. In them I have numerous friends who know my work, at least in part. In Japan, what is improperly called my O*euvres complètes* (Complete works) is also being published; a number of volumes have already appeared. I have been able to learn that students, especially in Kyoto, have been impressed, in a lasting way, it seems, by the views on immortality that I proposed to them. On the other hand, I know that even in India, that is to say in a land that I have not visited, there are professors who believe that, among contemporary European thinkers, I am one of those with whom they feel the most affinity. This is, moreover, connected to the relationship with Heidegger that Sartre seems to me to have totally ignored.

The conclusion that I believe I can draw from these experiences, which, unfortunately, have not been pursued as far as they should have been, is that my work is as little circumscribed as possible and that it reaches out, as I do through the best of me, towards an encounter with those very ones who are able, at first meeting, to appear the farthest and the most different from me. Hence the invincible horror that racism inspires in me.

I should nevertheless note with a mixed feeling of sadness and confusion that though I had the occasion, at least in the Corrèze, to talk with country people, I never came into contact with the working class. Not having done so is something I can only look upon as a failure, although I don't clearly see what I could have or should have tried to do in order to bring down the barrier I was up against on account of my own family background. Would I not have been able, for example, while there was still time, to belong to the Social Teams of Garric? I didn't refuse anything, but I would have had to do violence to a kind of timidity which has no doubt kept me from undertaking the necessary initiatives.

When I think about it, I believe that the social element, as it had been presented to us at the time of my studies, with Durkheim, or in a more mediocre fashion with Bouglé, struck a defensive chord in me.[1] To the one who upheld that society is more than the sum of its parts, I answered by saying "You are wrong." In fact it is a question of an algebraic formula where the individual aspects are cancelled out. I should have read, when it would have been helpful, some sociologists who would have been more philosophical, such as Max Weber, who was suggested to me too late, like so many other thinkers I ignored for such a long time.

Still there is no doubt that for some years social problems have awakened in me a growing interest, although their unsolvable and inextricable aspects appear most discouraging to me.

I haven't had the opportunity to speak about my election to the Academy of Political and Moral Sciences in 1952. I then filled the position left vacant by Émile Bréhier. Here I joined old friends such as René Le Senne, my dear cousin Pastor Marc Boegner, Daniel Halévy and Albert Rivaud who was one of my examiners for the agrégation. I was probably less active in the academy than I should have been, but on several occasions I tried to have it adopt a position on problems that appeared especially serious to me, as for example the embargo on arms destined for Israel. I am one of those who believe that the work of our academy should center itself more and more on current problems, by dedicating several meetings to them, as we did indeed do for the question of the elite, for lodging or more recently for what concerns individual freedom. I seriously think that, since it gathers in its circle jurists, economists, historians, moralists, and others, it is able to treat agonizing problems with insight that is more ample, more thought out and nuanced than what is usually provided. It also seems to me that there are more of us in the Academy who do view themselves this way. Some years ago it was my turn to become vice-president and then president. Unfortunately I had some setbacks,

1 Célestin Bouglé (1870-1940) was a disciple of Émile Durkheim (1858-1917), who was the driving force among early French sociologists. *Trans.*

some especially due to my poor eyesight, which was to get worse later, and so I thought I had to relinquish my turn. Perhaps I lacked courage at this time or even sinned through an excessive timidity which was one of my natural traits and which I have never generally been able to overcome. In any case, today it is much too late to take on these obligations just as it would be to try to become a member of the Académie Française, where I do have so many friends. Perhaps the word "friend" is not the one I should be using here; it is more a question of acquaintances. Among all these men whose hands I shake when I greet them, there is none with whom I am truly connected. And that is something I regret.

Indeed, at this moment, I have very few real friends left; and one could say, given my age, that that is in order. But how can one accept such a situation? The best, the most faithful ones no longer live in Paris, and I seldom see them. Of course, we do form new friendships. I would be over simplifying my situation if I said that I am losing everyone in my life. But these last years have been particularly difficult: three of those whom I love the most have died, one being Robert Garric. I particularly remember my dear friend Monique Picard with whom I spent so many pleasant hours in her house at Cabris that was a paradise for me. And also, of course, Monique Nathan who was my secretary for six years before being hired by the publishing house Le Seuil where she was to work so superbly. I don't think I have to picture them like some exhausted arrière-garde which hasn't been able to pursue its course, but rather as guides who have helped lead my own steps that have become more faltering.

23

I could not end this writing with a conclusion, or anything that might resemble it, because I have wanted what I have said, especially in the last part, to be faithful to life and its movement. It is possible, of course, that the reader may have been disconcerted at times by repetition. It was unavoidable owing to the spiral movement that here, as is so often the case, I felt obliged to follow.

Perhaps the end of my existence is quite near, although at the moment I am writing, nothing seems to indicate that. But when I reflect upon what this word "end" refers to, I see myself forced to observe that, whatever the aspect this end may in fact present, that of an accident or of sickness, there is not the least chance for this end to affect the character of a *resolution*, in the harmonic sense of this word. And yet, in my view, it is only the resolution that is important, the one resolution that would put an end to the dissonance and cacophony that wounds me day after day.

If *this resolution must come about*, it can only be within the context that is no longer that of the things of this earth.

If *this resolution must come about*, I have said: because here there is no place for one of these assurances, be it logical or technical, which commands human activity.

But, isn't the fact of raising this doubt, admitting this lack of certainty, the recognition that the axial effort of my entire life has perhaps been dependent upon some chimera?

I ask myself, and immediately an exclamation arises from the depths of my being: even if it turned out that what we call our existence finds a definitive closure upon our last breath, I would not deny, for all that, the movement that has carried me towards immortality ever since my childhood, and I note here how close I feel myself to the thought of Unamuno. And besides, on this point, thought takes back its rights, and the words "turned out" seem to indicate something nonsensical, for finally, I cannot imagine without some contradiction that I could find myself in a situation that might entail this negative observation, or even a demonstration that would replace it.

But, of course, the *nexus* where this exigency takes root can only be love and not some frenetic desire to live! And that is the reason why this demand can and must be looked upon as being incoercible.

This in no way means, of course, that there are not times—when the weight of age takes on too much importance, or when fatigue wins out—when the "let me fall asleep with the sleep of the earth"[1] of the poet is an exact translation of what is no longer a state of mind or of soul, but only the fatigue of an overworked body.

And, of course, how could I know what my last moments of consciousness will be like? The other day I talked about the feeling of panic which overcame me, in an inexplicable and sudden manner, at the thought of my death—that was perhaps imminent. How would I dare affirm that this anguish will not be my own, when I shall know that I will have to leave everything. And here "to leave everything" means above all to separate myself from those people I *hold on to* so strongly, and the thought of this separation is, literally, heartrending. It seems to me that the only recourse would be in the feeling of being literally *attendu* (*waited for- waited upon*). Rightly or wrongly, it seems to me that the English word is here more meaningful.

Perhaps you will be surprised, and I am also surprised up to a certain point, that here God is not mentioned but in truth understood on a deeper level.

I must bring out here what is doubtless one of the irreducible singularities of my position—should one say my philosophical position? I hesitate using this word. Here it is a question of something that is lived.

I believe I can say that those who are no longer of this world, but who live on in my heart, present themselves to me, always more

1 A well-known line from the poem *Moïse* (*Moses*) by Alfred de Vigny (1797-1863). *Trans.*

clearly, if not as intercessors, at least as mediators, such that the reunification I aspire to with all my being can only have its meaning in the light of Christ. The light of Christ: I sense a strange emotion in saying these words, because for me they have something unusual about them, but they mean that, for my spirit, Christ is less an object upon whom I would be able to center my attention than he is the Guide who lights the way, who can even take on a face, or more exactly a look. But that is precisely it, one does not look at, properly speaking, a gaze; one is penetrated by it and perhaps all the more so because one feels oneself gazed upon.

Several times, these last days, and again this morning, while listening to a program dedicated to the Patriarch Athenagoras, I was able to know to what extent a certain ecumenical Christianity remains unsurpassable for me.

I cannot contain my indignation when I hear talk about the book entitled *Ni Marx ni Jésus* (*Neither Marx nor Jesus*), that a fashionable featherbrain has just published.[2] What depths of incomprehension are revealed by such a declaration! Here I want to note the passionate adhesion I give to the pages on Jesus of Nazareth which figure in the last chapter of the book by Marcel Légaut, *L'Homme à la recherche de son humanité* (Man in search of his humanity), and that his brother was reading to me yesterday.

So I have the assurance that, if I remain conscious to some degree during my last moments, I shall express thanksgiving to the Resurrected Jesus while at the same time beg for his mercy for all the insufficiencies and omissions that have punctuated my long life.

I sometimes think—but, I admit, only rarely—that the infirmities which weigh upon my old age can at least take on a positive meaning, to the extent that I succeed—with difficulty I should add—in looking upon them as given to compensate for my failures and omissions. But this is more of a light than a thought.

And while waiting?

How could I not take as my own the question Arnauld asks Évelyne, in act 3 of *Les Coeurs avides*, which is also one of the key texts of my work: "On what do you live?" I believe I can say that I did not ask

2 The author is Jean-François Revel. *Trans.*

myself this question, so much did I feel myself to be creative, in the full meaning of this word, and after all, dramatic criticism itself was for me a kind of creativity. But my post as critic for *Les Nouvelles littéraires* was terminated two years ago, and besides I fear that the creative power which was manifest in my plays no longer inhabits me. So now what is the inner source that enables me to overcome well or not so well the sometimes desperate feeling of uselessness that accompanies the passage of time?

At most, I risk having the impression that nothing more can happen to me, except for an accident or some sickness, or that nothing can hold me back. But fortunately, there is the passionate interest that I have not only for my children and my grandchildren, but also for all those who are close to me, and even a strange curiosity for young people whom I only know by name. In brief, a persistent liking for people inhabits me like a hunger.

Nevertheless, that would still not be a sufficient motive to fight the *taedium vitae* which threatens us all, I think, at the end of our existence. I must still have the feeling of *serving*—in my case this word first of all means *listening*, but also *gathering together*.

After all, I am able, as this was the case in the past, to bring people together who, without me, would perhaps never have met. I think that here there is a need which answers a very deep need of my spirit, and of my heart: I should say that this demand is situated at a point where one and the other communicate. I am horrified by dispersion and waste. And, of course, this may be in part connected to an excessive taste for economy. But more deeply, it seems to me that it is the sign of a disposition for leaning towards spiritual kinship, towards a *choral* fashion of expecting that we be an ensemble, but each in his or her own place and in his or her own manner. *Choral*, I said, or *orchestral*; that is connected to the condemnation I have always had for equality, as such, because, in the final analysis, ignoring uniqueness and difference among individuals, it stifles them, as would death.

So it seems to me that today the motivation of my life is the fact of waiting day after day for the letter, the telephone call, or better still, the visit that will furnish me the opportunity to make a personal contribution, however small, to this Good that is unquestionably, and in every domain, an incarnate brotherhood.

I have already spoken somewhat about theatrical criticism: when I question myself about the place it has held in my existence, I am led to observations that may seem contradictory. If I consider my life according to the central perspective which was mine in this writing, I see myself forced to recognize, despite the passion with which I dedicated myself to it for so many years, that criticism will have been, after all, but a marginal part of this existence. But I must try at least to explain to myself why I gave myself to it with such ardor. Must I admit that it was for me, especially, a substitute and that I would have abandoned it, if my plays had been regularly performed, as after all, they should have been? That's possible, but nothing is less certain. Would it not be more exact to say that what I was looking for through the theatre was a more elaborate contact with different aspects of the reality that the life I lived did not give me access to?

This answer certainly contains a fragment of truth; but it also does not satisfy me absolutely, because it does not account for the fascination that the theatre—like music, of course—has exercised upon me since my early childhood. In the end, I have never done without it, since even today—although every professional obligation has disappeared—I feel the need to go see all the plays that seem interesting. One can also say, of course, that this is the expression of a persistent demand, that of being to the very end an attentive listener to what is happening in the world.

This demand, I agree, may seem unreasonable in an old man who would be better off, some might say, to begin his retreat from the world. But here I must strongly disagree: if there is an incoercible refusal in me, it is to fall back upon myself or to take refuge in the contemplation of some impersonal eternity. And here I remember the admirable pages where Chesterton speaks of this "flag of the world," around which men of good will assemble. *Coaevus universo*! I shouted out long ago. That is my world, I realize that I have always been in solidarity with it and will always be. I reject with horror an *acosmism* that would forever isolate me from it. I should probably add, and thus clarify a previous statement, that the immortality to which I aspire can only transpose, according to some unrepresentative modalities, both this creation and this service while alone conferring meaning and dignity to our life. But this creation and this service which are pursued beyond the narrow frontiers of our world can only be the approaches to the pleromatic unity of this *all in all* that is the resolution par excellence.

I would not be pleased with myself, however, to end this writing on such a perfect note. That would be to succumb to a temptation that I have fought from beginning to end.

Rather the final accent should be rightly placed on this rocky road, on the hesitant and staggering walk I have made during these difficult years: I cannot say enough how I feel myself dependent, and not only physically, but also morally, and how at times this dependence seems humiliating to me.

Three years ago circumstances allowed for Geneviève Boegner, the only surviving sister of my wife, to come live with me, keeping me from a solitude that, I feel quite well, I would not have been able to tolerate. Her presence is supportive, she reads to me, and we remember together the people whom we have loved so much. I don't know what would become of me if she died before I did.

I am far from forgetting the privileges which have been granted to me. My secretary, Denyse Lanoé-Mallet, who has been with me for fifteen years and whose qualities of order and delicacy I have so valued, lightens for me this burden of daily life which would seem to be so easily unbearable. For twenty-three years a Breton lady served me with dedication and almost became indispensable. Her health forced her to leave me. After a painful interval, we found someone who could give us every satisfaction. But the sense of the precariousness of all the conditions which assure my well-being has something painful about it. It is constantly sharpened by the news of death which comes to me: these last days, we learned about the death of an English friend who was very dear and at whose home I often stayed in London: she also died from the horrible sickness that took away my wife, her sisters and two of my dearest friends.

Every time it is the same shock before the incomprehensible, and I don't hesitate to say, the unjustifiable. Every attempt at rational justification in the name of I don't know what transcendent economy appears to me like some impiety. My friends in London have experienced, according to another rhythm, horribly accelerated, the very same trial that we went through in 1940 and in 1947. What a deep-seated feeling of fraternity is awakened by such similar experiences! It is through this feeling, it seems to me, and only through it, that such experiences open onto the spiritual, and that recollection worthy of the name becomes possible.

And here the inexhaustible sentence of my play *L'Iconoclaste* comes back to my lips: "Come now, you would not be satisfied for a long time with a world deprived of all mystery." This clearly means that the incomprehensible can shed light from the moment it becomes the place for authentic communion. If I am still a Christian, it is, I believe, in spite of everything, because I espouse this mystery of the Communion of the Suffering and of its being rooted in the life and person of Christ.

It is there, at this point attainable only with the greatest difficulty, that the highest music bursts forth. This is the music of the *Missa solemnis* and of the last *Quatuors* (*Quartets*). It is the music of the *Quintette à cordes* (*String Quintet*) of Schubert and of so many other works that I have passionately loved and that have always nurtured me. The hesitant and rather trembling meaning of my dramatic or philosophical effort will have consisted in translating into the language of thought, and more still into the language of existential dialogue, the kind of implicit assurance, and finally triumphant assurance, that these grand intercessors, as though anticipating the Revelation, will have granted me with the passage of time.

Biographical Note on Gabriel Marcel

Born in Paris, 7 December 1889.

Studies at the Lycée Carnot and at the Sorbonne.

Received the agrégation in philosophy in 1910.

Professor at the Lycée de Vendôme, the Lycée Condorcet, and assigned to Paris during the war, then at the lycée in Sens.

Leaves teaching in 1923.

Becomes a reader for publishing houses Grasset and Plon. While with Plon, in 1926, he initiates the series "Feux croisés" which features the works of foreign writers.

Drama Critic for the *Les Nouvelles littéraires*, contributor to *La Nouvelle Revue française* and other journals.

Awarded the Grand Prize in Litterature from the Académie française in 1949.

Elected in 1952 to the Academy of Moral and Political Sciences.

Received the Hanseatic Goethe Prize, awarded by the University of Hamburg, in 1956.

Received the National Grand Prize for Literature in 1958.

Received the Osiris Prize in 1963.

Received the Peace Prize awarded by the German Booksellrs in Frankfurt, September 1964.

Received the Grand Prize of the City of Paris in 1968.

Officer in the Order of the Legion of Honor. Received the Erasmus Prize, in Rotterdam, in October 1969

Grand Officer in the National Order of Merit in 1969.

M. Gabriel Marcel gave lectures in nearly all the large cities of Eastern Europe.

Was delegate to the Unesco Conference, Beirut, 1948.

Delivered the Gifford Lectures in Aberdeen in 1949-1950.

Gave lectures in Morocco, in 1951 and 1963, and in nearly all the large cities of South America, in 1951. He lectured in Canada in 1956, in Japan in 1957 and in 1966, and in the United States in 1961, 1965, and 1966.

He delivered the William James Lectures at Harvard University in 1961.

He received honorary doctorates from the University of Tokyo, De Paul University Chicago, and the University of Salamanca.

Selected Studies on Gabriel Marcel

Applebaum, David. *Contact and Alienation, The Anatomy of Gabriel Marcel's Metaphysical Method.* (Current Continental Research 214) Washington, D. C.: Center for Advanced Research in Phenomenology & University Press of America, 1986.

Bago, Jean-Pierre. *Connaissance et Amour. Essai sur la philsophie de Gabriel Marcel.* Paris: Beauchesne, 1958.

Bernard, Michel. *La Philosophie religieuse de Gabriel Marcel. Étude critique.* Le Puy: Cahiers du Nouvel Humanisme, 1952.

Berning, Vincent. *Das Wagnis der Treue. Gabriel Marcels Weg einer konkreten Philosophie des Schöpenferischen.* Freiburg: Alber, 1973.

Blain, Lionel A. *The Notion of Proof for God's Existence ijn the Early Writings of Gabriel Marcel.* Dissertation doctorale dactylographiée. Université catholique de Louvain, Institut supérieur de Philosophie, 1959.

Busch, Thomas W. *Circulating Being: From Embodiment to Incorporation*; *Essays on Late Existentialism.* New York: Fordham University Press, 1999.

Cain, Seymour. *Gabriel Marcel.* New York: Hillary House, 1963.

———. *Gabriel Marcel's Theory of Religious Experience.* New York: Peter Lang, 1995.

Chenu, Joseph. *Le Théâtre de Gabriel Marcel et sa signification métaphysique.* Paris: Aubier, 1948.

Cooney, William, ed. *Gabriel Marcel's Contributions to Philosophy: A Collection of Essays.* (Problems in Philosophy, Volume 18) Lewiston, NY: Edwin Mellen Press, 1989.

Corte, Marcel de. *La Philosophie de Gabriel Marcel.* Paris: Téqui 1938.

Davy, M. M. *Un philosophe itinérant, Gabriel Marcel.* Paris: Flammarion, 1959.

Gallagher, Kenneth T. *The Philosophy of Gabriel Marcel.* New York: Fordham University Press, 1962.

Gilson, Etienne, et al. *Existentialisme chrétien: Gabriel Marcel.* Paris: Plon, 1947.

Hanley, Katharine Rose. *Dramatic Approaches to Creative Fidelity: A Study in the Theatre and Philosophy of Gabriel Marcel (1889-1973).* Lanham, MD: University Press of America, 1987.

Keene, Samuel. *Gabriel Marcel.* Richmond: John Knox Press, 1967.

Le Thanh Tri. *L'Idée de participation chez Gabriel Marcel. Superphénoménologie d'une intersubjectivité existentielle.* Thèse doctorale. Faculté des Lettres, Université de Fribourg (Switzerland), 1959.

Miceli, Vincent P. *Ascent to Being. Gabriel Marcel's Philosophy of Communion.* New York: Desclée Company, 1965.

O'Malley, John B. *The Fellowship of Being: An Essay on the Concept of Person in the Philosophy of Gabriel Marcel.* The Hague: Nijhoff, 1966.

Parain-Vial, Jeanne. *Gabriel Marcel et les niveaux de l'expérience.* Paris: Seghers, 1966.

Pax. Clyde V. *An Existentialist Approach to God: Study of Gabriel Marcel.* The Hague: Nijhoff, 1972.

Prini, Pietro. *Gabriel Marcel et la Méthodologie de l'invérifiable.* Paris: Desclée de Brouwer, 1953.

Randall, Albert B. *The Mystery of Hope in the Philosophy of Gabriel Marcel (1889-1973), Hope and Homo Viator.* Problems in Contemporary Philosophy Vo.. 33) Lewiston, NY: The Edwin Mellen Press,1992.

Ricoeur, Paul. *Gabriel Marcel et Karl Jaspers. Philosophie du mystère et philosophie du paradoxe.* Paris: Temps Présent, 1947.

Schilpp. Paul A., ed. *The Philosophy of Gabriel Marcel.* (The Library of Living Philosophers, Vol. XVII). La Salle: Open Court, 1*984.*

Sottiaux, Edgar. *Gabriel Marcel, philosophe et dramaturge.* Louvain: E. Nauwelaerts; Paris: B. Nauwelaerts, 1956.

Troisfontaines, Roger. *À la rencontre de Gabriel Marcel.* Bruxelles: La Sixaine, 1947.

———. *De l'existence à l'être: la philosophie de Gabriel Marcel,* 2 tomes. Louvain: E. Nauwelaerts; Paris: B. Nauwelaerts, nouvelle édition, 1968.

Widmer, Charles. *Gabriel Marcel et le théisme existentiel.* Paris: Éditions du Cerf, 1971.

Philosophical and Dramatic Works Translated into English

The Philosophy of Existence. London: Harvill Press, 1949; New York: The Philosophical Library, 1949; Freeport, NY: Books for Libraries Press, 1969 reprint of 1949 edition. Includes: Introduction by Gabriel Marcel, "On the Ontological Mystery," "Existence and Human Freedom," "Testimony and Existentialism," and "An Essay in Autobiography."

Being and Having. Westminister: Dacre Press, 1949; New York: Harper and Row, 1965.

The Mystery of Being. Vol. 1. *Reflection and Mystery*. Vol. 11. *Faith and Reality*. London: Harvill Press, 1950-51; Chicago: Regnery/Gateway, 1960; Lanham, MD, University Press of America, 1984.

Homo Viator. London: V. Gollanoz, 1951; Chicago, H. Regnery Co., 1951; New York: Harper and Row, 1962; Magnolia, MA: Peter Smith, 1978.

Three Plays by Gabriel Marcel, A Man of God, Ariadne, and The Votive Candle (The Funeral Pyre). London: Secker and Warburg, 1952; New York: Hill and Wang, 1965. Includes Preface "The Drama of the Soul in Exile."

Metaphysical Journal. Chicago, H. Regnery Co., 1952; London, Rockliff Press, 1952, with essay "Existence and Objectivity" in appendix.

Man Against Mass Society. London: Harvill Press, 1952; Chicago, H. Regnery, 1952; Gateway edition, 1962; Lanham, MD: University of America Press,1985.

The Decline of Wisdom. London: Harvill Press, 1954; New York: The Philosophical Library, 1955; Chicago, H. Regnery, 1955.

The Philosophy of Existentialism. New York: The Philosophical Library, The Citadel Press Inc., 1956.

Royce's Metaphysics. Chicago: H. Regnery Co., 1956, 1975.

The Lantern in *Cross Currents*. West Nyack, New York, 1958.

The Existential Background of Human Dignity. Cambridge: Harvard University Press, 1963.

Creative Fidelity. New York: Farrar, Straus, and Co., 1964; reprinted: New York, Crossroads Press, 1982; New York: Fordham University Press, 2001.

"Desire and Hope" in *Readings in Existential Phenomenology*. Edited by Nathaniel Lawrence, Daniel O'Connor. Englewood Cliffs, N.J.: Prentice-Hall, Inc.,1967.

Philosophical Fragments (1904-1914) and *The Philosopher and Peace*. Notre Dame, IN: Notre Dame University Press, 1965.

Problematic Man. New York: Herder and Herder, 1967.

Presence and Immortality. Pittsburgh: Duquesne University Press, 1967. Includes *The Unfathomable*, the first act of an unfinished play (1919).

Fresh Hope for the World: Moral Re-armament in Action. Translated from the French by Helen Hardinge. Longmans, Green, and Co., Inc., 1960.

Searchings. New York: Paulist-Newman Press, 1967. Includes "My Dramatic Works as Viewed by the Philosopher" (1959).

Conversations Between Paul Ricoeur and Gabriel Marcel included in *Tragic Wisdom and Beyond*. Evanston, IL: Northwestern University Press, 1973.

The Existentialist Drama of Gabriel Marcel: The Broken World, The Rebellious Heart and an Introduction by Gabriel Marcel. ed. F.J. Lescoe, West Hartford, CT, McAuley Institute, St. Josepl's College, 1974.

Existential Background of Human Dignity (1961), Cambridge: Harvard University Press, 1963.

"An Autobiographical Essay" in *The Philosophy of Gabriel Marcel* (The Library of Living Philosophers, Vol. XVII). ed. P.A. Schilpp and L. E. Hahn, LaSalle, IL, Open Court, 1984.

Two One Act Plays by Gabriel Marcel: Dot the I and The Double Expertise. Translated by Katharine Rose Hanley. Introduction by Jean-Marie and Anne Marcel, Lanham, MD, University Press of America, 1986.

Two Plays by Gabriel Marcel: The Lantern and The Torch of Peace plus a previously unpublished essay "From Comic Theater to Musical Creation" by Gabriel Marcel. Lanham, MD, University Press of America, 1988.

Gabriel Marcel's Perspectives on The Broken World. The Broken World, A Four-Act Play followed by Concrete Approaches to Investigating the Ontological Mystery. Milwaukee: Marquette University Press, 1998.

The Unfathomable, an unfinished play. See *Presences and Immortality*.

Selected Works by Gabriel Marcel

Philosophical Writings

Published by La Nouvelle Revue Française, Paris:

Journal métaphysique, 1927, several editions.
Du refus à l'invocation, 1939, published again in the collection "Idées" underthe title *Essai de philosophie concrète.*

With Other Publishers:

Être et Avoir: Paris: Aubier, 1934; published again in the Livre de Poche collection, 2 volumes, 1970.
Homo viator. Paris: Aubier, 1947; later published with a text on *L'Homme révolté* of Albert Camus.
Le Mystère de l'être (2 vol.). Paris: Aubier, 1951. *Réflexion et mystère; Foi et réalité.* This second volumke was published as a softcover edition with Aubier in 1967.
La Métaphysique de Royce. Paris: Aubier, 1945.
Le Déclin de la sagesse. Paris: Plon, 1954.
L'Homme problématique. Paris: Aubier, 1955.
Présence et Immortalité. Paris: Flammarion, 1959. Published again in the Collection 10/18. Plon, 1968 (Union Générale d'Éditions).
Fragments philosophiques 1909-1914. Paris: B. Nauwelaerts, 1961.
La Dignité humaine. Paris: Aubier, 1964.
Paix sur la terre. Paris: Aubier: 1965.
Pour une sagesse tragique et son au-delà. Paris: Plon, 1968.
Coleridge et Schelling. Paris: Aubier, 1971.

Theatrical Works

Le Seuil invisible. Paris: Grasset, 1914. This volume includes *La Grâce* (5 acts);

Le Palais de sable (4 acts).

Le Coeur des autres (3 acts). Paris: Grasset, 1921, "Les Cahiers verts."

Un homme de Dieu (4 acts). Paris: Grasset, 1923, "Les Cahiers verts;" published again by La Table ronde in 1951.

L'Iconoclaste (4 acts). Paris: Stock, 1923.

Le Quatuor en fa dièse (5 acts). Paris: Plon, 1925.

Trois pièces. Le Regard neuf (4 acts); *Le Mort de demain* (3 acts); *La Chapelle ardente* (3 acts). Paris: Plon, 1931. *La Chapelle ardente* was later publshed by La Table ronde, with an unfinished first version titled *Le Sol détruit*, 1949.

Le Monde cassé (4 acts), Paris: Desclée de Brouwer, collection Les Iles, 1933. This volume contains a lecture titled *Position et approches concrètes du mystère ontologique. Le Monde cassé* was published again in *Paris-Théâtre*, 1952.

Le Chemin de crête (4 acts). Paris: Grasset, 1936.

Le Fanal (1 act). Paris: Stock, 1936.

Le Dard (3 acts). Paris: Plon, 1936. *Le Dard* was later published in a volume titled *Le secret est dans les îles*. Paris: Plon, 1967.

La Soif (3 acts). Paris: Desclée de Brouwer, collection "Les Iles," 1938; published later under the title *Les Coeurs avides*, La Table ronde, 1952.

L'Horizon (4 acts). Paris: Spes, 1945.

Théâtre comique. Paris: Albin Michel, 1947. This volume includes *Le Divertissement posthume* (1 prologue, 2 acts, 1 epilogue); *La Double Expertise* (1 act);

Les Points sur les I (1 act); *Colombyre ou le Brasier de la Paix* (3 acts).

Vers un autre royaume: Paris: Plon, 1949. This volume includes *Le Signe de la Croix*

(3 acts and 4 tableaux), published later separately by Plon in 1960 with an epilogue; *L'Émissaire* (3 acts), published again in *Le secret est dans les îles*, Plon 1967.

Rome n'est plus dans Rome (5 acts). Paris: La Table ronde, 1951; included in

Paris-Théâtre with *Le Monde cassé*, 1952.

Croissez et multipliez (4 acts). Paris: Plon, 1955.

La Dimension Florestan (3 acts). Paris: Plon, 1958.

Mon temps n'est pas le vôtre (5 acts). Paris: Plon, 1955.

L'Insondable (1 act) published in *Présence et Immortalité.* Paris: Flammarion, 1959.
Un juste (1 act) published in *Paix sur la terre*. Paris: Aubier, 1965.

Critical Works

L'Heure théâtrale. Paris: Plon, 1959.
Théâtre et Religion. Lyon: Éditions E. Vitte, 1959.
Regards sur le théâtre de Claudel. Paris: Beauchesne, 1964.

Index

Academy of Political and Moral Sciences, 172, 211, 231
Ackermann, Louise C., 53
Adoption, on, 113, 114
The Aeneid, 58
Alain, (Émile Chartier), 71, 81, 95-96, 160
Alliance française, 223
Anglo-American aviation, 206
Alexandre, Michel, 55, 81, 107-108
Allied invasion, 187
Allies, 95
Alsace Lorraine, 64
Alterman, Jean-Pierre, 22, 125-126
Ambiguity, 42, 52, 205
American politics, 212
Anouilh, Jean, 191
Antoinette, Marie, 62
Appell, Paul, 68
Annot, Madame, 99
L'Arbre (The tree), 71
Arishima, 229
Arisima, Akiku, 229
Armistice, 99, 110, 153, 161, 163, 188
Association of Professors, 229
Atheism, existentialism as, 192, 193
Athenagoras, 235
L'Attelage (The Yoke), 117
Augustine, St., 22, 123, 125
Aunt (Marguerite Meyer Marcel), 36, 41, 42, 43, 46, 47, 50, 51, 53, 57, 62, 67, 65, 66, 67, 92, 122, 149, 150, 153, 155, 227
Austro-Hungarian, 222
Autosuggestion, phenomena of, 182
Aymé, Marcel, 191
Audin, Maurice, 191

B. Madame, 153
Bach, Johann Sebastian, 57, 82, 176
Bachelet, Alfred, 57
Balkan Wars, 63
Baltic, 206
Barrès, Maurice, 85
Barth, Karl, 124
Baty, Gaston, 116
Beauregard, Abbé, 74
Beauvoir, Simone de, 188, 203
Becqué, Maurice, 185
Beethoven, Ludwig van, 57, 110
Being,
 mystery of, 12, 14, 15, 18, 20, 30, 57
 sense of, 9, 10, 11, 12, 40, 43, 87, 174
Bellay, Joachim du, 176
Berenson, Bernard, 80
Berger, Gaston, 102, 185, 227
Bergson, Henri, 51, 71, 83, 101-102, 118, 175
Berkeley, George, 84
Bernanos, Georges, 115
Bernhard, Prince, 221
Bérubet, Magdeleine, 138-139
Bidou, Henri, 116-117
Bibliothèque Nationale, 46
Billetdoux, François, 223
Biran, Maine de, 29, 81
Blain, Father, 85
Blacks, 178
Blondel, Maurice, 47
Blum, Léon, 132
Boasson, Marc, 108
Boegner, Alfred, 111, 181
Boegner, Anne. See Marcel, Anne Boegner
Boegner, Edmond, 111
Boegner, Geneviève, 111, 238
Boegner, Henri, 22, 111, 114, 169
Boegner, Jacqueline, 22
Boegner, Marc, 211, 231
Boeing, 227
Borne, Étienne, 215
Boucher, Maurice, 138
Bouglé, Célestin, 231
Bourbon Busset, Jacques de, 5, 30
Bovy, Berthe, 197
Bradley, Francis Herbert, 74
Brasillach, Robert, 36, 191

Bréhier, Émile, 231
Breitkopf, 82
Bro, Father, 181
Broken World, the experience of, 23, 122, 134, 146
Brunschvicg, Léon, 70, 140
Buber, Martin, 218
Buchman, Franck, 143
Bugbee, Henry, 212-214
Busch, Thomas, 11
Bultmann, Karl, 183
Bundestag, 206
Burgos, 204, 216
Butzow, Monsieur de 177

Caillaux, Joseph, 91
Carré, Jean-Marie, 87
Carlton Lake Collection, 56, 94, 221
Caslant, Eugène, 105
Catholic Church, 63, 124-126, 179-181
Catholicism, 22, 70, 124-126, 128, 181
Catusse, 48
Cazalis, Henri, 53
Centre dramatique de l'Est, 194-195
Cerisy-La-Salle Conference Center, 212
Chalory, 68
Chamson, André, 121
La Chapelle ardente (The Votive Candle), 37, 116, 117, 147
Chardonne, Jacques, 136
Charity, 13
Charles the Bold, 167
Chazel, Pierre, 156
Chausson, Ernest, 118
Chekhov, Anton, 120
Le Chemin de crête (Ariadne), 52, 140, 141, 142, 146, 196, 198
Chénier, Andr , 176
Cherry, Hélène, 142
Chesneau, 64
Chesterton, G.K., 237
Chrétien, J.-P., 30, 123, 178, 192, 195
Christ, Jesus, 19, 73, 117, 181-183, 235, 239
Christians, 54, 125, 162
Christianity, 86, 94, 111, 182-183, 230, 235
Clair, René, 192
Claudel, Paul, 71, 88, 120, 174
Clavé, André, 194
Clio, 98
Cocteau, Jean, 136
Le Coeur des autres (*The Rebellious Heart*), 17, 19, 35, 36, 113, 114, 121
Les Coeurs avides (Eager hearts), 196, 198, 199, 235
Cogito, 134
Coleridge, Samuel Taylor, 74-75
Colombyre ou le Brasier du la Paix (*Colombyre or the Torch of Peace*), 139, 145, 146
Colonna d'Istria, 21, 67-68
Combes, Emile, anticlericalism, 64
Companions of the Liberation, 163
Comical Element, of the, 146, 205
Commission of the National Committee of Writers, 189
Concentration camps, 167, 168
Congress of Philosophy, 140, 191, 222
Concrete given situation, of the, 52
"Les Conditions dialectiques de la philosophie de l'intuition," 88
Copeau, Jacques, 136
Coquelin, Aîné, 55
Combes, Émile, 63
Commission of the National Committee of Writers, 189
Commune, 132
Communists, 187, 189
Compton-Burnett, 116
Corneille, Pierre, 189
Courbaud, 70
Council of Paris, 163
Council of State, 46, 48, 52
Creativity, 9, 10, 13, 17
relation with receptivity or creative reciprocity, 141
Curel, François de, 85
Czar Nicholas II, 95

Daladier, Édouard, 149
Dallière, Louis, 124
Dane, Clemence, 120
Daniel-Rops, Henri Petiot, 151, 192
Le Dard (The sting), 52, 116, 138, 139, 140, 146, 196

Davids, Renée, 96, 98
Davy, Marie-Madeleine, 160
Death, 79, 80, 140, 152, 161, 165, 205, 206, 234, 238
Debussy, Claude, 82
Decroly, Ovide, 81
Degradation, of, 168, 171
Delannoy, Marcel, 177
Delbos, Victor, 81
Delhomme, Jeanne, 30, 195, 199
Delphi, 223
Descartes, René, 133-134
Desclée de Brouwer (publisher), 149
Despair/Hopelessness of, 146, 147, 159
Devêche, 197, 206
Devil's Island, 51
Dietz, Madame, 132
Dignity, 168
Divertissement posthume (The posthumous joke), 37
Domerat, 100
Dorst, 172
Doubt, 134
Drancy, 189
Dreyfus Affair, 43, 51, 52
Dreyfus, Alfred, 85
Dreyfus, Hubert, 213
Dreyfusards, 51-52, 132, 190
Du Bellay, Joachim, 176
Du Bos, Charles, 22, 115, 118-121, 124-126, 149, 169, 173, 175, 181
Dufet, 70
Duhamel, Georges, 133
Dukas, Paul, 82
Dumas, père, Alexandre 55
Durkheim, Émile, 231

East, 113, 206-207, 209-210, 217
Eastern Europe, 206
Education, his, 48, 49, 50, 54, 55, 66, 68, 69
Ehrenwald, Jan, 105
Eisenbudd, 105
L'Émissaire (The emissary), 42, 52, 128, 188, 196, 197
Engagement/Commitment, 190, 191
Epistemology, primacy of, 13
Erasmus Prize, 170, 210, 221
Ergaz, Doucia, 224
Estauni, Édouard, 102
Eternity, on, 80
Être et Avoir (*Being and Having*), 105, 128, 132, 158, 192
Euripides, 56, 223
Existence, 13, 73, 74, 86, 87, 23 237, 238, 239
Existentialism, 39, 74, 84, 86, 95, 122, 134, 168, 188, 191, 192, 193

Fabre-Luce, Alfred, 95
Faith, 13, 16, 85, 86
  idealistic faith, 85
  of grace, 140, 147
  Christian faith, 13, 16
  of the invisible world, 103
Le Fanal (*The Lantern*), 139, 140, 141
Fanaticism, 137, 146
Fascist, 188
Fatta, Marquis, 223
Fauré, Gabriel, 112
Fayard (publisher), 117
Ferrier, 197
Fessard, Gaston, 165
Feux croisés—terres et mes étrangéres (Crossfire—Foreign lands and souls), 120
Fidelity, 13, 16, 77, 78
Fidelity, creative, 127
Fischer-Diskau, Dietrich, 222
Le Figaro, 141, 198
Flaubert, Gustave, 53, 119
F.L.N. (Front de Libération Nationale), 191
Foëlz, Siegfried, 27, 206-209
Forster, Wilhelm, 131
Fouillée, Alfred, 67
French Republic, 202
French Revolution, 62, 203
Fourvière, 158
France-Culture, 142, 178
Franco, Francisco, 201-202, 204, 216
Franck, César, 82-83, 229
Franck, Henri, 21, 70-73, 82-83
François-Poncet, André, 195
Fraternity, 169, 175, 203, 225, 226, 238, 239

Fresnay, Pierre, 196
Free France, 153
Freud, Sigmund, 79
Freudianism, 105
Friars Preachers (Dominicans), 181

Garric , Robert, 121, 181, 229-230, 232
Gaulle, Charles de, 154, 160-161, 163, 166, 178, 186-187, 189
Gaullism, 163
Gautier, Jean-Jacques, 198
German Red Cross, 99
Germans, 99-100, 152, 187, 220
Gide, André, 71, 146, 172
Gifford Lectures, 194-195
Gilbert (American ambassador), 228
Gilson, Étienne, 29-30, 198
Gimel, 151
Giraudoux, Louis, 71, 120-121, 174
Goethe, Johann W. von, 19, 35, 71, 119-120, 130, 169, 220
Goethe Prize, 220
Goldman, Lucien, 220
Golsan, Richard, 188
Gomulka, Wladyslaw, 206
Gorce, Pierre de la, 167
Gouhier, Henri, 223
La Grâce (Grace), 45, 84, 113
Grasset (publisher), 46, 115, 174
Gregh, Fernand, 56
Gregorian chant, 124
Gregory of Nyssa, Saint, 14
Grenier, Jean, 156
Grieg, Edvard, 57
Grgec, Radovan, 210
Grosjean, Pastor, 143
Grotzer, Peter, 76
Guéhenno, Jean, 121
Guilloux, Louis, 121

Hadamard, Jacques, 51, 100
Halévy, Daniel, 86, 121, 167, 231
Hébertot, Jacques, 139, 197-198
Hegel, Friedrich, 9, 64
Hegelian, 24, 75, 108, 133, 205
Heidegger, Martin, 15, 172, 193, 212, 218, 220, 230
Henriot, Émile, 198
Herold Verlag, 222
Hervieu, Paul, 195
Hirt, Éléonore, 141
Hitler, Adolf, 95, 131-132, 149
Hitlerism, 219
Hocking,W.E., 21, 72, 211-214
Hofmannsthal, Hugo von, 221
Holy Spirit, 144
Homais, 53
Homer, 223
Un homme de Dieu (*A Man of God*), 52, 121, 142, 194, 195, 196, 198, 199, 211, 219
Homo Viator, 29, 59, 161, 193
Hope, 13, 158, 159
Horace, 170
L'Horizon (The horizon), 117
Humanism, 167, 169,170, 171, 172, 173
Humbert, Pierre, 156
Hungarian Chamber, 63
Husák, Gustav, 210
Husserl, Edmund, 134
Husserlian, 134, 212
Huxley, Aldous, 121

Ibsen, Henrik, 51, 56, 142, 195
L'Iconoclaste, 38, 78, 105, 116, 183, 239
Idealism, 9, 23
Imagination, 20, 38, 59, 102
L'Immoraliste (*The Immoralist*), 71
Incarnation, 152
Indians of Amazonia 228
d'Indy, Vincent, 111
L'Insondable (*The Unfathomable*), 38, 89
Intersubjectivity, 17, 21, 23, 72, 87, 92, 93, 105, 106, 120, 143, 225
Intuitions, 87, 88, 104, 105
Inventories, 63,
  Church and State, 63,
  State Inventories 63
Ionesco, Eugène, 205

Jaloux, Edmond, 116
James, William, 168, 213
  William James Lectures, 168
Jankélévitch, Vladimir, 220
Jarring, 217

Jaspers, Karl, 12, 102, 128-129, 193, 217
Jesuit Scholasticate of Fourvière, 158
Jesuits (Society of Jesus), 158
Jews, 178-179, 189, 211, 216-217
  Statutes against Jews, 189
Joachim du Bellay (Lamentation of the hopeless person), 177
Joan of Arc, St., 141, 161
Jolin, Stephen, 24, 206
Jouvenel, Bertrand de, 171
Jouvenel, Marcelle de, 185
Jouvenel, Roland de, 185
July Monarchy, 63, 167
Un juste (The just one), 38, 89, 90, 107, 108
Justice, 189, 190, 191, 202, 203
Julliard, 138
Jung, Carl, 105

Kant, Emmanuel, 9, 11, 14, 169
Kantian ethics, 168
Kaplan, Alice, 191
Kierkegaard, Søren, 12, 73, 192
Kemp, Robert, 139, 141, 198, 205
Kemmel, Mont, 108
Kiefe, Robert, 174
Kojima, Professor, 229
Krantz, Paul (Eric Noth), 138-139

Lahor, Jean, 53
Lalande, André, 70
Lamartine, Alphonse de, 177
Lanoë-Mallet, Denyse, 238
Lanson, Gustave, 69
Laurent, Jeanne, 23, 135-136, 194
Lavelle, Louis, 192
Lawrence, D.H., 121
Lecomte du Nouÿ Prize, 172
Le Seuil (publisher), 38, 45, 84, 147, 195, 232
Légaut, Marcel, 155, 179, 182, 235
Légaut, Maria, 55
Légaut, René, 182
Léon, Xavier, 70, 90, 132, 140
Lenôtre, Théodore Gosselin, 62
Leopardi, Giacomo, 53
Leriche, 98, 100-101
Le Senne, René, 102, 192, 231
Lévy, Roger, 115
Liberation of France, 36
Lichtenberger, Henri, 130
Lion, Jeanne, 85, 114, 116
Lived experience, 23, 114, 171
Louis XVI, 62
Love, 154
Lubac, Henri de, 133, 158, 181
Lucas-Montigny, 47
Lucretius, 190
La Lumière sur la Montagne (The light on the mountain), 56

McCormick, Peter, 206
Malraux, André, 119, 121
Mallarmé, Stéphane, 80
Man, Paul de, 119
Marcel, Anne, 70, 114, 187
Marcel, Madame Jules, 125
Marcel, Marguerite Meyer (aunt to Gabriel Marcel and second wife of his father Henry Marcel), 41, 47, 50, 51, 57, 62, 65, 66, 67, 92, 122, 149, 150, 153, 155, 227
Marcel, Henry (father of Gabriel Marcel), 43, 46, 47, 48, 50, 51, 52, 53, 54, 56, 57, 61, 63, 64, 66, 67, 72, 76, 92, 116, 122, 151, 152, 157, 167, 225, 226
Marcel, Jacqueline Boegner (wife of Gabriel Marcel), 21, 22, 110, 112, 113, 123, 124, 125, 137, 145, 151, 153, 154, 155, 157, 158, 165, 176, 177, 181, 187, 192, 194
Marcel, Jean-Mari, 70, 113, 114, 153, 187, 202, 236
Marcel, Laure Meyer (mother of Gabriel Marcel), 41, 42, 46, 47, 53, 152
Maréchal, Joseph, 127, 154
Marie-Antoinette, 62
Maritain, Jacques, 115, 126-127, 137, 201
Maritain, Raïssa, 137
Marivaux, 55
Martiny, Dr., 185
Massignon, Louis, 181
Marx, Claude-Roger, 116

Marx, Karl, 204, 235
Marxism, 204, 215, 217
Marxists, 187
Mauriac, François, 22, 121, 123, 178, 191, 201
Maurras, Charles, 190
Maurice, Dom, 20, 33, 37-38, 47, 54, 85, 138, 185
Mediation, 143, 144
Menander, 56
Mendizabal, José Antonio, 201
Merle, 151
Metaphysical Institute, 185
Metaphysical Journal, 39, 82, 93, 94, 95, 101, 104, 105, 113, 118, 119, 123, 134, 183, 222
Méta-problématique, 140
Meyer, Madame (maternal grandmother of Gabriel Marcel), 52, 63, 65, 91, 110, 151, 172
Meyer, Aline, 52
Meyer, Édouard, 70
Meyer, Ernest, 52
Meyer, Madame (maternal grandmother of Gabriel Marcel), 52, 64, 66, 92, 111, 152, 173
Meyer, Madeleine, 52
Middle East, 217
Michelet, Edmond, 151, 158-159, 163, 178
Mignet, Auguste, 62
Ministry of National Education, 150
Mirabeau, 47
Missions Évangéliques (Evangelical Missions), 111
Molière, 65,
  Molière's Alceste, 46
Mon testament philosophique, 222
Mon temps n'est pas le vôtre (My time is not yours), 146, 147, 196, 206
Le Monde, 16, 20, 22-23, 33, 122, 134, 136, 140-141, 146, 171, 198-199
Montaigne, Michele de, 29, 71, 170
Montherlant, Henri de, 121
Moral Rearmament, 144-145, 212, 214-215, 231
Le Mort de demain (Tomorrow's dead), 37, 109, 147
Mounier, Emmanuel, 131, 154, 168
Moussorgsky, Modest P., 210
Moüy, Pierre de, 58
Mozart, Wolfgang Amadeus, 57, 221
Music, importance of, 22, 40, 47, 56, 57, 58, 82, 83, 175, 176, 177
La Musique dans ma vie (Music in my life), 222
Mystery, 169, 239
Le Mystère de l'être (*The Mystery of Being*), 17, 33, 223

Nano, 98-99
Nathan, Monique, 232
Nationalism, 100
Nature, 172, 173, 213, 217
Nazism, 139, 219-220
Nazi, 202, 219
Nerval, Gérard de, 177
New Testament, 182
Nietzsche, Friedrich,12, 220
Nobel Laureats, 217
Nussbaum, Robert, 81
Nouÿ, Lecomte de, 172
Novels, 116
Nyssen, Father, 218

Objectification, 19, 33, 34, 35, 56
Objectivity, 13
Occupation, 187, 202, 211
  German Occupation, 187
Old Régime, 62
Old Testament, 182
Oratory, 211
d'Ormesson, Vladimir, 130
Orthodox Church, 180
Other, the, 12, 13, 23, 32, 41, 208
  being with, 91, 159
  disappointment, 40)
Ottaviani, Cardinal, 215
Ozeray, Madeleine, 141
Oxford Groups, 143-145, 214

Pacifism, 130, 146
Le Palais de sable (The sand castle), 45, 84-88
Paléologue, Maurice, 116
Parain-Vial, Jeanne, 176, 195

Parapsychial/Prophecy/Mediation, 21, 97-101, 105, 143, 144, 184, 185
Participation, 13
Pascal, Blaise, 29, 183, 192, 198
Pascal's Wager, 183
Paul, St., 182
Paul VI, Pope, 204
Paulhan, Jean, 39, 118, 146, 189
Pavel, Toma, 210
Peace Prize, 220-221
Péguy, Charles, 141
La Porte étroite (*Strait is the Gate*), 71
Le Porte-glaive (The sword bearer), 78
Position and concrete approaches to investigating the Ontological Mystery, 122, 133, 158
Post-modernism, 9, 10, 11, 23, 24
Personification, of God, 182
Personalism, 168
Personality, of, 136
Pétain, Marshal, 153-154, 161, 188-190
Le Petit Garçon (The little boy), 43, 44, 45, 46, 158
Pfeil, Dr., 219
Phenomenology and its existential turn, 12
Philosophical Fragments, 85, 86
"*Philosophie de l'épuration* ... "(The philosophy of cleansing), 189
Picard, Monique, 232
Piercy, Major, 77
Pilinsky, Janos, 210
Pirandello, Luigi, 37, 141
Pius XII, Pope, 179
Planchon, Roger, 223
Plato, 84, 118, 223
Plon (publisher), 30, 108, 115, 120, 192
Plotinus, 118
Poe, Edgar Allan, 80
Poher, Alain, 160
Poincaré, Raymond, 95-96, 130
Poliana, Iasnaïa, 120
Pompidou, Georges, 191
Poncet, André François, 195
Popular Front, 132
Poulet, Georges, 76
Pozzi, Catherine, 177
Presence, 13, 105
Prieur, Jean, 185
Prini, Pietro, 104
Problem, as distinct from mystery, 133, 193
Prokofiev, Serge, 60
Protestants, 181, 196
Protestant Week of Theatre, 196
Protestant Reformation, 126
Proudhon, Pierre Joseph, 204
Proust, Marcel, 7, 21, 49, 72, 94, 173-175
  Bergotte, 173
  Du Côté de chez Swann, 49, 174
  À la recherche du temps perdu, 173, 175
Psalms, 182
Purge, 187, 188

Quartet in F#, 38, 105, 118, 136, 198

Racism, 230
R., Madame, 97-98, 100
Ransom, Harry, Research Center, 56
Red Cross, 38, 90, 92, 97-99
Reformed Church, 124, 181
Reflection, 10, 12, 13, 14, 15, 16, 18, 20, 23, 33, 34, 170, 171
Le Regard neuf (The new look), 20, 37, 38, 44, 113
Renaissance, 170
Renan, Ernest, 53
Renouvier, 70, 168
Responsibility (see also Engagement/Commitment, & Participation), 43, 87, 125, 204
Resolution, of, 233
Revelation, 181, 182
Rex Party, 188
Resistance, 117, 153, 158
Resurrection, 182-183
Revel, Jean-François, 235
Ridel, Madame, 119
Ricoeur, Paul, 15, 24, 203
Rilke, Rainer Maria, 120
Rivaud, Albert, 231
Rivière, Jacques, 115
Rivière, Isabelle, 115
Roche, Denis, 120

Roger, Maurice, 30, 54, 115, 223
Romains, Jules, 138
Rome, 98, 179, 191, 198-199, 215, 222-223
Roman Catholic Church, 124-126, 179-181
Rostand, Edmond, 55
Rougemont, Denis de, 122
Rousseau, Jean-Jacques, 170
Royce, Josiah, 9-10, 21, 72, 110, 213
Ruf, Wolfgang, 218
Russian language, 210, 224

Saint-Simon, Claude Henri de Rouvroy, 223
Salignac-Fénelon, Bertrand, 174
Sankt Benno Verlag, 206
Sarraut, Albert, 131
Sartre, 20, 38-39, 102, 119, 188, 192-193, 199, 212, 218, 230
Sartrian, 172
Scheler, Max, 120, 203
Schelling, F.W. Joseph von, 9, 74
Schiller, Friedrich von, 120
Schloesing, Émile, 70
Schnee, Werner, 138-139
Schnitzler, Arthur, 221
Schoningh (publisher), 76
Schopenhauer, Arthur, 70
Schubert, Franz, 19, 225, 239
Schumann, Robert, 37, 57, 225
Self, the, 92, 144, 205
  forgetfulness of, 151
  condemnation of, 155)
Sentis, Michel, 215
Le Seuil invisible (*The Invisible Threshold*), 38, 84, 147, 195
Le Signe de la croix (*The Sign of the Cross*), 157, 196, 197
Six Personnages en quête d'auteur (Six Characters in Search of an Author), 37
Situation, character of, 42, 53, 89, 103
Semprun, Jorge, 201
Slavic, 210
Siegfried, André, 27, 187, 206-209
Social Teams, 230
Society, of (see also Justice), 61, 62, 231
La Soif (*Thirst*), 139, 146
Sophocles, 56
Sora, Michel, 210
Sorrow/suffering (see also Despair), 57, 165
Sorbonne, 68-70, 107, 115, 130, 138, 186
Souffrance et Bonheur du Chrétien (Suffering and happiness of the Christian), 123
Soviet, 149, 209
Soviets, 204
Spanish Civil War, 201
  Basques, 202
  Catalans, 202
  Republicans, 201
Spencer, Herbert, 53, 62
Spes, 117
Spinoza, Baruch, 73, 172
Stockman, 51
Stravinsky, Igor, 49
Subconscious, 197
Subjectivism, 87, 173
Supervielle, Jules, 177
Swinnerton, Frank, 120
Swiss, 55, 155

Taine, Hippolyte, 53
Tardieu, André, 130
Tépéneag, 210
Theatre, its relation with Philosophy, 117, 118, 137, 138, 148, 194, 197, 198, 199, 200, 238
Thibon, Gustave, 155, 169
Thomas Aquinas, St., 127, 182
Thomism, 126
  Neo-Thomism, 127
Thureau-Dangin, Paul, 167
Time, 75, 76, 169, 222
  here-now, the event, 75, 218
  the then, 75
  discontinuity of, 76
Tocqueville, Alexis de, 63
Touvier, Paul, 188, 191
"*Tragique et Personnalité*" (*Tragic and Personality*), 37
Treaty of Versailles, 107
Trévise, Duchess de, 119
Trois Épis, 144

Truth, 35, 41
the light of truth caused by Death, 161

Ulbricht, Walter, 206
Unamuno, Miguel de, 234
Unforeseeable/Unverifiable/Invisible, 102, 103, 104, 127, 153
Unesco, 197
Union of Women of France, 92
Universal Exposition, 139
U.S.S.R., 157

Valéry, Paul, 122, 171, 174, 177
Vichy, 154, 156-157
Vietnam War, 212
Vigny, Alfred de, 53, 234

Wackrill, 49
Wagner, Richard, 57, 82, 86, 130
Wagnerian, 57
Wahl, Jean, 91, 191
Warcolier, Rhine, 103
Wassermann, Jakob, 120
Watteville, Robert and Diane, 143
Weber, Max, 231
Weil, George-Denis, Mr. and Mrs., 174
Weil, Louis, 150, 155, 174 ?
Weil, Simone, 150, 155, 174 ?
Weiss, Louis, 115
Westerners, 222
Whitehead, Lord Alfred, 212
War, on, 64, 94, 95, 96, 108, 130, 146
Wladmir d'Ormesson, 130
Wolf, Hugo, 221
World War I, 40, 70, 75, 81, 88-89, 96, 99, 102, 167, 171, 196, 209, 213, 221
World War II, 21, 39, 65, 94, 106, 121, 129, 143, 146, 169, 188, 197, 209, 211, 222
World Wars, 121-122, 147

Places

Aigle, 47
Ain, 156
Aix-en-Provence, 47, 90, 138
Algeria, 161, 191
Algiers, 189
Alsace, 112, 195
Alsace-Lorraine, 64
Amazonia, 228
Arc de Triomphe, 163
Ardéche, 124, 156
Ardennes, 97
Argentat, 151
Arpajon, 153
Athens, 223
Austin, 56, 94, 221
Austria, 91, 95, 141, 221
Austria-Hungary, 63

Balkans, 63
Bamberg, 219
Basel, 129
Battle Abbey, 76
Bayreuth, 219
Béarn, 73
Beirut, 197
Belgium, 146, 167, 188, 198
Berlin, 206
Blonay, École Foyer des Pléiades, 81
Bois des Corbeaux, 111
Bodiam Castle, 76
Bonn, 219
Bosnia, 63
Boston, 213
Boulogne, 113
Bournemouth, 76
Brazil, 176, 229
Porto Alegre, 176
Brigue, 91
Brittany, 139, 173
Brigue, 91
Brittany, 139, 173
Brive, 151
Brussels, 141, 188, 199, 227
Buenos Aires, 207
Budapest, 131
Burgos, 191, 201, 204, 216-217
Caux, 144-145, 214
Cabris, 232
Champex, Lake, 75
Charleroi, 92
Charmes, 124

Chemin des Dames, 100
Chicago, 24, 191, 213
Chiers, 99
Chile, 227-228
Clermont-Ferrand, 154-155
Cleveland, 214
Cobourg, 196, 218
Coimbra, 224
Cologne, 218
Colombey-les-Deux-Églises, 160, 163, 166
Cordillera, 228
Corrèze, 151-152, 155, 167, 176, 197, 230
Cuzco, 228
Czechoslovakia, 149, 222

Devil's Island, 51
Dolomites, 141
Dresden, 27, 206-208
Drôme, 155
Dubrovnik, 224

Eastern Europe, 206
England, 84, 188, 194-195
English Channel, 159, 173, 212
Ehrenwald, 105
Eisenbudd, 105
Élysée Palace, 166
Emmaus, 182
Epidaurus, 223
Essen, 188
Europe, 61, 64, 115, 122-123, 206, 213, 218, 222, 225

Finland, 48, 149
Flueli-Ranft, 91
Forez, 153
Fossé, 97-99
France, 9, 36, 53, 59, 63, 76, 83, 90-92, 95, 112, 121, 130-131, 133, 136-139, 143, 150, 153, 158, 162, 172, 177, 188-189, 191, 193, 198, 204, 209, 212, 215, 220
  Sisteron, 47
  Sorbiers, 176
Frankfurt, 133, 175, 220-221
Fribourg, 193, 218
Fuji, 229

Gdánsk, 204
Gdynia, 204
Geneva, 74, 130, 156
Germany, 76, 91, 95, 128, 130, 157, 173, 188, 196, 199, 206-207, 209, 218-221, 223
Gimel, 151
Goleferanci, 77
Göttingen, 219
Greece, 223

Hakone, 229
Harvard University, 168
Haute-Loire, 156
Heidelberg, 219
Herefordshire, 77
Hernösand, 49
Hofkirche, 208
Holland, 194, 223
Homburg, 173
Hong Kong, 207
Hudson River, 213
Huancayo, 228
Hungarian, 63, 131

Idaho, 213
Isonzo, 101
Isle d'Yeu, 188
Israel, 216, 231
Italy, 112, 195, 204, 223-224

Japan, 191, 218, 228-230
  Inland Sea, 229

Kiel, 219
Kremlin, 204, 210
Kyoto, 229-230

La Paz, 228
Lake Geneva, 74
Lake Huron, 212
Lake Sarnen, 91
Leipzig, 206
Lebanon, 218
Le Peuch, 151, 156, 167
Le Moyne College, 36

Leningrad, 216-217
Lichtenberger, 130
Ligneyrac, 158
Lille, 192
Lima, 227-228
Limoges, 155
Loetschberg, 91
London, 104, 142, 161, 175, 199, 238
Lucas-Montignys, 47
Luléå, 49
Lyons, 7, 154-155, 157-158

Madrid, 201, 216
Maelar, 57
Mackinaw, 145, 212
Machupicchu, 228
Mackinaw, 145, 212
Maisons-Lafitte, 197
Marburg, 219
Marseilles, 133, 137, 143, 199
Martigny, 75
Merle, 15
Merlée, La, 154
Meudon, 137
Meyssac, 151
Ministry of Education, 94, 156
Missoula, Montana, 213
Milan, 176
Montana, Switzerland, 145, 156,
Montmédy, 99
Montpellier, Le Peyrou, 156
Montserrat, 201
Morgat, 139
Morocco, 218
  Fez, 224
  Marrakech, 224
Mont Kemmel, 108
Mont Pélerin, 76-77
Munich, 149, 219
Münster (Westphalia), 195
Musées Nationaux, 46

Nantes, 197
Nazareth, 235
Netherlands, 198, 221, 223
New Hampshire, 72, 211
New Mexico, 121
New York City, 207, 213
Noirétable, Loire Valley, 152
Normandy, 187
North Africa, 159, 189
Norway, 48
North America, 10, 102, 213, 218, 228-229
Notre-Dame Cathedral, 161-162, 166, 187

Old World, 213
Oregon, 213

Paris, 4, 30, 48-49, 55, 63, 71, 73-74, 82, 85, 91-92, 99, 112-115, 117, 122, 125, 131, 133, 138, 140, 142, 149-150, 152-154, 156-157, 161, 163, 168, 172, 176, 182, 187, 195, 197-199, 207, 209, 213, 215, 222, 227, 232
Peru, 228
  Upper Peru, 228
Peterhof, 95
Pontigny, 118
Pirna, 207
Pittsburgh, 214
Poland, 204, 206
Prague, 112, 160, 209
Provence, 139

Rhine, 95, 103, 130-132, 138, 149, 218
Rhineland, 218
Rocky Mountains, 213
Rome, 98, 179, 191, 198-199, 215, 222-223
Rotterdam, 210, 221
Ruhr, 130
Russia, 101, 216-217, 224

Saint-Léonard, 76
Saint-Wolfgang, 141
Saltsjön, 48
Salzburg, 141, 221
Sancerre, 153
San Francisco, 214
Sardinia, 77
Serbia, 91
Sens, 36, 89, 109, 112-113, 195
Serbia, 91

Sendai, 229
Sens, 36, 89, 109, 112-113, 195
Sicily, 223
  Agrigente, 223
  Monreale, 223
  Taormina, 223
  Palermo, 223
Slavery, 178
South Africa, 168
South America, 102, 218, 228
Spain, 61, 202, 224
  Andalousia, 224
  Avila, 224
  Castilla, 224
  Cordoba, 224
  Granada, 224
  Salamanca, 224
  Segovia, 224
  Seville, 224
Spes (publisher), 117
Stockholm, 46, 48-49, 57, 174
Suga-Quin, 229
Sully, 153
Switzerland, 47, 90
  Taunus, 173

Tel-Aviv, 216
Tokyo, 176, 214, 227, 229
Toledo, 224
Treviso, 101
Tréminis, 47
Trevise, 119
Trieste, 101
Tübingen, 219
Tunisia, 153
Tyrol, 141

Udine, 101
United States, 15, 139, 168, 212-213
University of Chile, 227
Unterwald, 91
Urubamba, 228
Utrecht, 105, 194, 223

Valais, 91
Valpariso, 227
Vendôme, 81, 87
  Lycée de Vendôme, 81
Venice, 101
Versailles, 107, 119, 126, 174
Vevey, 76
Vienna, 199, 209, 222
Vienna Burg Theater, 222
Vietnam, 212

Washington, 213
West Germany, 219

Zurich, 76
Zwinger, 208

Plays and Characters

Le Coeur des autres:
  Rose Meyrieux 36, 113
  Daniel Meyrieux 19, 35, 113, 114
  Jean 36
Les Coeurs avides:
  Arnauld 235
  Évelyne 235
Le Chemin de crête:
  Ariane Leprieur 85, 140, 142
Le Dard:
  Béatrice 146
  Werner Schnee 139, 146
L'Émissaire:
  Ferrier 197
  Antoine Sorgue 42, 128
Un Juste:
  Bernard 108
  Raymond 90, 107, 108
La Grâce: Françoise 85
  Gérard 85
  Olivier 85
Un homme de Dieu:
  Claude Lemoyne 196
  Edmée 196
Le Monde cassé:
  Geneviève (Forgue) 33, 135
  Christiane Chesnay 23, 33, 34, 135, 136, 146
  Laurent Chesnay 23, 135, 136
  Dom Maurice 33

Mon Temps n'est pas le vôtre:
Alfred Champel 146
Le Palais de sable:
Moirans 85, 86, 87
Clarisse 85, 86, 87, 88
Le Petit Garçon:
Philippe Crozant 43, 44, 45
Colette Crozant 44
André Rimbert 43, 44, 45
Geneviève Rimbert 43, 44, 45
Le Mort de demain:
Antoine Framont 166
Jeanne (Framont) 113
Jean 36
Le Regard neuf:
Maurice Jordan 20, 37, 38
Jordans 113
La Soif:
Arnauld Chartrain 146
Rome n'est plus dans Rome:
Marc-André 198
Pascal Laumière 198
Le Signe de la Croix:
Tante Léna 197

Theatres in Paris

Comédie-Française, 55, 140
Théâtre de l'Ambigu, 113
Théâtre de la Madeleine, 136
Théâtre Montmartre, 36, 112
Théâtre de l'Oeuvre, 195
Théâtre des Arts, 116, 139
Théâtre Hébertot, 139
Théâtre des Deux Masques, 139
Théâtre des Mathurins, 113
Théâtre du Montparnasse, 195
Théâtre du Vieux-Colombier, 116, 141, 198
Brussels: Théâtre du Parc, 141
Dublin: Gate Theatre, 136
Bibliothèque Nationale, 46
Boulevard de Beauséjour, 175
Collège de France, 53, 83
École des Beaux-Arts, 195
École des Mines, 64
École Militaire, 98
École Normale, 71
Faubourg Saint-Germain, 174
Invalides, 162, 166
Lycée Condorcet, 94
Lycée Louis-le-Grand, 150
Notre-Dame Cathedral, 161-162, 166, 187
Saint Augustine Parish, 125
Saint-Marcel, Temple de, 176
Schola Cantorum, 111
Lion de Belfort, 114
Panthéon, 162, 166
Passy, 131
Place de l'Étoile, 110
Place de l'Opéra, 132
Place Malesherbes, 176
Plaine-Monceau, 152
Quai de l'Horloge, 121
Rue Boulard, 115, 118
Rue Budé, 120
Rue Chamlonas, 113
Rue Émile-Dubois, 114
Rue Général-Foy, 43
Rue Meissonier, 43, 57, 152
Rue de Prony, 96
Rue de la Tombe-Issoire, 114
Rue des Réservoirs, 119, 122
Rue de la Chausée-d'Antin, 82
Rue des Mathurins, 70

Printed in the United States
By Bookmasters